M000195256

Broken not Shattered

Broken not Shattered

RITA POTTER

SAPPHIRE BOOKS PUBLISHING
SALINAS, CA.

Broken not Shattered
Copyright © 2021 by Rita Potter
All rights reserved.

ISBN - 978-1-952270-22-2

This is a work of fiction - names, characters, places, and incidents are the product of the author's imagination or are used fictitiously. Any resemblance to actual persons living or dead, business, events or locales is entirely coincidental.

All rights reserved. No part of this publication may be reproduced, distributed, or transmitted in any form or by any means, including photocopying, recording, or other electronic or mechanical methods, without written permission of the publisher.

Editor - Kaycee Hawn
Book Design - LJ Reynolds
Cover Design - Fineline Cover Design

Sapphire Books Publishing, LLC
P.O. Box 8142
Salinas, CA 93912
www.sapphirebooks.com

Printed in the United States of America
First Edition – April 2021

This and other Sapphire Books titles can be found at
www.sapphirebooks.com

Dedication

For Terra: Forever, please.

For Maxine: Gone but never forgotten.

Acknowledgements

I would like to thank Chris and everyone at Sapphire Books for giving me the chance to make my dream a reality. I will never forget the Sunday afternoon when you called to give me the news. I was so impressed that you spent over an hour answering all my questions, never making me feel as if you wanted me to shut up and get off the phone.

Thanks to my editor, Kaycee, who patiently dealt with this comma-challenged author. Not only did your recommendations make my writing better, you also saved the readers from having to read the word, "said", 750 times more than was necessary. And thanks for the email exchanges that made me feel like a person, not just a job.

Thanks to my now retired high school English teachers. Mrs. Cleland, who may never know the impact she had on a teenager struggling with herself. And Mrs. Wright, who braved reading a lesbian romance, sex scenes and all, in order to make this a better book.

Thanks to Kristy 2.0, who is traveling the writer's journey with me. I look forward to the day I read my name in your acknowledgements.

Thanks to the team that has walked beside me for so many years in my "day job": Gene, Laurie, Barb, and Alicia. We've been through everything together. I wouldn't have the time or energy to write if it wasn't for you guys. You've had my back, you've been my family, and most importantly, you've made me laugh, no matter what the situation.

Thanks to my family. To my mom, who instilled the love of reading and learning in me. To my brother, who taught me how to be competitive, since I kicked his butt in everything we ever played. To Mom and Dad Stetz, who has cheered me on and entrusted their daughter to me.

Thanks to Kourtney, for being my beta reader, marketing guru, ping pong buddy, book club participant, and best friend. Even though it hasn't always been easy, it's been worth it.

Thanks to Maxine, who is gone but not forgotten. You were the inspiration for this book, and my best friend, until the big C took you from us. But you left me with the most valuable gift anyone could give, when I inherited Kristy 1.0 and the best man I have ever known, her husband Mike.

Thanks to Chumley, the cat. I was afraid if I didn't add him here, he wouldn't let me use his pictures on my website or my social media posts anymore. If anything will make me go viral, I'm sure it will be him, not my writing.

Thanks to Terra, my wife, who makes everything in my life possible and better. People always say that relationships are hard, but being with you has always been easy. You've been my biggest supporter, while also being courageous enough to give me honest feedback in my life and my writing, which has made me a better person and author. For the past twenty years, you've let me shine and pursue all my crazy ideas, while you quietly bring the steadiness and stability I need. Now that we've been married for over six years, one day I might actually ask you to marry me.

And finally, I would like to thank the readers, who I hope will learn to love my characters like I do.

PROLOGUE

A lex McCoy stumbled down the hallway, only partially awake. The pounding persisted and grew in its urgency. Not thinking to flip on the light, she swung the door open and looked into the dim corridor. Her senses were suddenly alert when she saw Jill Bishop's distorted face. Jill smiled, but the effort caused her to wince.

Alex led Jill inside, making sure to secure the deadbolt behind them. In the living room, she turned on the table lamp to examine Jill's face. She wished she hadn't. Alex tentatively reached out and touched Jill's cheek. Jill closed her eyes at the light touch of Alex's fingertips.

"We need to get you cleaned up." Jill nodded.

Alex guided Jill to the bathroom and helped her ease onto the closed toilet seat. Jill slumped against the tank, her arms hanging limply at her sides. Alex grabbed a washcloth, ran it under the faucet, and wrung out the excess water.

Turning back to Jill, Alex steadied her trembling hands, not wanting to inflict further pain. She lightly brushed Jill's dishwater blonde hair away from her face before wiping around her dark brown eyes. Alex discovered she could not wash away all the red. She took a deep breath as she cleaned the blood from under Jill's nose, then rinsed the rag and moved to

Jill's lips, causing Jill to flinch when the cloth brushed against the scab that was forming.

After Alex finished cleaning her face, Jill tried unsuccessfully to stand. Alex offered her arm for support, which Jill used to pull herself up. Once Jill was on her feet, she twisted a couple times, trying to remove her shirt; finally, she yanked at her sleeve, and her face went white. Her breath caught, and she grabbed the sink. Alex moved quickly and wrapped her arm around Jill's small waist, easily supporting her full weight. Jill leaned against Alex, her head resting on Alex's chest. She took several deep breaths before her breathing evened. Alex offered to help with her shirt, and Jill nodded. Alex gripped the bottom of her blouse and lifted it slowly, trying not to brush any part of her skin. Alex grimaced when she saw the angry red welts accenting the older purple and green bruises covering Jill's torso. Trying not to stare at the damage, Alex helped her raise the shirt over her head.

In order to regain her composure, Alex turned away under the pretense of preparing the shower. She adjusted the temperature and flicked her hand under the jets to ensure the water was warming. Satisfied that it was, she opened the linen closet, pulled out a fresh towel, and draped it over the shower rod. Alex looked back as Jill was sliding her sweat pants down her narrow hips. Alex's eyes widened when she saw the dark red blotch on Jill's panties. Bile rose in her throat, but she forced it down. Jill stood naked and exposed, like a battered child. Alex wanted to comfort her, but didn't know how, so she stepped forward and brushed a bloody wisp of hair from Jill's eyes.

Jill stepped into the shower, and Alex picked up her discarded clothes. She left the room and hurried to the half bath. She barely had the toilet lid up before she lost the contents of her stomach. She stood over the toilet bowl for several minutes in case her stomach decided to rebel again. She flushed the toilet, splashed cold water onto her face, and ran her hand through her short hair. When she glanced in the mirror, she was surprised by how pale she looked.

She angrily took the bloody clothes into the laundry room, wishing she could burn them. Instead, she treated the blood with stain remover and threw them into the washing machine. She scrubbed her hands vigorously in the utility sink, erroneously believing blood covered them.

Alex could still hear the shower running when she went to the kitchen. She opened the pantry door and scanned the bottles. She located Jill's favorite Pinot Grigio, and pulled it from the wine rack. She positioned the corkscrew over the top of the bottle and twisted. Still shaken, she missed her target and the spiral dug into the cork at an unnatural angle. Alex swore as she struggled to straighten the opener, so it would grip the cork enough to allow her to remove it. After some maneuvering, the cork popped out without leaving any remnants behind to fall into the wine. She emptied the bottle into two glasses and swirled the liquid to ensure it was free of debris.

When Alex returned to the bathroom, Jill was finished in the shower. Jill had slipped on Alex's thick terry cloth bathrobe and looked small and frail as she wrapped it around herself. Without a word, Alex handed her one of the glasses. Jill's hand was shaking when she brought the glass to her lips and the liquid sloshed against the sides. A thousand vise grips tightened around Alex's chest when she looked at the shattered woman in front of her. Alex knew anger was the last thing Jill needed, so she choked down her rage and moved closer. She looked at Jill tenderly and tentatively reached out her hand. Jill responded by clutching Alex's hand, but she still didn't speak. Alex led her from the bathroom into the bedroom. The covers were askew from where Alex had been asleep not long ago. Jill stiffened when the two reached the bed but said nothing. Jill obediently got in, her demeanor suddenly making Alex uneasy. What little life Jill had left in her eyes flickered out, and she opened her robe.

"God, no." Alex was unable to find any other words. She wrapped the robe tightly around Jill and covered her with a soft blanket.

Chapter One

Six Months Earlier

"Miss, you're holding up the entire line. You're gonna have to give me more money or put something back." The young salesgirl looked at Jill with contempt and rolled her eyes at the man next in line. "This might take a while," she said loud enough for patrons at the surrounding registers to hear. The man glared at Jill, removed his items from the counter, and brushed past the tall woman standing behind him.

Jill reddened. "Um, I'm sorry," she stammered at the retreating man. Turning to the woman behind the counter, she repeated, "I'm sorry. I thought there was more money in here." She held up an envelope with $150 written in neat print across the center while the other hand unconsciously twisted her hair.

"Well, apparently you were wrong. You only gave me $100, and your bill comes to $148.18. Do you wanna give me a credit card for the rest?"

"I don't have a credit card," Jill responded as she shuffled through the bags, pulling items out.

"No credit card," the loud-mouthed salesgirl practically shouted, drawing more attention. "Who doesn't carry a credit card?"

"Well, my husband, he—" Jill started and

stopped mid-sentence, wondering why she felt the need to explain herself to this abrasive young woman. She certainly didn't want the children witnessing her humiliation.

"It's okay to put my dolly's new dress back; she won't mind."

"It's okay, honey; you don't need to worry about it. I'll take care of it." Tears threatened to surface, but Jill choked them back. She would not let this woman humiliate her, especially in front of the girls.

"I'm going to have to void this order," the sales-girl said, hitting the switch on the pole with more gus-to than was necessary. The flashing light was like an arrow pointing at her, accentuating her humiliation. Her eyes remained downcast as she sorted through the items she'd pulled from her bags. She tried to do the math in her head, the whole time feeling the cashier's eyes boring into her. Jill's focus was on her task, and her hair cascaded around her face, blocking her vision.

"Here, that should cover it." The woman behind her reached out, offering something to the cashier.

Jill stopped what she was doing, brushed her hair back, and lifted her eyes in the direction of the voice. She looked into the warmest brown eyes she had ever seen. The woman had a chiseled face, almost handsome, but the eyes softened her features. The look nearly brought tears to her eyes again, but instead she reacted with a shy smile.

"What do you want me to do with this?" the clerk responded, wrinkling her nose and holding up several crumpled bills.

"Stop harassing this poor woman and her children and complete her sale." The woman's warm eyes turned to steel when she looked at the clerk, but the warmth returned when she looked back at Jill.

"Of course, yes," the clerk stammered and quickly started punching keys on her register.

"You might want to turn out that light."

"Sorry, yes." The saleswoman fumbled for the switch and flipped off the light.

"It's not me you should be apologizing to," she said, the authority in her voice evident.

Jill was shocked when the cashier turned to her and mumbled an apology. Jill pushed her hair behind her ear and simply smiled. She finished putting the rest of the bags in her cart and quickly left the register. She found an inconspicuous nook against the wall and gathered the girls around her. Jill watched the stranger complete her sale and turn toward the door.

"Excuse me," Jill said softly.

The woman looked her way and smiled. Her intense brown eyes twinkled.

"I want to get your address." Jill twisted her hair as she spoke.

With a subtle flick of her eyes, the woman motioned to the salesclerk, who was watching their exchange with interest. The stranger approached Jill, put her hand on the cart, and, without a word, led them toward the exit. Obediently, Jill followed with the girls in tow.

"I'm sorry. I didn't mean to act all James Bond on you back there. I just wanted to wipe that superior grin off her face. I didn't think she needed to be involved in any more of your business."

"Thank you so much; that was very kind of you. I want to get your name and address so I can send you the money I owe you." Jill looked up from her groceries only once before quickly looking down again.

"Don't worry about it. Next time you see someone in need, just pay it forward, then your debt to me will be paid in full."

Jill looked up again and shuddered when her eyes met the kind eyes looking back at her.

"Are you okay?"

"Yes," Jill said softly. "I'm afraid I haven't been having the best of luck lately, and you know what they say about the kindness of strangers. You helped renew my faith in people today."

"That's all the payback I could ever want." The woman paused, seeming to weigh whether she should say more. "I sensed something back there. I mean…I couldn't help but notice that the world seems to be weighing on you, so I thought maybe I could ease it in some small way."

"You did; thank you." Jill unconsciously smoothed the wrinkles in her well-worn coat.

"Sorry; I'm making you uncomfortable. My friends say I should stop saying whatever comes to my mind. I didn't mean to intrude. I should be going. I hope your day gets better." With that, the woman turned and walked away.

"Wait," Jill shouted before the woman could turn the corner. *What in the world had gotten into her? She didn't talk to strangers, let alone shout down the street at one.* Jill unconsciously reached for the girls' hands when the stranger turned around and walked back toward them.

"Is everything okay?"

"I'm sorry; it's just that I never got your name." Jill fidgeted with her hair.

A broad smile broke across the woman's face, and she laughed. Jill's cheeks reddened.

"Hey, I'm sorry, it's okay. I'm not laughing at you." She lightly reached out and touched the arm of Jill's coat. Jill looked down at the hand and felt herself reacting again. *When was the last time someone had been so kind, someone who wanted nothing from her?* She managed a smile and hoped her eyes did not betray her.

"I had a flashback from one of those stupid old TV shows." She flashed a smile at Jill. "Do you remember the Lone Ranger? At the end, someone would always say, 'Who was that masked man?' Then someone else would say, 'You don't know who that was? That was the Lone Ranger.' It just struck me as funny. I guess it doesn't take much to amuse me, huh?"

"So, who is this rescuer of shoppers in distress?" Jill surprised herself with the playful comeback.

"Alex. Alex McCoy. And you are?"

"Jill," she mumbled.

"I'm sorry, I didn't catch that."

"Jill," she said with more force.

"It's nice to meet you, Jill. Now you won't have to think of me as that mysterious stranger." Alex winked and ran her hand through her short dark hair.

"I just wanted to…well, to thank you again for your kindness. The girls and I, well, I, well, we appreciate it. Don't we, girls?"

Two sets of eyes looked up, but said nothing.

"Shy and quiet, just like their mom, huh?"

"Um, well, this is Jenna and Trina. Say hello, girls."

Two tiny voices muttered hello in unison. Alex

knelt in front of them and introduced herself. Jill was shocked when the girls began to talk to Alex when she asked them about their dolls. She looked down at the scene, a smile parting her lips. It was nice to see the girls talking to Alex, since they were always shy and withdrawn around others.

When Alex finished the conversation with Jenna and Trina, she stood and looked at Jill. She opened her mouth to speak, but stopped. Jill noticed the hesitation, so she looked at Alex questioningly. When Alex still didn't speak, Jill added, "Was there something you wanted to say?"

Alex blushed. "Well, no…it was stupid."

"Don't they say there are no stupid questions?" She smiled and added, "But I guess they don't say the same about statements, so I guess you better ask a question." *What was up with her? Was she really bantering with a woman she just met?*

"Okay then." Alex laughed. "You've convinced me to stick with my original question. I just have to warn you, it popped into my mind out of nowhere. I'm not usually into propositioning strangers on the street."

Alex's eyes got big, and Jill tried not to smile at Alex's obvious discomfort. "What is wrong with me? You would think I just learned how to speak English. I did not mean propositioning. I better leave you ladies to your day, before I say something else stupid or inappropriate."

There was a charm about Alex's floundering that oddly put Jill at ease. Even though Alex exuded an air of authority, Jill sensed the vulnerability underneath. Jill was curious about what question could possibly have Alex so flustered. "No, please. I believe that you're not into propositioning strangers. I promise, we won't be offended by your question."

"Okay, but please don't feel obligated in any way to say yes; it was just something that came to mind on a whim. I'm not even sure where it came from." With a nod, Jill encouraged Alex to continue. "Well, I was on my way to the park to get some ice cream, and I wondered if you ladies would like to join me?"

Jill hesitated, knowing they needed to get home soon. At Jill's hesitation, Alex held up her hand. "No need to say anything more. I understand in this day and age you can never be too careful."

"No, it's not that. We just don't have a lot of time." Jill looked at the girls' hopeful faces and realized she felt the same. "But it is a beautiful Indian summer day, and ice cream season will be coming to an end soon."

"So, is that a yes or a no?" Alex asked.

"Why not! But we can't stay too long. Ice cream and a round on the swings, then we need to get home," Jill said to the girls.

"All right," they said at the same time.

"All right," Alex mimicked, her eyes twinkling. "Let's get your groceries in your car before we go."

Jill pointed behind her. "We walked. We only live three blocks back in Whispering Winds."

"I used to have a friend that lived there. I haven't been there in years, but her apartment was really nice."

"They're okay. Unfortunately, the elevator rarely works, and we live on the fourth floor. I guess it beats going to the gym."

"Hey now, what do you have against gyms?"

"I'm sorry." Jill reached for her hair and shifted her eyes to the ground.

Alex put her hand on Jill's arm and waited for her to look up. Alex's eyes still held their warmth, but they also showed concern. "I'm sorry; I didn't mean to scare you. I was teasing. I work at the gym a couple blocks down from the park. It was a stupid joke since you didn't know that."

Jill smiled, appreciating the ease in which Alex offered an apology. Too many people thought apologizing showed weakness, so they rarely did it. Jill looked at Alex, noting she certainly didn't look weak. She was several inches taller than Jill and had broad shoulders that tapered into a thick, but much smaller waist.

"Is that the big gym with the pool, the one with the really weird name?"

"That's the one. So, are you just going to take your cart down to the park then?"

"That's my plan."

"I'll race you," Alex said to the girls. Before Jill could protest, the three raced around the corner, heading for the park at the end of the block. Jill jogged the short distance to the corner and watched the three run ahead. Jill marveled at the effortless stride that kept Alex running alongside the girls. The last forty yards, Jenna began to pull away from her younger sister. Jill gasped when Alex plucked Trina from the sidewalk and, without breaking stride, lifted her to her shoulders. She heard Trina's delighted squeal as they closed the gap on her big sister. With ten yards to go, Alex moved beside Jenna and slowed her pace, timing it so they all burst across the imaginary finish line at the same time. Alex set Trina down and fell to the ground, feigning exhaustion. The girls followed suit and crumpled next to Alex.

Alex and the girls were lying on a bed of leaves, giggling and panting when Jill arrived pushing her cart.

"I can't believe you just did that," Jill said.

"I'm sorry." Alex jumped to her feet.

"No, I, I...I didn't mean it that way." Jill faltered and backed up a couple steps. Her shoulders hunched, and she drew into herself, making it look as if her coat were swallowing her.

Alex started to step forward, but stopped. Instead, she stood very still and spoke slowly and softly. "I didn't mean to upset you."

Jill looked through the hair that had fallen across her face. With only a slight hesitation, she pushed the hair behind her ear and looked directly at Alex. She straightened her coat and tried to formulate a response.

"It's okay." Alex gave Jill a reassuring smile. She put out her hand, palm up. Jill was stunned when she felt herself step forward and take Alex's hand. The warmth felt good on Jill's cold fingers. "Your hand is an ice cube." Alex lightly put her other hand on top of hers. Jill noticed that Alex held on loosely and wondered if she sensed Jill's skittishness.

"Cold hands, warm heart," Jill responded. Her shoulders were beginning to relax and a smile parted her lips.

"I'm not sure what that says about me." Alex laughed, still holding Jill's hand.

"I'm starting to wonder about you. I started out thinking you were the Lone Ranger, but it turns out you just may be Wonder Woman. You picked Trina up like she was a sack of potatoes and never broke stride."

"I'm not allowed to talk about my secret identity." A twinkle played in Alex's eyes as she released Jill's hand. "Should we get our ice cream? I'm not sure your hands are cold enough, yet."

Jill immediately missed the warmth of Alex's hand, but enjoyed Alex's playfulness. "You're lucky I'm an ice cream junkie." Jill noticed the look of surprise on Alex's face. Despite her oversized coat, she knew it was evident that she was too thin. "Don't think I'm naive. I know you're trying to lure me with ice cream, so I'll forget my quest to discover your identity."

"Busted," Alex chuckled.

༄ ༄ ༄ ༄

It was late in the season, so the park was surprisingly empty despite the gorgeous day. Most of the vibrant orange and red leaves lay on the ground; few remained in the trees. The ice cream vendor would be closing for the season in another week, and snow would cover everything in due time. For today, with the temperature being so perfect, they could pretend it was a late summer day if they ignored all the obvious signs of late autumn.

Jill struggled to believe she was in the park with a complete stranger, eating ice cream and swinging. She was unsure what had come over her, but she hadn't laughed this much in years. Alex put her at ease, the awkwardness of earlier long forgotten. Their conversation was effortless, which was even more surprising. Jill couldn't remember the last time she sat with a friend, talking. She couldn't actually call Alex a friend, since they just met, but there was an undeniable connection. The comfortable feeling must be loneliness, she reasoned, and the exhilaration was because of the crisp fresh air.

Once their ice cream was eaten, the girls abandoned them to explore the rest of the playground. Jill and Alex lazily continued swinging and soon discovered they shared a love for old television shows. The talk eventually turned into a spirited game of trying to stump the other with obscure television trivia.

"I give up." Alex put her hands in the air in surrender. "You're putting me to shame."

Jill laughed and pumped her legs, trying to get more height.

"Oh, now you're trying to beat me at swinging, too. I won't go down that easily." Alex pumped her powerful legs as well.

Jill felt alive as she soared higher and higher. She lifted her face to the sky, letting the warmth of the sun and the chill of the rushing air massage her face. For the first time in years, she felt completely carefree and wished this moment could go on forever. After several minutes, it was obvious she was reaching greater heights because of her smaller size.

"You might beat me in height, but watch this." Alex jumped from her swing. She landed, raised her hands above her head, and hopped forward like a gymnast sticking the landing. "Nailed it."

"I'm only giving you a seven-point-five. The landing was good, but the form in the air had a lot to be desired. Arms and legs were flapping everywhere, not much grace."

"Man, tough judge. Let's see if you can do any better."

"Here goes." Jill launched herself from her perch

and felt incredibly free as she soared through the air. The exhilaration was short lived when she realized she had been higher than she thought and would soon hit the ground. When she landed, she continued running forward trying to right herself. Her feet were moving too quickly and they threatened to tangle, which would surely send her crashing to the ground. Just when she started to stumble, Alex stepped in front of her, arms outstretched. Jill's forward momentum caused her to drive toward Alex's body; however, the hard impact she expected never came. Somehow, Alex was able to give ground, yielding enough to steady Jill and gently pull her against her chest. Jill's body relaxed as she leaned into the embrace, making no effort to let go. Alex was the first to move and tentatively backed away, her hands still holding Jill on each side.

"Are you okay?" Alex asked.

"Uh, yeah," Jill stammered. She was unnerved by how right it felt wrapped safely in Alex's arms, but at the same time, she didn't care and wanted to fall into them again. Jill returned to the moment when she noticed the panicked look on Alex's face.

"Hey, I'm okay, really." She tried to say more but giggled instead. Every time she went to speak, a new wave would start. The laughter was contagious, and soon Alex joined her.

As their laughs intensified, they dropped to the ground, landing in a pile of leaves. Jenna and Trina, worried that they were missing out on the fun, came running. They piled on top of Jill, who playfully rolled them in the leaves. Alex sat back and laughed as the girls tried to get the best of Jill. Eventually, Jill noticed and whispered to them. Without warning, Jill sprang and tackled Alex, pushing her onto her back. While

Jill lay on top of Alex, Jenna and Trina climbed on the pile.

"We have you pinned. Are you ready to surrender?" Jill lowered her voice, trying to sound menacing.

"Never; a superhero doesn't give up this easily." Alex wiggled around, but made no real attempt to get free from the bottom of the heap.

"Say uncle, before we squish the breath out of you," Jill teased.

"Who says I won't squish you?" Alex wrapped her arms around all three, growled, and pretended to squeeze them hard, but exerted little pressure.

"No fair, we're on top, we should get to win." Jill pouted.

"Okay, fine. Uncle." Alex had a wide smile on her face.

"Okay, girls, looks like this one is a wimp. We better let her up before she starts crying." When she rolled off Alex, she caught a glimpse of her watch and let out an audible gasp.

"Oh God," Jill said. "Girls, we have to get home."

❧ ❧ ❧ ❧

An internal war raged inside Alex as she watched Jill frantically pick at the leaves that clung to her coat. It was almost as if she were fearful of the leaves. There was an innocence and genuineness about Jill that drew Alex to her, but at the same time, there was something about Jill that haunted Alex. At times, an unmistakable guardedness would descend, and the light in Jill's eyes would fade. Alex found she wanted to make Jill laugh, just to see the life dance back into her lovely brown eyes.

Alex wondered what caused such an abrupt change. Maybe rolling around like a couple of school kids embarrassed Jill, or maybe she sensed Alex's reaction to her, and it made her uncomfortable. Whatever the reason, Alex knew the afternoon was about to come to a sudden end.

A wave of sadness washed over her when she realized that she may never see Jill again. *Would Jill find it weird if she asked her to meet again sometime?* She was unable to give it any more thought because of the rushed activity around her. The girls scrambled to get their coats, a panicked frenzy guiding their actions. *What was she thinking?* Jill had two small children; for everyone's sake, she needed to savor the moment, but want nothing more.

"Thank you guys for a fun afternoon," Alex said formally.

"I'm sorry that we have to run off, but my husband will be home soon, and I have to have his supper on the table."

"I need to get back to work anyway." The word husband cut into Alex, solidifying her decision to say nothing more.

"I'm sorry we kept you." A guarded look returned to Jill's face and she played with her hair.

"Maybe I'll see you around sometime." Alex wished she could take it back, until she saw the hope that flickered in Jill's eyes.

"That would be nice."

"Goodbye, Jenna and Trina. It was nice meeting you. You take care of your mom." Alex knelt to get down to the girls' level. They both ran over and hugged her.

"Goodbye, Jill." Not knowing what else to say,

Alex turned away.

"Don't I get a hug too?" spilled out of Jill's mouth.

Alex smiled broadly and the light danced in her eyes. She stepped forward and wrapped her arms around Jill. Alex didn't want to let go but was afraid of Jill's reaction if she held on any longer. She forced herself to end the embrace, but failed to notice she was the first to let go.

"Take care." The tightness in her chest made it difficult for her to speak. Without another word, she turned and started down the sidewalk.

"Goodbye," she heard Jill say from behind.

Jill was putting away the last of the supper dishes when Steve walked into the kitchen, opened the refrigerator door, and pulled out another beer. He paused to look at her, his eyes making their way up the length of her slender body. His eyes stopped at her breasts before he finally looked up. She hated the way he leered at her, but preferred his focus to remain on her body, so he wouldn't look at her face. She intentionally wore her hair long, so it would partially cover her eyes, giving her a sense of invisibility.

"You're awfully quiet tonight." He popped open his beer. "You didn't have much to say at supper."

"I guess I'm just a little tired."

"So, how was grocery shopping?"

"Just fine." She put the last plate on the shelf and the cabinet door rattled as she closed it. She turned back and never saw the back of his hand until it connected with her cheek. Her back banged against the counter, and she crumpled to the ground.

"Don't lie to me, bitch." He towered over her. "Where did you get the money?"

The realization dawned on her; he had shorted the envelope. *How could she have been so stupid?* He was too meticulous to have made an error. He had set her up, and now she was going to pay for it. It would do no good to tell him about Alex and her kindness; it would probably make things worse. Before the next blow, she readied herself by disconnecting her mind from the moment. Her body still felt his fists, but her mind retreated to the safety of the park. The violence continued as she replayed the events of the afternoon in her head.

She didn't know how much later it was when she came to on the kitchen floor. She crawled to the couch and wrapped herself in a blanket, trying to stop the shivering that wracked her body. A smile crossed her lips before she fell asleep, her mind and body back in the park, feeling the sun and Alex's arms warming her.

❧❧❧❧

Jill was confused when she felt the coldness on her cheek and reached up to explore the source. She winced at the pain the movement caused, and the memories came flooding back. *She was getting too old for this.* Her body was only thirty, but it felt like it was eighty. She felt the warm hand stroking her hair. She squeezed her eyes shut tighter, so the tears would not escape. Slowly, she opened her eyes and saw Jenna holding an ice pack to her cheek and Trina gently caressing her hair. She smiled, or at least tried.

"Good morning, my two angels. What are you

doing up so early?"

"It's not early," Jenna said, the relief apparent on her face.

"What time is it?"

"It's almost ten o'clock."

Jill was startled and abruptly sat up. Pain left her seeing black and drove her back down onto the couch. Fear registered on the girls' faces and they quickly resumed their posts.

"I'm sorry. I'm just a little under the weather," she lied. *As if they believed her.* These two had seen too much in their young lives.

"It's okay. We be nurses," Trina answered, kissing Jill on the forehead.

"What would I do without you guys?"

"Did he find out about Alex and the park?" Jenna asked.

"No, honey, that's our secret. You don't need to worry about it; I'll be fine."

Chapter Two

"I'm going to get some lunch," Alex said when she ducked her head into Sarah's office.

"Sure." Sarah smirked and propped her feet on her desk. "How long are we going to keep up this charade?"

"What charade?"

"The one that I pretend to be ignorant, and you pretend not to notice I'm pretending."

"What do you mean?" Alex asked.

"How long have we been friends?" Sarah didn't wait for an answer. "You still think you can fool me. This time I can't claim that I have a special way of reading you. You're an open book. Every day for a week, you leave at the same time, taking special care to get your little spiky hair all spiked up. You change out of your sweat clothes and put on your jeans and a nice shirt. Then you sprinkle on a little cologne and walk out of here with that goofy look on your face. And every day you come back from lunch, looking like someone ran over your puppy."

"Is it that obvious?" Alex asked.

"No, I'm just a good guesser." Sarah rolled her eyes. "I'm worried about you."

"Why?"

"Umm, let's see…she has two small children and a husband. Do you really want me to go on?" Sarah answered.

"Oh," was all Alex managed, not bothering to call Sarah on her sarcasm. She looked down at the ground, feeling guilty and embarrassed.

"You haven't exactly had the best track record with women. We've been saying for years that you need to pick a different type, but we certainly weren't talking about a married straight woman."

"I know."

"I'm not trying to beat you up, just worried about you. That's what friends are for, you know."

"I know. I don't know what my problem is. I can't get her out of my mind. I know it's wrong, and I know I'm stupid. But I don't know what else to do." Alex's despair was palpable.

"You're not stupid." The look on Sarah's face softened. "Go on and get some lunch. I'll hold down the fort."

"Thanks." Not knowing what else to say, she left Sarah's office.

❧❧❧❧

Jill's breath caught in her throat when she yanked on the vacuum cleaner that was wedged under the couch. She was starting to mend, but her body reminded her she wasn't completely healed. Jill needed to keep moving and finish her chores before Steve got home from work. She knew her body well enough to know she was not in any shape to take another beating like the one she endured the week before. Even though she knew it wasn't the best choice, she was saving the most difficult task until last. She had given up trying to deceive herself as to why she was taking this chance, but in her mind, it was well worth the risk. Her entire body ached, and the afternoon was going to be excruciating. A smile still played on her lips when she left the apartment.

The temperature had dropped by nearly thirty degrees since last week. She could see her breath, which was a reminder winter was just around the corner. She hated winter in the city, especially since she walked or took the bus wherever she went. The store was only three blocks away, but her coat was threadbare and did not provide the protection she needed. Several of the buttons were missing, so she pulled the coat as tightly as she could around herself. She knew if she put on a little weight, it might act as insulation, but it was difficult eating when her stomach was constantly in knots. *There would be no enjoying the park today*, she thought. She found herself going back to that day often in her mind, a place to be happy. A place to escape.

❧❧❧❧

Alex picked at the remains of her sandwich and dejectedly searched the crowd once again. Last night before falling asleep, her thoughts were full of various scenarios of how she would meet up with Jill. When she woke up this morning, something told her today would be the day. She floated through her morning on autopilot, unable to remember what work she accomplished, if any. When she left the gym, she firmly believed her instinct was firing on all cylinders, and today would be the day. As she watched the hurried shoppers, she realized her imagined clairvoyance was simply faulty logic. She'd met Jill one week ago today.

Something in the way Jill behaved convinced her she would follow a strict routine, which meant she should be grocery shopping again today.

Alex had been picking at her lunch for nearly an hour, staring out the window at the market across the street. She saw several shoppers enter the store, and watched the same people leave, pushing carts full of groceries. *Great, I'm officially a stalker*, she thought. She tossed her half-eaten lunch back into its bag and angrily crumpled the top closed. Two teenagers, who had been eyeing her table for the past ten minutes, looked at her hopefully. She would have felt guilty for her lack of consideration, had she not been so disheartened.

She made her way to the restroom, trying to convince herself she should forget Jill. She had been trying to convince herself of this all week, but just about the time she had herself persuaded, a scene from the park would flash in her mind, and she would be back where she started. She chastised herself for acting crazy. If Sarah were in the same situation, Alex would be lecturing her endlessly about the stupidity of her attachment to a married woman with two kids. Not just a married woman with kids, but also a woman she spent time with only once. She would question Sarah's stability, just as she was questioning her own.

≈≈≈≈

Jill's stomach was still doing flip-flops and had been since she woke up this morning. She was unsuccessful at convincing herself the odds of running into Alex were slim at best. Try as she might, the optimism repeatedly silenced the pessimism. By the time she ap-

proached the store, despite her soreness, there was a
spring in her step. She had to laugh at herself when a
moment of dejection hit her. *Had she really expected
Alex to be standing outside the store, just waiting? Yep,
that was exactly the way it played out in her mind.*
She'd watched too many movies and read too many
fairy tales. God knows life doesn't happen that way,
especially not hers.

Jill's eyes darted from face to face as she scanned
the busy lunch crowd. She walked slowly, making sure
to check out the people on both sides of the street. She
reached the front of the store; no sign of Alex. She
was still hopeful. Maybe Alex would be inside; after
all, that is where they first met. She had forgotten how
cold it was outside until the warmth blasted her when
the door slid open. Jill stopped just inside and rubbed
her hands together to warm them. She tried to appear
casual as she took in the room, but her heart was
racing. The only familiar face was the nasty cashier
who had harassed her last week. Even though what
she needed was at the front of the store, she decided
to make a pass through the rest of the aisles.

❧ ❧ ❧ ❧

Alex emerged from the restroom with fresh de-
termination. While waiting in line for a stall, she had
plenty of time to give herself a stern lecture. She reminded herself of all the things she would tell Sarah,
had Sarah been the one to lose her mind like this.
Even though she felt the lecture had done her good,
Alex immediately began examining the crowd as she
made her way through the eatery. *Okay, so she would
need a few more lectures, but they could wait for later.*

She was sure Sarah would help her out on that front.

The man in front of her threw open the door and a blast of cold air slammed into her, making it difficult to catch her breath. Despite the cold, Alex took her time crossing the street, her eyes continually returning to the area around the store. She paused when she got to the front of the building; an internal battle raged. Should she go back to work and give up this adolescent game, or would she always regret not going in?

❦❦❦❦

By the time Jill made it to the last aisle, the spring was gone from her step and a slow plod took its place. She didn't have time to feel sorry for herself. She needed to get on with her chore, or she would never be done in enough time. Jill forced herself to pick up the pace as she approached the checkout counters. Her bad luck continued; the mean cashier was the only one without a customer. *What the hell,* she thought. *She felt lousy enough, she might as well wallow in it a little more.* Jill stepped up to the counter and unconsciously reached for her hair. Recognition slowly registered in the clerk's eyes. She glanced behind Jill to ensure there were no reinforcements.

"Hi." Jill tried to sound friendly, hoping to neutralize the rude woman. The cold stare that greeted her caused her to look down at the money in her hands.

"Yes," the clerk responded.

"I need to purchase ten bags of salt, but will only be able to take two at a time. I'll need to return for the rest."

"Well, I guess you'll have to buy two now, come

back and buy two more, and so on." The clerk gave Jill a smug smile.

"But that will take so much more time. Could I please just buy them now and have them set aside?"

"Do we look like Nordstrom? You're in a discount store. We don't do that kind of thing here." To emphasize her point, she looked toward the salt, and suddenly stopped. "Ya know, I think we could probably do that for you."

Jill had been shuffling her money, not wanting to look at the hateful woman. Without lifting her head, she cautiously raised her eyes. The clerk had turned from Jill and was punching in the transaction, muttering that she would get a stock boy to pull the salt and put her name on it. Jill stared at her with a puzzled expression, but the woman continued to focus on the register. Jill turned toward the salt display, trying to figure out what had caused such a change of heart. Her eyes widened when she looked at the pile.

※ ※ ※ ※

Alex hesitated for only a second before pushing through the door. She had come this far; she might as well go in before she gave up her stalker ways. *This was it, though*, she promised herself. Alex looked toward the checkout lines, and her heart skipped a beat. She couldn't suppress the silly grin that tugged at the corners of her mouth. She was unsure how to approach, so she jumped up onto the pile of salt, letting her legs dangle. She watched the sneering salesgirl talk to Jill.

Jill hurried over to the salt pile. Alex nonchalantly remained on her perch, trying to exude a sense of cool. Her exterior did not match the excitement that fluttered inside her body. Despite the differences in demeanor, both sported similar grins.

"We need to stop meeting like this," Alex joked.

✂ ✂ ✂ ✂

Jill started to speak, but instead she stammered. She felt exposed and was afraid Alex would see through her. *What would Alex think of her if she found out their short time in the park had meant so much to her? Would Alex be able to understand if she knew Jill had survived the last several days by replaying moments from their time together over in her mind? Alex would undoubtedly think she was pathetic or crazy.* Jill's enthusiasm drained. A cold blast of air hit her when the outside door opened. The cold and fear of exposure caused her to draw her coat closed and wrap her arms around herself.

"How have you been?" Jill asked with no affect.

Alex's smile faded, and Jill was sure it was her cold demeanor that had extinguished it. Alex ignored Jill's question. "I've been hoping to see you again."

"Really?" Jill felt a sense of hope returning, but didn't want to appear too eager.

"Actually, I've been keeping my eye out for you all week. I've been across the street for over an hour having lunch, just hoping that you would be here. And well, I finally gave up and was heading back to the gym when something told me I had to look one last time."

"I'm glad you did." Jill wanted to say more or at least smile, but her fear caused her to remain stoic. Jill knew Alex sensed her guardedness, but hoped she could also feel Jill's deep yearning for connection. She saw the internal struggle raging in Alex's eyes, and felt guilty that she was causing it.

"I had a really nice time last week," Alex said, the caution in her eyes replaced by the familiar warmth. "I can't count the number of times I thought about you and the park, and without fail, it made me smile. Then I was afraid that I would never see you again. I kicked myself for not getting your last name or phone number. The thought of never seeing you again, never talking to you again, was just something I wasn't willing to accept. This might sound strange, but I missed you." Alex's eyes widened. "Oh God, I told you my friends accuse me of saying much more than I should. I'm sounding like a crazy stalker, aren't I?"

"No," Jill answered. She reached out, put a reassuring hand on Alex's arm, and looked into her eyes, the same eyes she had seen so many times in her mind the past week. The kindness she saw there made it easier for Jill to say, "I was hoping to see you too."

"Seriously?" Alex asked, her eyes lighting up.

Jill took a deep breath and pushed through the fear. "I've thought about the park, too. I wish I could tell you how much I enjoyed myself, but I'm afraid I'm not as good with words as you are. I was scared to death you would ride off into the sunset, just like the Lone Ranger, and be the mysterious stranger I never saw again."

Another blast of cold air rushed in; she shivered and hugged her coat tighter against herself. Alex removed her own coat, put it over Jill's shoulders, and drew it closed in front. Despite the intimate nature of the gesture, it seemed perfectly natural. The coat still held Alex's body heat, and Jill immediately felt warmer.

"Thank you." Jill rewarded Alex with a shy smile. "Aren't you going to get cold?"

"I'll be fine. I have a lot more padding than you do. Besides, your coat doesn't look thick enough for this weather."

"I guess it has seen its better days."

"It seems we are being watched." Alex gestured toward the clerk who was staring with interest. "Would you like to get a cup of coffee to warm you up?"

Reality returned and Jill frowned. "I'm sorry; I can't." She wanted to hug Alex when she saw the disappointment on her face. "I'd love to, though," she continued, hoping to save the moment. Alex looked at her, but said nothing. "You see, I have to get ten bags of salt up to my apartment before my husband gets home from work."

"Holy shit, what kind of monstrous water softener do you have?"

"It's not for a softener. My husband puts it in the back of his truck. I guess it helps weigh it down for the winter."

Alex's eyebrows drew together and a puzzled look crossed her face. "Why doesn't he just stop at the store on his way home?"

"He's really busy." Jill fidgeted with the zipper on Alex's coat and looked at the salt pile when she spoke.

"I can help you load the truck, then there will be plenty of time for coffee."

"I don't have the truck."

"How are you planning on getting them back to your apartment then?"

"That's my wagon." Jill pointed to a small children's wagon next to the salt. "I just have to take several trips. No big deal." Jill hoped she was convincing in her carefree attitude.

"At least you won't have to lug them up four flights of stairs."

"Good memory. But actually, I do. He wants me to put them in the apartment. He's afraid someone may steal them if I leave them outside." Jill reached for her hair and began winding it around her finger.

"You're already freezing, and it's not getting any warmer out there." Alex's eyes narrowed and she scowled. "That shit's heavy too."

"I'll warm up once I get moving." Jill shuffled from one foot to the other, and reached for her hair. She felt defeated, but didn't want Alex to see her distress. She knew Alex was staring at her, so she needed to do or say something to divert the attention.

Alex opened her mouth to speak, but instead put her hand on top of Jill's cold hand. Jill looked up and felt a flicker of hope return. "I've got an idea." Alex pulled a cell phone from her pocket. "I'll call in the cavalry. We'll get the job done in no time, and then you'll have time for coffee."

Jill's first thought was to refuse the help. *What if Steve found out*? Instead, she smiled and asked, "What do you have in mind?"

Alex hit speed dial, and Jill could hear the phone ringing on the other end. "Leave it to me. I have…"

"Hey," Alex said into the phone. "I need some help. Can you send a couple of the girls over? Actually, I need three. They need to be lifters." Alex listened for a moment before speaking again. "I ran into Jill, and she needs to get ten bags of softener salt moved from the store up to her apartment…I'm pretty sure it's three blocks, hold on."

"Jill, how far do we have to go?" Alex asked.

"Umm, you're right, three blocks," Jill answered.

"Yep, confirmed three blocks. Sarah, have them bring the van. There's no sense trying to carry this shit that far. She only has a little Radio Flyer…You're the best. We'll be out front waiting for them. Thanks again."

"Piece of cake." Alex had a huge grin on her face. "Sarah will round up a few of the girls working out in the gym, and they can get a natural workout. What time does your husband get home?"

"Around 5:30."

Alex glanced at the clock on the wall. "It's not even 1:30. We'll have plenty of time to get coffee. We better get out there; those girls move fast."

Jill slipped out of Alex's coat and held it out to her. Alex shook her head. "No, I want you to wear it; you still look cold." Alex took the coat from Jill and held it out, so Jill could slip her arms into it.

"But we're going outside; you'll be cold."

"I'll be fine. Stop arguing with me and help me with this." Alex continued to hold the coat out in front of her.

Jill stepped back, putting her arms out behind her. Not only was Jill enjoying the warmth of the coat but also the feeling of comfort it brought. She was unaccustomed to someone being concerned about her needs and was surprised how good it felt.

Alex awkwardly tried to help Jill on with her coat. Jill giggled. "Alex, I'm afraid I don't bend that way." Alex muttered an apology and tried again. Jill twisted her right arm back and it went in easily. Alex was making a clumsy attempt at her left arm which was much more challenging. Jill did everything she could to assist, and somehow her arm finally slid into the sleeve. Alex looked dejected when Jill turned to thank her.

"Why the sad look?" Jill asked.

"I was trying to make you feel better, but I just managed to twist you up."

"You do make me feel better." Jill patted Alex on the arm and smiled. Alex gave her a half smile, obviously unhappy with her lack of grace. Impulsively, Jill wrapped her arms around Alex and hugged her. Alex returned the hug. When they separated, the twinkle was back in Alex's eye and a huge smile was on her face.

"Now I know why I didn't play with dolls when I was a kid. Putting their clothes on was beyond my skill set."

Jill laughed as they headed for the door.

❧❧❧❧

The big, white van with the bright multicolored letters that read Sal-Rexah Gym rounded the corner. Alex never got tired of seeing their vans driving through the city. She waved her arm at the approaching vehicle. The van pulled up, the side door opened, and two very athletic women leapt out.

"Where's the goods?" one of the women asked, hitting Alex on the upper arm.

"Inside. We need ten bags." Alex started to thank the women but was distracted when a tiny woman jumped from the driver's seat. "Sarah, I wasn't expecting you," Alex said, shooting her a look. The look was lost on Sarah, who had already bypassed Alex and was making her way toward Jill. Alex hurried after her.

"You must be Jill. I'm Sarah. It's good to meet you." Sarah extended her hand to Jill.

"It's so nice of you guys to come and help out a total stranger." Jill took Sarah's outstretched hand. Alex looked on, marveling at how such a small woman could convey such confidence. Jill had at least three inches on Sarah, but somehow Sarah seemed to be the bigger of the two.

"No problem, we're happy to help." Sarah laid on the charm. Alex glared at her and decided she would kill her later. Jill was obviously causing her not to think clearly. She should have known Sarah would never pass up the opportunity to spy on her. Afraid Sarah would say something to embarrass her, Alex bolted into the store to help the girls.

After the last bag was loaded, Alex approached Sarah and Jill, who were deep in conversation. "Uh, excuse me, guys, we're all loaded and ready to roll."

"So soon? We were just getting to know each other." Sarah said, with a devious twinkle in her eye.

"You can get to know each other in the van." Alex frowned at Sarah, who continued to ignore her.

Sarah laughed, put her arm around Jill, and led her to the passenger seat. "She is such a crybaby. She hates it if she's not getting all the attention. I hope she doesn't throw a tantrum, since I'm having you ride shotgun."

"Do you think she'll still take me out for coffee?" Jill was obviously already comfortable with Sarah.

Sarah looked back at Alex, who was pretending to pout. In a loud whisper, she said to Jill, "Little secret, she's a big pushover. Her growly tough-girl act is just a front."

"Don't make me come up there," Alex said from the back of the van.

"Be quiet back there; we're trying to have a conversation."

Alex knew Sarah was here to size up Jill, and Alex was helpless to prevent it, so she sat back in her seat and closed her eyes.

❧❧❧❧

Sarah pulled up in front of a large brick apartment building. Jill got out of the van and fumbled with her keys. Fear gripped her. *What if someone saw them unloading the salt and told Steve?* She was being paranoid. Steve never talked to anyone in the building, except Mrs. Harrison, who she knew would never tell him anything.

Sarah opened the side door, and Alex and the two women spilled out. Alex climbed into the cargo area of the van and grabbed two of the forty-pound bags. She handed one to each woman, who lifted it as if it were a jug of milk. Sarah was next in line, and Jill brought up the rear. Alex plucked two more bags off the floor and handed one to each of them. Jill didn't expect the searing pain that shot from her ribs all the way to her shoulder blade. The pain caused her to gasp and drop the salt to the sidewalk. Alex leapt from the van, and Sarah dropped her salt and put her hand supportively on Jill's back.

"Are you okay?" Alex asked, placing her hand on Jill's back as well.

"Yes." There was no conviction in Jill's voice. The pain seared down her back, but she reached down to pick up the salt again. This time she braced for the agony that she knew would come.

"Whoa, you're not going to carry that." Alex stopped her and gently rubbed her back.

"We can get it," Sarah added. "What did you do to yourself?"

"I'm so clumsy. I fell down the stairs last week," Jill lied. "I didn't realize I was still sore until I picked up the bag. I don't want you guys doing all my work. Let me help."

"It's not gonna happen." Alex picked up both bags and started toward the apartment complex. Sarah followed Alex's lead and guided the empty-handed Jill toward the front door.

Chapter Three

I can't thank you enough. You and your friends are lifesavers," Jill held her mug in both hands as she sipped her coffee. "Sarah is such a sweetie. How long have you been friends?"

"I'm so not telling her you said that. She's arrogant enough." Alex shook her head and smiled. "We met our freshman year in college." Alex squinted and looked toward the ceiling as she did the math in her head. "Means we've been friends for fifteen years. Damn, that makes me feel old."

"How did you meet?" Jill blew on her coffee before taking another sip.

"Do you really want to hear all the boring details?" Alex smiled as she remembered the day.

"Every last one."

"You asked for it," Alex said and launched into the story.

She earned a full academic scholarship to the University of Michigan and was thrilled to be leaving her small-town life far behind. The campus housed twice as many people than lived in her entire hometown, so it didn't take long for her to become overwhelmed. Many times, she wondered if she had made the right decision, but a free education wasn't something to pass up. Besides, she was trapped, since she didn't want to, or for that matter, couldn't return home. Despite Jill's questions, Alex danced around the issue of her family and continued her story.

The first semester was pure hell. Alex's room assignment was with "Buffy" and "Muffy" or at least that's what she called them. Fifteen years later, for the life of her, she couldn't remember their actual names. They were typical sorority girls, whereas Alex certainly was not. They were never mean or unkind, but they looked at her most of the time as if she were an alien. The feeling was mutual. Most everyone on the floor was cut from the same cloth, so she spent most of her time in the library. This resulted in her making excellent grades, but unfortunately, there was nobody to share her success with.

At first, she resigned herself to her fate, figuring she would study hard, get through college, and then her real life would begin. She spent three long weeks alone, while Buffy and Muffy were off enjoying the holiday with their Mumsie and Daddy. It was the Friday before classes were to begin for second semester; the weather was unseasonably warm, so she decided to get outside and take a walk. She came upon a spirited game of four-on-four basketball, so she stopped to watch. Before long, she noticed that there was an extra player waiting to get into the action. She wasn't sure what possessed her, maybe it was the three weeks of near solitude, but she approached the stranger and asked if they needed another player. The stranger, as it turned out, was Sarah. She eyed the much larger Alex suspiciously, sizing her up. From that day on, Alex teased Sarah that her "little-man syndrome" almost ruined their friendship before it even started. The desire to get into the game won out, so Sarah accepted her offer.

The girls were highly competitive, but still a lot of fun. For the first time in months, Alex felt happy. The game was nearing its completion when Sarah drove the lane. Alex stood poised her arms raised high, her five-foot, nine-inch height dwarfing Sarah. She went to move her hand to block Sarah's shot and was stunned when Sarah lowered her shoulder and drove into Alex's gut. Despite her greater bulk, the impact caused Alex to give ground and lose her footing. Sprawled out on the court, she saw the basketball swish through the hoop. The other players scrambled, clearly expecting a confrontation after such a blatant foul. Never one to back down, Sarah stood over Alex, puffing up, as much as someone five-foot-two could muster. From the ground, Alex looked up at the little spitfire in front of her and surprised everyone when she grinned. "Nice shot," was all Alex said. Sarah extended a hand and helped Alex to her feet. From that moment on, they were friends.

"Oh God, the visuals. I would love to have seen your face when you realized she was going to level you." Jill laughed.

"All I remember thinking the moment before she hit me was, *oh no she's not*. Then bam, she did. It shocked me how hard she hit me. I swear I saw stars. I always tell her she steamrolled me the first time we met, and she's never stopped."

"Are you two a couple?" Jill asked.

"No. God no," Alex answered.

"I'm sorry. I didn't mean to offend you. I just thought…" Jill trailed off, fidgeting with her hair.

"No offense taken." Seeing Jill's discomfort, Alex didn't want her to think she was completely off base. "We are lesbians though, if that's what you're asking."

"I'm sorry. I don't know what's gotten into me. I don't normally ask people such personal questions." Jill's face reddened to match her already crimson neck.

Jill looked down at the napkin she was fidgeting with and tore it into strips. Her shoulders rounded, and Alex could almost see her retreating into herself. Alex broke the silence. "I'm probably stepping way over my bounds, but can I tell you what I think?"

"Go ahead." Jill looked up briefly but shifted her eyes back to her hand holding the napkin.

"I don't think you feel comfortable with too many people." Jill nodded and Alex continued. "But unless I'm delusional, I believe you're comfortable with me."

"You're not delusional. It just seems weird." Jill smiled and looked into Alex's eyes. "We just met, but when we talk, it seems so easy. And you're right. I'm not comfortable with many people."

"It's just my charm and personality."

"That must be it." Jill laughed. The waitress stopped at their table and refilled Jill's cup. After she left, Jill asked, "Did you ever think of dating Sarah?"

"Man, you are full of tough questions. Once I answer this one, it's your turn." Alex took a drink from her cup before answering. "I would be lying if I said neither of us ever thought about a possible relationship. There were times in the first couple of years that one or the other of us would be interested, but thankfully it was never at the same time."

"Why do you say it like that?"

"Sarah's my best friend and I love her dearly, but it never would have worked out. Luckily, Michelle saved us from crossing the line."

"Michelle?" Jill reached for her hair and unconsciously wove it between her fingers.

"Is talking about all this lesbian stuff making you uneasy?"

"No, of course not." Jill gathered up the strips of napkin, wadded them into a ball, and threw them onto her saucer. "So, tell me about Michelle."

Alex had spent a lifetime gauging people's reactions to her being a lesbian, but she was having trouble reading Jill. She wasn't getting the usual sense that Alex being gay was unnerving her, but there was something that seemed to be bothering Jill. Alex was so lost in her thoughts that she realized she'd forgotten the question. "I'm sorry, could you ask me that again?"

"I asked you about Michelle," Jill replied.

"Ah, Michelle. She is probably the kindest, most generous person I know. She's an incredible woman."

"How long have you been together?" Jill reached for her hair and spun it, while she waited for Alex's response.

"No! No, Michelle and I aren't a couple," Alex practically shouted. Alex was embarrassed by her overreaction. *Why did it matter if Jill thought she was in a relationship with Michelle?* "She's Sarah's partner, has been since our junior year in college."

Jill let out her breath. *Did Jill just sigh in relief?* Alex chastised herself for trying to read more into Jill's breathing than was warranted. Jill smiled. "After that reaction, I think I need to hear this story."

"Okay, but this is the last one. It's your turn next. I met Michelle at a party and asked her out. After I picked Michelle up, I realized I'd forgotten my wallet, so we stopped by the apartment I was sharing with Sarah."

"I'm thinking this is not going to end well for you."

Alex pretended to scowl before continuing. "Sarah was there with her date having a beer, so they asked us to join them. Now keep in mind, that afternoon Sarah was adamant that I stay away from the apartment because she was planning on getting lucky. I figured I would just slip in and get my wallet."

"Oh God, you didn't interrupt something, did you?"

"No, thankfully," Alex answered. "But it did surprise me when Sarah invited us to have a beer. Surprised me even more when she suggested that all four of us go out."

"How did her date react?

"I think it surprised her more than anyone." Alex laughed. "I'm pretty sure she was thinking they were destined to end up in bed that night. But instead, we ended up closing down the clubs. We spent the whole evening laughing and dancing, but in hindsight, I should have noticed that Michelle spent more time dancing with Sarah than she did me."

"What about Sarah's date?"

"She was actually being pretty cool, until we drove home. I think she still thought she would end up spending the night with Sarah. But as soon as we got in the car, Sarah said we should drop her date off first because her apartment was the closest."

"Ouch, seriously?"

"Yep, seriously. Sarah was clueless." Alex shook her head as she remembered. "From the moment she met Michelle, I don't think anyone else existed. She certainly didn't notice her date."

"But Michelle was your date, so how did that work out?"

"It didn't take her long; in fact, it was when we were driving back to our apartment after dropping Michelle off. In typical Sarah fashion, she jumped right to the point and said, 'Michelle is a knockout. I think I just might be in love. Can I ask her out?'"

"No!" Jill bit her lip.

"Go ahead, laugh; everyone else does."

"That's brutal."

"And the rest, as they say, is history." Alex laughed along with Jill.

"You poor thing," Jill patted Alex's hand. "It was pretty big of you to say yes."

"I knew from the beginning. The chemistry just oozed off them. Sarah couldn't have stayed away from Michelle. She would have tried for me, but in the end, she would have failed, and it would have ruined our friendship. Wait until you meet Michelle, then you'll understand. They still have this insane chemistry thirteen years later."

Jill started to ask another question, but Alex held up her hand. "Enough of my stories, it's my turn to ask the questions. How old are the girls?"

"Jenna just turned eight and Trina is four." Alex liked how Jill smiled and the warmth that radiated from her eyes at the mention of the girls.

"So, you've been married for quite a while." Alex didn't want to hear about Jill's marriage, but figured it was only polite to inquire.

"Yes." Jill didn't elaborate.

"What does he do for a living?" Alex tried to think of the most benign questions she could, not wanting to think about Jill's husband.

"He's in sales."

"Where did you meet?"

"Choices. I was working part time as a weekend receptionist at the drug and alcohol center. Unfortunately, I needed a supplement to my full-time job to meet the bills."

"He was a patient?" Alex tried to hide her surprise.

"No, his sister was."

Alex studied Jill's face but asked no further questions. She hoped Jill would elaborate on her own, but she didn't. The withdrawn look was back on Jill's face, and her eyes were distant. Her answers were robotic and monosyllabic. Alex struggled with where to go next with the conversation, not wanting to lose the connection she felt earlier.

Alex reached out and touched Jill's arm, which seemed to bring some life back into her eyes. "No more questions, just tell me anything."

"Anything? How about I tell you about the time I decided to take my dad's car for a spin, when I was five?"

"I'm intrigued."

When Jill told stories about her childhood, she was animated and had Alex laughing so hard her stomach hurt. Jill's eyes danced, especially when she spoke of her dad.

"Your childhood sounds amazing."

"There was always plenty of laughter and love in our house." Jill smiled, but she seemed far off.

"How fortunate for your husband and children." Alex was trying unsuccessfully not to be envious of him.

"My dad would have loved you. They both would have, but him especially. You have the same playfulness that he did," Jill said, not commenting on

Alex's earlier statement. "He would have been right there rolling around in the leaves with us."

"That explains it."

"Explains what?"

"I was afraid you were embarrassed by our juvenile behavior."

"Are you kidding? My dad taught me to never lose my childlike wonder. He complained that too many adults had sticks lodged up their butts. Mom was always swatting him because he'd go up behind people and pretend he was trying to find the stick."

"I'm liking him more and more."

"What about your family?"

"Not much to tell." Alex wanted to change the subject, but she didn't want Jill to think she was rude. "My family is nothing like yours was; we were never really very close." Before Jill could ask another question, Alex waved the waitress over.

"What can I do for you?" the waitress asked, smiling at Alex.

"I think we should splurge today. Can we get a look at your dessert menu?"

"Sweetie, you came to the right place for dessert." She pulled a thick menu from her apron and set it in the center of the table. "I'll give you a couple minutes to look this over."

The previous conversation was forgotten while they pored over the menu, finally settling on sharing a double chocolate brownie delight.

The next two hours flew past. They shared stories, talked about current events, and got embroiled in another game of television trivia. The contest was closer this time, but Jill eventually prevailed.

"One of these days I'll get you," Alex said in defeat.

"I'm up for the challenge." Jill looked at her watch. "Unfortunately, I really need to get home. It's after four o'clock, and I told Mrs. Harrison that I would try to get the girls by 4:30."

"I don't want to leave the next time to chance, so can I get your phone number?" Alex asked. She was puzzled when she thought she registered fear in Jill's eyes.

Jill quickly recovered and responded, "I'm hard to reach. I haven't caught up with the times and gotten a cell phone, and Steve uses the phone a lot for business. Why don't you give me your number? It would be easier."

Alex asked the server for a pen and wrote her number on a napkin. Alex watched Jill's eyes scan the number several times.

"Afraid you might lose it?"

"Yeah," Jill stammered. "The girls are constantly picking stuff up and taking it to their rooms. So, I just memorize numbers and throw them away." The explanation seemed strange to Alex, but she didn't press.

They made their way to the door and stood to the side out of the way of the other customers. Alex was ill at ease, not sure how to end their time together. Jill fidgeted with her hair, and Alex shuffled from foot to foot. Their small talk soon tapered off, and they stood looking at one another.

Surprisingly, Jill spoke first. "Alex, I had an amazing time today. Talking to you is so easy. I can't remember the last time I laughed this much. I hope we can do it again soon."

"I'd like that." Alex smiled. She didn't want the

time to end, but she knew it had to. "I guess we have to say goodbye, huh?"

"I'm afraid so." Like the time in the park, Jill initiated the hug. Alex felt her heart flutter when she drew Jill against her. When she released Jill, she thought she saw tears in her eyes, but decided it must just have been the way the light was reflecting off them.

꧁꧂

Alex knocked on Sarah's door, but didn't wait for an answer before pushing in. Sarah was sitting at her desk, hunched over her computer, frowning at the spreadsheet in front of her. Her shoulder-length blonde hair was messed up, a look Alex had seen many times before. Whenever Sarah worked on a difficult problem, she constantly ran her hand through her mop of hair. Her naturally curly hair usually had an untamed look anyway, but now it looked as if she didn't own a brush.

"Man, you look rough," Alex teased.

"I've been staring at this damned screen for over half an hour, and I still can't find the error. For once, your visit is a welcome relief."

"Gee, thanks, you're always so complimentary."

"That's what friends are for."

"So?" Alex said.

"So…What?"

"You know what. What do you think of her?"

Sarah seemed to be measuring her words carefully, which was highly unusual for her. "I'm a little puzzled because she's not exactly what I expected. The way you have been mooning about her, I was expecting Heidi Klum."

"What's that supposed to mean?" Alex looked

down at Sarah, the wrinkle in her forehead deepening.

"Sit down; you're making me nervous."

"Sorry." Alex pulled up a chair and sat.

"She's just different than the women you usually choose. That's not all bad, looking at your track record. Maybe a change of pace is a good thing."

"How is she so different?"

"Are you serious?" Alex looked at her, perplexed, so Sarah continued. "Nothing against Jill, but you always go for flashy women. She's just a little...a little plain. Well, except for her body, nothing plain about that." Another blank look crossed Alex's face. "Oh God, don't tell me you didn't notice her body."

"Well, no, not really," Alex answered. Her answer was only partially true. She hadn't paid much attention to what Jill's body looked like, but she did know how it felt in her arms. Thinking about it brought a goofy smile to Alex's face. She wanted to hide it before Sarah noticed, so she continued. "Does that mean I'm getting old? I honestly couldn't tell you if she has big boobs or small ones."

"Trust me, they're nice," Sarah said. Alex reached across the desk and playfully slapped her.

"Hey, keep your eyes to yourself, or I'm telling Michelle."

Sarah rolled her eyes and ignored Alex's threat. "So, if you haven't noticed her boobs, what in the world are you looking at?"

Alex looked toward the ceiling and smiled, seeing Jill in her mind. "The only thing I've seen since the first time I met her. Her eyes."

"Oh God, this is not good. You are so far gone. Hello, have you forgotten? Married. Children. Ring a bell?"

"I know. You probably think I've lost my mind. Hell, I think I've lost my mind."

"I don't want to be a downer, but what happens when she finds out you're gay?"

"That's one thing I don't have to worry about. She already knows." Alex tried to exude more confidence than she felt.

"You told her?" The surprise registered on Sarah's face.

"Well, kind of. She asked me,"

"Just like that, she asked if you were gay?"

"No, actually, she asked if we were a couple."

"Oh God, I would have loved to have seen your face." Sarah laughed and put her hand on her head. "When do you see her next?"

"I don't know."

"Well, are you going to call her and ask her out?" Sarah back-peddled. "Well, I guess you don't ask a married woman out. I mean are you going to ask her to meet up again?"

"I can't."

"Spill."

"She didn't give me her number, but she took mine."

"Let me get this straight, she found out you were gay, then she wouldn't give you her phone number."

"It's not like that. She doesn't have a cell phone and she's hard to get in touch with."

"You know, it would be best if she didn't call."

"I know," Alex admitted. She also knew it wasn't what she hoped for.

Chapter Four

Alex stuck her head in Sarah's office. "I'm going to get a bite to eat."

Seeing the look on Alex's face, Sarah said, "With Jill?"

"Yep." Alex's smile grew bigger.

"You've been seeing quite a bit of her." Sarah said it as a statement, not a question.

"Yep."

"It's Friday, so it's her laundry day?"

"Yep."

"Which means a two-hour lunch at the laundromat with her?" Sarah was already accustomed to Alex's patterns.

"Yep."

"You're on a dangerous path."

"Yep."

"But you are too stupid to care right now."

"Yep."

"And you will expect me and Michelle to pick up the pieces when you fall."

"Yep."

"Well, I know a way to wipe that goofy grin off your face. Don't forget you promised Michelle that you would go to Denise's party with us tomorrow night."

"Yep," Alex answered, the smile never leaving

her face.

"Oh God, you are in trouble if you are still smiling after that."

"Yep."

Sarah laughed. "Get the hell out of here before you really start to get on my nerves."

"Yep," Alex answered, her smile bigger than ever.

☙ ❧ ☙ ❧

Alex popped the last soggy bite of sandwich into her mouth. Good thing they hadn't brought hot food, or it would have been cold long ago. Soggy food she could deal with.

"I think we've learned a valuable lesson. We need to order cold food when we go out to eat together because we talk too much for hot food," Jill said, as if reading her mind. Jill was dressed in a tattered sweat suit, but in Alex's eyes, the outfit was as good as any Vera Wang or Versace. Jill's well-worn attire, in many ways, added to her appeal. It was unpretentious and gave Jill a natural, girl-next-door look.

"You don't mind the soggy bread?" Alex asked.

"It's not my favorite, but I'm not here for the food." Jill's answer held a hint of flirtation.

Alex knew she should avoid the bait but couldn't resist. "Why are you here then?"

"The ambiance," Jill said, with a devious smile.

Alex laughed and looked around at the bustle of the laundromat. There were several newspapers scattered haphazardly on the table, joined by a collection of mismatched socks, and the surface was so grimy it appeared brown, which Alex suspected was once white. She had all but tuned out the children running around screaming, while their mothers watched the loud soap opera displayed on mounted televisions in every corner.

"And here I thought it was the company."

"Well, that's not so bad either." Jill smirked at Alex. Those were the looks that melted Alex and made her want to spend more time with Jill. In those moments, all Jill's guardedness was gone, which allowed their genuine connection to thrive.

Jill glanced at her watch, which Alex had grown accustomed to. She'd stopped taking it as an indication of Jill wanting to end their time together.

"You're not going to be able to afford such lavish lunches if I keep taking you away from your job."

Alex glanced up at the clock on the wall that read seven o'clock, the same time it registered all the time. "What time is it, anyway?"

"Nearly two-thirty. Are you going to be in trouble at work?"

"No, no problem. I'll work late tonight." Alex gathered up the remnants from her lunch and stuffed them into the bag they'd pushed off to the corner of the table.

"It's Friday night, no big plans?" Jill followed Alex's lead and tidied the table in front of her.

"Not tonight, those are for tomorrow night." Alex grimaced. She unconsciously held the bag out for Jill, so she could discard her garbage.

"For someone with big plans, you don't look too thrilled." Jill threw the wad into the bag, and then began picking up the tiny crumbs that remained on the table. Alex wanted to laugh. The tables around them were covered in crumbs – not just crumbs, but whole chips and sticky chocolate smeared on the surface, but the area in front of Jill was now pristine.

"Sarah and Michelle are dragging me to some stupid party. I'd much rather curl up with a good book, but Michelle caught me in one of my weaker moments. So, it's too late to back down now." Alex crumpled up the bag and took it to the nearby garbage can, careful to avoid the children that were running through the aisles.

"A party sounds like fun," Jill said when Alex returned to the table.

"It wouldn't be so bad, but Michelle, the matchmaker, is setting me up on a blind date; I hate blind dates," Alex whined. She felt a shift in Jill, but it wasn't her normal guardedness. "What's that look for?" Alex asked.

"Oh, nothing." Jill twirled her hair around her finger. When Alex looked at her suspiciously, she continued. "I'm just surprised none of the blind dates have worked out."

"And why is that?" Alex said a little louder than she intended in order to be heard over the washing machine clanging nearby. She didn't think commercial washers went out of balance, but this one certainly seemed to be. "Is that yours?" Alex nodded her head in the direction of the noise.

"Nope, I never use that one; she's temperamental. Anyway, back to your blind dates."

"Damn, I thought you'd forget." The washing machine suddenly went still, and Alex glowered at it.

"Obviously, the washing machine is interested in your dating too." Jill laughed. "Seriously, you're just so, well, so sweet. I figured someone would have snatched you up."

"I should hire you as my publicist, and then

maybe I wouldn't be single." Alex rubbed her chin. "Let's just say I've made a career out of bad choices."

"Meaning?"

"I've always said that I've only made one good choice when it comes to women, and then Sarah snatched her from me." As if on cue, the washing machine lurched twice before going quiet. "See, the washing machine even thinks I'm pathetic. The sad thing is, unfortunately, it's true."

"No, you've just had a string of bad luck, but here comes lucky thirteen. This might be your year."

"Maybe so." She couldn't help smile at the irony; what if the good woman she met this time happens to be straight? Alex quickly lifted her eyes to the sky and thought, *fate, you don't like me much, do you*?

"So, tell me about your bad choices." Jill looked down at the table and picked up a crumb that Alex couldn't see.

"Oh no, that's a story for another day or another ten days. I want you to leave here today still thinking well of me. Once you hear what a pathetic mess my love life has been, your opinion of me is sure to go downhill."

"I don't think you have anything to worry about." Jill gave Alex's hand a reassuring squeeze.

"Besides, I'm talking too much. I want to hear more of your stories."

Jill fiddled with her hair only a couple times as they talked; Alex hoped that was a sign that she was becoming more comfortable. When Alex asked questions, she noticed Jill said little about her personal life, at least the present, and next to nothing about her husband, which was fine by Alex. The only thing she seemed willing to talk about were the girls. Her face glowed when she spoke of them. *Maybe she's not happy in her marriage*, Alex thought hopefully and then felt guilty. For starters, she wanted nothing less than complete happiness for Jill. Secondly, even if she were unhappy with her husband, she was still a straight woman.

⊱⊰⊱⊰

Jill refused Alex's offer to help take her laundry home, as she always did, fearful that Steve might get home early from work. He sometimes did on Fridays, but he never let her know ahead of time. He liked to keep her off balance. She felt tense Friday evening, knowing she had more than forty-eight hours of being constantly on guard. By Monday, she was exhausted, and her nerves were raw. She quickly pushed him from her mind, preferring to think of the afternoon she spent with Alex.

She needed to be careful when she got home. Last night, she caught Steve eying her suspiciously and realized she was too buoyant for him not to notice. She covered it by telling him how much fun she had with the girls, baking cookies that afternoon. This seemed to satisfy him, but she knew she needed to watch herself in the future.

Her mind wandered to the conversation about Alex's blind date. She couldn't deny the topic upset her. *Why?* she wondered. She struggled for an explanation and finally settled on one that eased her mind. She was simply concerned about her time with Alex. If Alex started dating, she would have less time for her friendship with Jill, if she had any time for her at all. Jill would be shut out while the new relationship occupied nearly all of Alex's waking moments. It was comforting finally to have a friend. She had gone so many years alone. The thought of losing the budding friendship terrified her.

Jill refused to think about any of her other feelings. Like how often she saw Alex's chiseled face and penetrating eyes in her mind. How much she enjoyed watching the self-confident way Alex carried her muscular body. Most disturbing of all was how much she longed to be in Alex's arms, whenever she felt scared or alone. These concerns were thoughts for another day. For now, she would savor the happiness that hadn't been a part of her life for so long. It didn't matter that Alex was a woman or a lesbian, for that matter. The only thing that counted to Jill was that Alex made her feel special and cared for. Before she arrived home, she was through with doubts and placed them in the far corner of her mind.

Chapter Five

B y the way, I forgot to tell you, you're inviting us up for a nightcap," Michelle said, when she pulled to a stop in front of the gym.

"I was afraid you were going to say that." Alex shook her head and looked at Sarah. "I thought I was going to make a clean getaway."

"Right! With Michelle around, you really believed that?"

"Would you be interested in a nightcap?" Alex said in her best formal voice.

"I thought you'd never ask," Michelle shot back.

Michelle and Sarah held hands as they followed Alex. Though Sarah claimed to be half an inch taller, standing side by side Michelle had at least an inch on her. Despite being similar in stature, they were polar opposites when it came to coloring. Sarah's hair was blonde, whereas Michelle's hair was so dark it appeared almost black. Without a tan, Sarah's skin was naturally pale, while Michelle's olive skin looked tanned year-round. Sarah had ice blue eyes, while Michelle's eyes were so dark it was difficult to see where her irises began and her pupils ended.

Alex opened the side door and made her way up the steep steps. She preferred to use the gym entrance to get to her apartment, but at night it was simpler to use this entrance. The hall showed all the character old buildings shared, which was a stark contrast to the ultra-modern look inside her apartment. She'd completed most of the work herself, in her spare time. She'd done an incredible job of hiding, or at least masking, the architectural design and materials that gave away the age of the building. The space age look was consistent throughout the apartment, culminating in a futuristic kitchen done in black and stainless steel. Alex loved the space she created for herself and sought refuge here, whenever the world became too difficult for her to handle.

"Beer or wine?" she asked her guests.

"Do you have any more of that merlot?" Michelle asked, sitting down on the plush white loveseat. Sarah plopped down beside her and propped her feet on the coffee table.

"Wine doesn't bode well for me, does it?"

"Whatever do you mean?" Michelle flashed Alex a cheesy smile.

"This isn't a ten-minute drink, and then me-shoving-you-out-the-door kinda moment, is it?" Alex didn't wait for a response because she already knew the answer. She pushed through the kitchen door that swung both ways. Alex opened a bottle of merlot, poured her friends a glass, and twisted the cap off a beer for herself.

She knew it was only a matter of time before Michelle quizzed her about Jill, since Sarah shared everything with Michelle. She knew her behavior tonight only served to hasten the interrogation. There was nothing wrong with her blind date, but Alex had absolutely no interest. This hadn't gone unnoticed by Michelle or her date, for that matter. Alex had done a lousy job of pretending to have a good time.

Everything the woman said or did, she compared to Jill. Every mannerism or gesture measured against Jill. Sarah and Michelle would argue that her date was hands down more attractive than Jill, but they didn't know what to look for. Her pale blue eyes were lifeless compared to Jill's lively brown eyes.

"Here you are." She handed her friends their drinks. She sat down in her favorite recliner and pulled the lever for the foot rest. She stretched out and got comfortable. "Let the inquisition begin."

"What the hell are you trying to do to yourself? Do you want to fuck up your life?" Michelle asked.

"Do you think you could be a little more direct? I'm afraid I missed your point since you were so subtle." Alex took a long drag from her beer and tried to look pensive.

"Seriously, what's going on with you? You have us worried," Michelle said, softening her approach.

"I have myself worried. I wish I could get you guys to understand."

"Try." Michelle ran her finger along the rim of her wine glass.

Alex took another long pull from her beer and sighed. "I'll start with the obvious. I haven't had much success on the relationship front, as you guys well know. I pick the wrong women every time. How often have you guys had to pick up the pieces? It's been nearly three years since Kristen, and we all know how that ended. I made a vow after that, never again. I seem to do the best with casual dating, and, for the most part, it's worked for me."

"I see the big 'but' coming," Michelle said to Sarah.

"But." Alex smiled. "I've been doing some soul

searching, and I don't like what I see." Alex held out her hand with her palm down and moved it slowly, as if she were running it over a flat surface. "I'm always even keeled, no ups and no downs, just a flat line. Do you know what a flat line means?" Alex tilted her head back, taking in more of the cold beer before continuing. "It means you're dead and most of the time that's how I feel inside, dead. When was the last time you guys saw me really feel anything, good or bad?"

Sarah and Michelle looked at each other, as if willing the other to respond.

"That's okay; it doesn't require an answer. I know what the answer is, and I don't like it." Alex lifted her beer to her lips again, nearly finishing it. "I'm numb and have been for years. Sure, I laugh and joke around and even have a good time, but nothing ever touches my heart, until recently."

"But—" Michelle started to say.

Alex held up her hand and continued. "I know all the buts. I do. For right now, I don't care. The first day I met Jill, I don't even remember what we were talking about, but I looked in her eyes and I felt something. Do you want to hear something pathetic? I didn't even know what the hell it was. I felt my chest suddenly clench, and my first thought was I'd overdone it in the gym. Do you get that? It's been so long since I've truly felt something that I didn't even recognize what it was. It was as if my heart hadn't beat for years; then all of a sudden, a faint little beat happens, then another and another. And I have to tell you, it felt good."

Tears welled in Michelle's eyes. "Oh, Alex. Why didn't you tell us?"

"Because until that moment, I didn't know." Alex's eyes were full of sadness. "I would have told you if I'd known myself. After what happened with Kristen, a switch flipped, and I stopped feeling anything."

She smiled sadly at her friends. "What I didn't realize was once you stop feeling the bad stuff, you don't feel any of the good things either." Alex stopped and finished her beer. She put her hand over her heart and patted her chest a couple of times. "All of a sudden I feel something in here. My chest feels like it's expanding and opening up, and I like it. Am I making any sense? Do you guys understand?"

"I think so," Sarah answered for the couple. She turned to Michelle, who nodded.

"I know you're worried about me and I know I may be setting myself up for a huge heartbreak, but it beats the alternative, which is feeling nothing. I look in her eyes, and I feel something. I see her smile, and I feel something. I hear her voice, and I feel something. I make her laugh, and I feel everything." Alex had a far-off smile, obviously seeing Jill as she spoke. "Once I get used to feeling again, I hope I can put our friendship into perspective. Then maybe I can put my new found ability to feel to good use, preferably with a lesbian." Alex twirled the empty bottle in her hand, peeking into the bottle to ensure there was nothing left. "I don't need to hear all the cautions or the pitfalls; I know them already. I just need you guys to support me and try to understand."

"Always," Michelle said. She got up, went into the kitchen, and returned with another beer. "I think you could use this." She handed it to Alex.

"We've got your back," Sarah added. Michelle sat back down, and Sarah snuggled against her side.

"I know. I've never doubted you guys, and I never will. I'm going to ask you for something that is going to be very hard for you. Especially you, Michelle." Alex winked at Sarah.

"I don't like hard," Michelle whined. "But go ahead and give it to me."

"Please don't try to protect me. Don't try to cushion me from a fall. The only way you keep me safe is to clip my wings and not let me fly at all. But I want to fly, and Jill makes that happen. I'm going in with eyes wide open. I just want to feel again."

"Looks like she's ready to leave the nest," Michelle said to Sarah, fluttering her hand over chest, acting as if she were trying to stop from crying.

"Does that mean we're gonna suffer empty nest syndrome?" Sarah asked, ignoring Alex.

"I'm afraid so, honey," Michelle joked. "But don't worry. They always come back when they need something."

"Okay, enough you two. I'm breaking out the cards. You've crawled around inside my head enough for tonight."

"I have one more thing to say before you change the subject."

"Of course you do." Alex looked toward Sarah.

"Don't look at me. You know she always gets the last word. How do you think we've stayed together for so long?"

Ignoring Sarah, Michelle said, "I need to meet this woman."

Alex groaned. "How did I not see that one coming?"

❧ ❧ ❧ ❧

Jill lay on the couch, only half watching the television. She'd been tossing and turning, unable to sleep, so she finally gave up and went into the living room. All evening, her thoughts kept returning to Alex, wondering how the blind date was going. Try as she might to be happy for Alex, she was fighting a losing battle. Repeatedly, she tried to picture what the woman looked like but dismissed each image as not right. Then she would try to imagine Alex on the date. She would see the interactions but soon replace the images with scenes from the time she spent with Alex. She gave up worrying about what her thoughts signified, nestled down further on the couch, and let herself relive the time she spent with Alex.

Chapter Six

Sarah and Alex were going over the latest financial statement when Alex's phone vibrated. *Would Jill be calling this soon on a Monday morning?* Not wanting to take the chance, she pulled it from her belt clip.

"Hey Jill," she said, the smile evident in her voice.

Sarah looked at her and rolled her eyes. "Get out of here; I have work to do." Sarah smiled. "And tell Jill hi for me," she added loud enough for Jill to hear. In a softer voice, she said, "And give her a big hug and kiss for me too."

"Shut up," Alex said to Sarah.

"Why can't she say hi to me?" Jill asked defensively.

"No, that's not what I was telling her to shut up about." Alex shot Sarah a dirty look. Sarah laughed and pretended to flip through the papers in her inbox.

"I didn't hear her say anything else."

"She was just being a smartass. Just ignore her; that's what I plan on doing." Alex sneered at Sarah before she turned away. "We'll go into my office where it is more pleasant." Alex went to the door and heard Sarah laugh before she slammed the door in mock outrage. Alex gave Jill a narrative of the sights and sounds and even some of the smells, as she walked down the hall to her office. "Okay, we're safe in my office now." She plopped down in her well-worn desk chair and put her feet on her desk.

"Were you guys working on something important? I didn't mean to disturb you."

"Nothing that we can't do later."

"Well, in that case, how did it go?" Jill said in a singsong voice.

Alex searched her mind, trying to remember if she'd forgotten something important. Jill normally didn't call this early on a Monday, and definitely didn't sound so exceptionally perky. Not coming up with an answer, Alex asked, "How did what go?"

"Saturday?" Jill waited for an answer, and when Alex didn't respond, she added, "The blind date."

"Oh, that. I forgot all about it." If only Jill knew how true this was. Since Saturday night, there was only one woman Alex thought about.

"No love connection?"

"I'm pretty sure there wasn't even a like connection," Alex joked. "Michelle says I'm an awful date, and she doesn't know why she keeps trying to fix me up."

"I can't imagine you being anything but sweet and charming."

"Maybe next time she should set me up with you. You appreciate my delightful personality." Alex couldn't believe the words slipped from her mouth before she could censor them. She could feel her face redden; she was thankful they weren't face to face.

"You're a fabulous date. Michelle took you out of your element by dragging you to some boring party. I'm sure your date would have seen you in a much better light if you took her to a swank laundromat."

Alex was glad that Jill seemed not to have

noticed her faux paus. She was also happy that Jill sounded more like herself, and had dropped the strange cheerfulness. Alex didn't have time to dwell on it because their banter intensified. They began creating a more and more outlandish blind date scenario as they talked. Alex was laughing so hard that tears streamed down her cheeks, and at one point Jill snorted. This sent the pair into another round of laughter. Eventually, they switched topics and fell into an easy conversation, which seemed to happen every time they talked.

Nearly half an hour later, Jill said, "I have to get Trina ready to go downtown for her school placement tests."

"Remember, Wednesday we're having lunch with Sarah and Michelle."

"I'm looking forward to it."

≈≈≈≈

Alex was just about to hang up the phone when she heard someone pick up.

"Hello," the strange voice said.

"Hi, may I speak to Jill?"

"I'm sorry. I'm afraid you have the wrong number," the elderly voice said.

Alex looked at her phone. *How could that be?* It was the same number Jill always called from. There was no chance she dialed wrong since the number was stored in her phone.

"Um…I'm sorry to have bothered you." Alex started to hang up.

"Wait, you must be Alex."

"Yes." Alex was surprised that the woman knew

her name.

"I'm Alice Harrison, Jill's neighbor. She's told me so much about you. She's always so happy after she talks to you. The dear deserves a little happiness in her life. You know what I mean?"

Alex was speechless, unsure what to say, but it didn't seem to matter to Mrs. Harrison, who continued talking for several minutes about how wonderful Jill and the girls were. Alex noticed that Mrs. Harrison said nothing about Jill's husband, which coincided with the way Jill handled him, as well. Mrs. Harrison offered to check if Jill was next door, but Alex assured her it wasn't necessary.

Alex was frowning at her phone when Sarah walked in.

"Did it pee on the carpet?" Sarah asked.

"Huh?"

"Your phone. The way you're looking at it, I thought maybe it did something wrong."

Alex laughed. "No. Something weird just happened. I tried to call Jill to check and see if she likes Thai food, since I know that's where Michelle really wants to go. You know how busy the place gets, so I figured I should make reservations. When I called Jill, this old lady answered. It turned out to be her neighbor. But for some reason, whenever Jill calls, she's been calling from there."

"Hm, that's odd," Sarah said. Alex thought she was going to say more, but she remained silent.

"What aren't you saying?"

"Nothing." Sarah deliberately backed toward the door. "I need to make a couple calls before lunch." She turned and abruptly left.

Alex stared at the spot Sarah vacated. *What the*

hell was that about? First, Mrs. Harrison and now Sarah's bizarre behavior. Alex was looking forward to their lunch, so she pushed the thoughts from her head.

࿐ ࿐ ࿐ ࿐

Jill's stomach was in knots when she left her apartment. She was both excited and apprehensive. Alex had been so sweet when she invited her to lunch with her friends. Alex seemed afraid she might say no and part of her wanted to. She was afraid she wouldn't know what to say, and Alex's friends would hate her. The other part of her was excited to be out to lunch with friends like a regular person.

She tried styling her hair differently the last couple of days, attempting to make it look a little less stringy. Steve didn't allow her to go anywhere to get her hair done or even get it cut for that matter. She trimmed it herself with her sewing scissors. There had to be a way to give her hair more body, but she'd yet to figure it out. Despite her best efforts, she was disappointed in the results. She'd considered putting makeup on, but was afraid that somehow Steve would find out, and she wouldn't be able to explain why she wore makeup to the grocery store. She wore her one nice sweater, but figured she could explain wearing it because of the bitter cold.

By the time she arrived at the gym, her hands were numb from the cold and her face hurt. She should have asked Alex to pick her up, but she was embarrassed to admit she didn't have enough money for lunch and a cab. She looked at her watch and saw she was ten minutes early, but she certainly wasn't going to kill time outside in this weather. Besides, it would be nice to spend a little time alone with Alex before they met up with Sarah and Michelle. Alex would put her at ease and make her feel less self-conscious. Jill approached the woman sitting behind the reception desk and smiled.

"I'm here to see Alex," she said.

The woman smiled. "Sure, just a second." She picked up the phone. "Jill is here to see you." It wasn't lost on Jill that the receptionist used her name, even though she hadn't provided one. "She'll be right with you."

Alex was there almost immediately, a big smile lighting her face. Her face fell when she got closer to Jill. "Oh my God, did you walk here?"

"Well, yes," Jill stammered and reached for her hair.

"Jill, you look like you're freezing. Your face is bright red, and you're still wearing your thin jacket. Plus, you're not wearing gloves." Alex took Jill's hand and sandwiched it between hers. The warmth immediately soaked into her hands. "Give me the other one; this is unacceptable. We would have picked you up if I knew you weren't going to take a cab. I wanted you to see the gym, but we could have swung by after lunch." Alex continued to mutter as she moved in closer and rubbed Jill's hands.

Jill looked at Alex and started to laugh; the woman behind the desk laughed too.

"What?" Alex asked.

"I'm fine. You don't need to fuss over me." Jill looked around the lobby and noticed the couple who were leaving staring in their direction, as well as the three women who had just come in. "You're causing a scene in the middle of the lobby."

"Hey, Alex, how come none of us get such good personal service?" one of the women teased. "You've never rubbed all over me before."

Alex's face reddened, and she seemed to notice the other people in the room for the first time.

"Me neither," another one joined in. "Do we have to pay a special membership fee to get the works? Jane, can I get that application?" she said to the receptionist.

Everyone laughed. "Very funny," Alex said. "Come on, Jill. I'll show you my office, so we can get away from this crowd."

Alex, still holding Jill's hand, started to lead her away when one of the women called after them, "Hey, Alex, what kind of personal training do you do in your office? We want an application for that, too."

Alex kept walking, pretending not to hear them. Jill giggled. After they turned the corner, Alex gave Jill an embarrassed smile. "I'm sorry."

"No need to apologize. It's fun seeing the calm, cool, and collected Alex rattled." Jill smirked and squeezed Alex's hand. Jill was surprised they were still holding hands, and even more surprised that it seemed so natural. "I think those ladies were serious, Alex. I think they'd be happy to get a private session with you."

"What? No."

"You really didn't notice they were flirting, did you?" She searched Alex's face for any sign of false modesty and found none. Alex was oblivious to the women's flirtation; Jill found the innocence endearing.

"They were just screwing around. They didn't mean anything by it."

Jill responded with a smile. She tried to ignore the sense of satisfaction she felt as she walked down the hall with Alex.

Alex opened her office door and gestured for Jill to enter. Jill walked into the brightly lit office, taking in the décor. It was a picture of contrasts. One side was starkly professional, almost cold. The desk, furniture, and equipment were black or silver. Everything on the desk was neatly arranged, and the file folders were methodically stacked and sorted by color. On the other side of the room, there was an overstuffed couch and two cushy chairs, all bright blue. The well-worn furniture looked as if it got frequent use.

Alex took Jill's coat and gestured toward the inviting corner. She hung the coat in the closet and emerged carrying a fuzzy gray blanket. Alex wrapped the blanket around Jill's shoulders and steered her to the couch. Before sitting, Jill slipped off her shoes and took the blanket from her shoulders. She sat with her feet underneath her and pulled the blanket up to her neck.

Alex looked at the chairs and then back at the couch. Jill noticed her indecision, so she patted the space next to her. Alex sat down stiffly, leaving two feet between them. Jill threw some of the blanket over Alex and, in doing so, closed the gap. Jill shivered again from the draft she created when she let Alex under the blanket.

"You're still cold." Alex moved a little closer to Jill.

"Unfortunately, once chilled, it takes a long time to warm me back up." Jill shifted so their bodies touched. "You seem to be generating plenty of heat though, so I should be fine."

"I've always been hot-blooded." Alex remained sitting ramrod straight with her hands on her lap.

"Why so stiff?" Jill linked arms with Alex and felt Alex relax beside her. "Much better."

"You should have plenty of time to shake off the cold, since I had you come half an hour early. I knew you would be more comfortable if you had a chance to settle in before being bombarded by Sarah and Michelle."

"It's frightening how well you know me already."

"Is that a bad thing?"

"No, not at all. I'm just not used to it. It's a little scary," she answered honestly.

Jill was resting her head against Alex's shoulder, and they were deep in conversation when Alex's office door flew open. A small, dark-haired woman burst into the room and stopped short when she noticed the two sitting on the couch covered with a blanket. Her eyes widened momentarily when she took in the scene, but she quickly recovered. Jill immediately knew this must be Michelle.

"Knock much?"

"Just wanted to keep you on your toes," Michelle shot back. She walked to the couch and extended her hand. "Hi. You must be Jill. I'm Michelle."

"Nice to meet you." Jill took Michelle's hand, while unconsciously running her other hand over the blanket.

"This crazy woman walked six blocks in this weather, no hat, no scarf, and no gloves. She had to be thawed before we take her out in the cold again."

"Six blocks. It's below zero out there. What were you thinking?" Michelle looked at Jill with concern. She pulled keys out of her pocket and flipped them to

Alex. "Looks like you better bring the car around for us. We'll get to know each other while you're gone." Michelle looked at Jill and winked.

Ignoring Michelle, Alex turned to Jill and asked, "You warmed up now?"

"Yes, thank you."

"Okay then, your chariot will be outside in a couple minutes."

❧❧❧❧

Jill was having the time of her life. Sarah and Michelle immediately made her feel at ease. They told stories about Alex's past exploits, most of them embarrassing. Jill joined in and told them about the women who were propositioning Alex at the gym. Alex good-naturedly handled the ribbing and seemed happy that Jill was having a good time. At times, Jill felt self-conscious and struggled to maintain eye contact. As the meal went on, she got lost in the camaraderie and forgot her nervousness.

"Now that I have the historians here, I want to hear the real story of why you're still single," Jill said to Alex.

"Do you have about three days?" Michelle said.

"She's been trying to psychoanalyze me for years. I keep hoping she'll give up."

"Like that'll ever happen," Sarah said. "So, what do you want to know, Jill?"

"What about your last relationship?" Jill immediately regretted her question when she saw the fleeting look of pain cross Alex's face. "You don't have to if you don't want to. I shouldn't pry."

"You're not prying. I'll trust you with my ugly

secrets."

Jill felt the weight of Alex's words and felt guilty. Alex was entrusting her with personal information while Jill kept her life hidden from Alex.

"Trust me; it's all been ugly," Sarah piped in. "But Kristen was the ugliest of the ugly."

"What happened with Kristen?" Jill asked.

"I caught her in bed with one of the yoga instructors from the gym." Alex's tone was the same as if she'd said, "I had a ham sandwich for lunch."

Jill looked at her, searching for some kind of emotion, but found none. "I'm sorry." Jill didn't know what else to say.

"Those yoga instructors sure can bend," Alex joked.

"What did you do?" Jill felt bad for Alex and couldn't find the humor, despite the attempt at levity.

"I fired her."

"That's not what I meant."

"I know," Alex said softly.

❧ ❧ ❧ ❧

Jill listened intently, as Sarah and Michelle took over the story, detailing the rise and fall of Alex's relationship with Kristen. They'd been together for nearly three years, so initially they tried to mend the relationship. It was over within two months. It wasn't that Alex couldn't forgive her. Other than it being a blow to her ego, Alex didn't much care about the affair. Alex became painfully aware that her relationship with Kristen was superficial, just like all her previous relationships. They all followed the same pattern. They started with an irresistible sexual attraction but never developed into the type of relationship she craved. For a while, the sizzling sex would sustain the relationship, but without any emotional connection, it soon lost its appeal.

Alex fooled herself into believing they had a deeper connection; in hindsight, she knew it wasn't true. When she met Kristen, she was tired of the same relationship pattern and vowed it would be different. The only difference was Alex settled and denied how empty the relationship made her feel. Kristen was as superficial as they came. Her only concern was money, possessions, and social status. All their conversations centered on one of those three things, and if Alex tried to discuss something more, Kristen became bored and changed the subject back to her favorite topics. Michelle and Sarah hated her. They double dated twice, but it was so awkward that Alex never tried again. After Kristen, she swore off relationships and went through a period of sex with no attachments. When this proved unfulfilling, she gave up dating and preferred to spend time with her friends, occasionally accepting a blind date from Michelle.

"Would it be wrong to tell you that I'm shocked?" Jill said. Sarah burst out laughing, and Alex shot her a look. "Oh God, I didn't mean it that way. The person you guys have been describing isn't the Alex I've gotten to know. I'm confused."

"Trust me, honey, we all are." Michelle patted Jill's hand. "What she says she wants and what she finds are always two different things."

"What do you want?" Jill looked directly into Alex's eyes.

Alex looked down at her own hands. "Someone I can talk to and laugh with. I want to be able to share everything." Alex patted her chest a couple times and looked back at Jill. "I want someone I feel here first. I don't want someone I lust after, but someone who touches me much deeper."

"You'll find her, Alex. If you're the person you are with me, I can't imagine you not finding her." Jill saw the vulnerability in Alex's eyes and wanted to comfort her, but sensed it would make Alex uncomfortable. "I have to ask you, though. Do you act differently with women you're attracted to?"

Sarah choked on her drink, practically spitting it across the table. "Sorry, went down the wrong way," Sarah managed to croak.

"I don't know," was all Alex could muster. Jill gave her a look that said *cop-out*, so Alex continued. "Well, I haven't with you." Alex froze and Sarah and Michelle looked at her wide-eyed. Alex stammered on, "I do with Sarah and Michelle, too. I guess you could say I have it with my friends."

"There's your answer," Jill said. "You need to be friends first, and then the rest will develop later."

"I think you may be right. I keep develop-ing friendships with unavailable lesbians or straight women. I guess it's time to find some new friends."

The words stung Jill, but she tried unsuccessfully to hide her reaction. Alex must have seen it because she continued. "I didn't mean you. I'm thinking more along the lines of out with the old."

"Hey now," Sarah said, feigning outrage.

"Fine, I'll keep all three of you. I'll look for love some other time."

Jill felt relief wash over her but tried to ignore it. She refused to analyze how much she enjoyed spend-ing time with Alex. "Good, I'm getting kinda used to having you around."

"Enough of the psychoanalysis. The more important question is, what are we having for dessert?" Michelle said, rescuing Alex.

After a lengthy debate, they agreed to disagree. The argument came down to a clash of wills between Alex and Sarah. Both had their favorites and neither was prepared to budge. They settled on ordering both desserts, the fried bananas and the sticky rice pudding with mangos. Jill didn't think either sounded good, but was willing to try anything.

Jill marveled at the exquisite desserts the waiter left on their table. The fried bananas were covered in a honey glaze and generously topped with whipped cream. Jill was surprised by the unique contrast in tastes. The banana was bitter, but was offset by the cloying sweetness of the toppings. When it came time for Jill to try the sticky rice, Alex carefully loaded the spoon for her. She took a generous scoop of rice and doused it with coconut milk from the moat surrounding the dessert, then she selected a large piece of mango and placed it on top. Jill described the sticky rice as rice pudding with an attitude.

Sarah protested that Alex was cheating, trying to sway Jill's opinion. Jill wisely refused to choose a favorite, but kept taking another bite under the pretense of trying to come to a decision. Alex smiled broadly, as she watched Jill sample the desserts.

⚜ ⚜ ⚜ ⚜

"God, I hate this weather. It wreaks havoc on my hair." Michelle tried to put her hood up without flattening her hair.

"You have such pretty hair. I wish I could get mine to look a tenth as good as yours. How do you get so much body? I messed with my hair this morning, and it turned out like this." Jill pointed to her head and shook it.

Michelle reached out to touch Jill's hair, and Jill flinched and closed her eyes. In an instant, Jill opened her eyes, knowing her reaction had been out of place.

"I'm sorry, knee jerk reaction," Jill stammered.

Michelle and Sarah exchanged a quick, imperceptible glance before Michelle said, "Quick reactions, you'd be good in the martial arts. Now, let me take a look at your hair, it looks like it has some potential." This time, Jill let Michelle touch it without reaction.

⁂

"I think you're right, Sarah. How do we tell Alex?" Michelle asked.

"We don't."

"What do you mean, we don't?"

"We don't have enough to go on. What if we're wrong?"

"Did you see how she flinched when I went to touch her?"

"That doesn't prove anything. We have to be sure before we say anything. Alex will be devastated, or worse, she may go after the son-of-a-bitch. That's all we need, her riding in like some white knight."

"I know you're right, but I'm no good at sitting around and doing nothing. I like her. I like her a lot, and I'd set out not to. She's falling for Alex too, you know?"

"Damn it, Michelle, you don't know that."

"Cut the outrage." Michelle took Sarah's hand and looked into her eyes. "We both love Alex and don't want to see her hurt. But they care about each other; there's no denying it."

Michelle's heart broke when she saw the pain in her partner's eyes. Before Sarah could respond, Michelle sat down in Sarah's lap and kissed her tenderly on the lips. She ran her hand through Sarah's long blonde hair and the kiss intensified. Sarah broke off the kiss.

"Whoa, time out. You're trying to distract me, you trollop."

Michelle laughed. "Guilty as charged. You know I can't stand to see you upset."

"I'll have to remember that." Sarah kissed Michelle again. Her lips made their way down Michelle's neck.

Michelle moaned. "We need to finish our conversation about Alex. Besides, you need to stop. We don't need someone from the gym walking in on us."

"I'll lock the door." Sarah brushed her fingers over Michelle's hardened nipple.

Michelle jumped out of Sarah's lap. "That was mean. Now I'm going to walk around sexually frustrated for the rest of the day. Don't plan on getting supper when you get home. You'll have something else to take care of before you eat."

"I could take care of it right now." Sarah slowly licked her lips and eyed Michelle. "I don't think it's good for you to walk around with all that pent-up frustration. Lock the door. I can make it nice and quick."

Michelle hesitated, but the throbbing between her legs was almost unbearable. Reluctantly, she turned and locked the door. She smiled when she felt Sarah's body push up against hers and Sarah's hand move inside the front of her pants. This wouldn't take long, she knew. She reached back and rubbed the crotch of Sarah's jeans while she enjoyed Sarah's fingers. After thirteen years, they knew each other's bodies, knowing exactly how to bring the other to a quick release. At times, they could spend hours in bed, teasing and slowly bringing each other to climax. Today was not one of those days. Soon Michelle was breathing heavily and temporarily forgot the hand that was pleasuring Sarah. Michelle put both arms against the wall and spread her legs further, so Sarah could hit the right spot. Within thirty seconds, she was having a silent orgasm, wanting to scream out, but knowing there were people beyond the door. Sarah held her up from behind, her legs rubbery.

Michelle turned and kissed Sarah hard, pushing her back toward her desk chair. Sarah fell into her chair, the kiss never broken. Michelle fumbled with Sarah's zipper as Sarah pressed against her. When Michelle took too long, Sarah groaned and moved Michelle's hand away so she could undo her own pants. Once unzipped, Michelle pulled Sarah's jeans and underwear down around her ankles and dropped to her knees in front of Sarah. Desire burned in Sarah's eyes; unconsciously, she raised her hips from her chair and thrust toward Michelle's waiting mouth. Michelle's tongue slid inside Sarah, thrusting in and out several times. Sarah put her hand on the back of Michelle's head and gently urged her tongue higher. Michelle lingered a bit longer, feeling Sarah's need. She looked up into Sarah's eyes, right before she flicked her tongue over Sarah's clitoris. Sarah stiffened and gasped, rising from her seat further. It took only a couple more quick passes of Michelle's tongue before Sarah had an explosive orgasm. Sarah laid her head back in her chair and took several deep breaths before pulling her pants up.

"Now that we are a little more relaxed, do you think we can talk sensibly?" she said, kissing Michelle.

"Okay, where were we? I want to tell her and you don't. Is that the gist of it?"

"You make it sound so black and white." Sarah grimaced and rubbed her forehead. "It's complicated. It's not that I don't want to tell her. I just think we have to be one-hundred percent sure before we do. If we're wrong and do something that destroys their relationship, Alex may never forgive us. That woman means a lot to her."

"That woman's name is Jill, and she is not the enemy."

"I know. I'm sorry. I like her, too. That's part of the problem," Sarah admitted. "The thought of some asshole hitting her turns my stomach. However, the thought of her letting some asshole hit her, also turns my stomach. What turns my stomach the most is what Alex might do if some asshole is hurting her."

"I know it's not a good situation, but it's the situation we're faced with. We have to play the hand we're dealt."

"Yes, but what if she's looking for a way out and just using Alex? Maybe she has her sights set on the gym."

"That's ridiculous. She doesn't even know you guys own the gym."

"She could have figured it out from the name, you know. Sal-Rexah."

"Oh for God's sake, nobody could figure it out from that. She probably thinks some sheik owns it or something."

"I know. We just need to be certain, is all."

"Fine, you win. But you have to make me a promise when the time comes that we are certain, Alex has to know." Michelle realized she'd said when, not if, but didn't want to draw attention to her mistake. In her heart, she feared *when* was going to be the correct word.

"Deal!" Sarah said and kissed Michelle again.

Chapter Seven

"Jill, I'm getting tired of these few stolen moments," Alex said, several weeks later. They managed to see each other as often as possible, but it never seemed like enough time. Jill called her every day during the week, sometimes more than once. When she could, she would sneak over to Mrs. Harrison for a quick call on the weekend. Alex never asked why she only called from Mrs. Harrison's, nor let Jill know that she'd discovered the secret.

"I'm sorry," she mumbled, casting her eyes down. The angry red scrapes down one side of her face coupled with the sadness in her eyes made her look defeated.

"No, I didn't mean it that way. Don't look so sad." Alex reached out and gently touched Jill's damaged cheek. "You and the girls need to be more careful when you play. It seems like you are always getting hurt."

"I know." Jill quickly changed the subject. "So, what did you mean?"

Alex pulled a flyer from her pocket. "The gym is doing a ten-week swimming program for kids. I thought maybe Jenna and Trina would be interested. It's every Monday and Wednesday. Isn't that a coincidence?" Those were the two days they rarely saw one another since Jill had no excuse to leave the house.

"You had some say on the days, didn't you?"

"Me?" Alex feigned innocence.

"I'm not sure Steve will let them sign up." Jill's face dropped. Alex's smile disappeared, too.

"Oh," was all she managed to say.

"I'll work on it," Jill said, trying to lighten the mood.

≈≈≈≈≈

Jill kept the flyer in her coat pocket for several days, making her plans. Alex had not mentioned it again, and Jill knew she wouldn't. Early in their friendship, Alex invited her to several places, but after so many rebuffs, she stopped. Friday at the laundromat was the most time they had together. It was the highlight of Jill's week, but she felt guilty. Alex spent half her day there, then worked late on a Friday night to make up for it, but she never complained. Jill would feel better about it if they were at least going somewhere interesting. If she could find a way to get Steve to go along with the swimming, she would be able to see Alex twice a week at the gym. She wondered if that meant Alex would no longer spend the morning with her at the laundromat.

Jill strategically placed the flyer on the kitchen counter. She was careful to make it look haphazardly thrown down next to the recycling bags. She made sure she was in the kitchen, putting the final touches on the supper when he came in. She heard the front door close and voices in the living room.

"I'm home," Steve said, walking into the kitchen. He didn't seem to be in one of his moods, which was the first necessity for her plan to work.

"I'm just finishing up supper. It'll be on the table in a minute." She felt his eyes on her back but tried to keep herself from tensing. "Do you want milk or tea with your meal?"

She heard him moving around behind her and hoped her assessment of his mood was correct. She didn't want to be blindsided.

"Milk," he said absentmindedly. He was obviously distracted, looking at something. "What's this?"

"What?" She turned to look at him.

"This." He held up the flyer.

This was the critical point in her plan. She had to feign disinterest. She squinted to show she was puzzled and walked toward him. "What is that?"

"That's what I'm asking you," he said, the irritation evident in his voice.

"Can I see it?" She knew better than to reach for something without his permission.

"Here." He handed her the flyer and eyed her suspiciously.

She looked at it for a couple seconds. She had read it so many times she could recite it word for word, but she could not let him see that. Her eyes scanned the paper as she pretended to read.

"Oh, I'm sorry. I forgot to throw that away. Some woman was handing them out in front of the grocery store." She turned and started to throw the flyer into the garbage. She didn't realize she was holding her breath until she heard him speak.

"Wait."

"What?" She turned back to him, trying her best not to show the hope on her face.

"Let me see that again." She handed him the paper and watched his lips move as he read. "Did you read this?"

"Well, yes. That's why I was going to throw it away. You know how much I hate the water." She said the line she'd been practicing all day.

"You'd deprive the girls of learning how to swim because of your own fears? Isn't that selfish of you? You know my sister and I were fish when we were kids, so they have it in their genes."

It was time to move to phase two of her plan. She needed him to believe her opposition and sell that she was angry with herself for forgetting to throw the flyer away.

"Isn't it two afternoons a week? I wouldn't have time to fix you much of a supper by the time we got home."

"I'm sure you could get everything prepped before you left. I think you're just making excuses."

She could tell it was working, so she threw out a couple more excuses, making sure not to sound argumentative. Jill saw the seed growing in his mind as he shot down every excuse.

"It's settled then. I'll give you the money so you can go to the gym tomorrow."

"Whatever you want." She looked dejected; it took everything she had to show the opposite of what she felt. She wanted to jump in the air or do a happy dance, but instead she took the flyer from him and put it on the refrigerator.

Chapter Eight

Y ou need to come down here, now," was all
Sarah said.

"Shit. I'm on my way," Michelle said and hung
up the phone.

Fifteen minutes later, she burst into Sarah's office.

"You made good time." Sarah looked up from
the papers on her desk. Michelle chose not to mention
that the papers were upside down.

"Tell me it's not Jill, and you were just dying to
see me."

"I wish I could."

"What is it this time?"

"A big shiner. Jenna accidentally kneed her
while they were wrestling."

"I see." Michelle sat down heavily in the chair.
Her small frame made a surprisingly loud bang when
she landed.

"When do we tell her?" Sarah asked.

"I've been thinking about it." Michelle hesitated.

"Uh oh, why don't I like the sound of this?"

"I've changed my mind."

"And when did this happen?"

"A while ago."

"Why didn't you talk to me about it?" Sarah tried
to hide the hurt in her voice.

"Denial. I started to believe. No, I wanted to believe that we were wrong, and we would never have this conversation. I was afraid talking about it would make it happen. Please, don't be mad."

"I'm not mad; how could I be? You've got me wrapped around your little finger," Sarah said, trying to lighten the mood. Her face grew grim. "I wanted to believe, too."

"I want to talk to Jill and give her the opportunity to tell Alex herself." Sarah started to protest, but Michelle held up her hand. "We've gotten to know Jill. I've grown to really like her, and I know you have, too. It seems like a betrayal to do this without giving her the chance. It's not right. We may lose her friendship, and she definitely will never trust us again."

"Do you think it will matter after this? We'll probably never see her again."

"You don't mean that, and I certainly hope you don't want that. Or you're not the woman I fell in love with." Michelle tried to keep the anger from her voice.

"Ouch. What if I meant it?"

"You don't," Michelle said matter-of-factly. Michelle was shocked to see tears streaming down Sarah's face. Sarah was not one to show emotions, even with her. Michelle jumped from her chair and went to her partner.

"Sweetie, talk to me. What's going on?" Michelle put her arm around Sarah.

"I'm afraid for Alex. I've thought about this a million times. What if somebody was hurting you? I'd flip out and want to do something stupid. Alex will too. I'm scared for her, Michelle."

"I know. I'm scared for both of them, but I refuse to believe there's not a way to fix this."

"That's why I love you – always the optimist," Sarah hugged Michelle and let her tears flow.

❧❧❧❧

"Can't it wait until later?" Alex said. "The girls will be done in half an hour."

"Sarah needs to talk to you about the Florida deal, now! That's what she said," Michelle answered. "I'll keep Jill company."

"Fine, I'll go." Alex smiled at Jill. "I'll be right back."

"Take your time. I'll catch up with Michelle." Jill said. Michelle was acting strangely, and Jill's radar was up.

"I need to talk to you. Let's go somewhere more private." Jill simply nodded, and fought back the panic rising in her. Michelle yelled to the instructor that they would be in the equipment room if anyone needed them.

"Please, sit down." Michelle pulled up two chairs.

Jill lowered herself tentatively, while Michelle sat down across from her. Jill searched her face for clues. Michelle's eyes darted around the small room, and looked everywhere but at Jill. The normally polished and composed Michelle appeared to be rattled, and Jill's heart sank.

"What's going on, Michelle?"

Michelle looked up, finally making eye contact with Jill. Tears welled up in Michelle's eyes, but she still didn't speak.

"You know, don't you?"

"Yes," Michelle answered, letting out a deep

breath that she had apparently been holding.

"And?"

"Alex needs to know." Michelle spoke the words that Jill dreaded hearing. Her stomach lurched, and she cast her eyes to the ground. Her hands rested in her lap, and she was surprised when tears bounced off them. She was crying and hadn't known. Michelle knelt in front of her and put her hands over Jill's.

"When?"

"Soon. Do you want me and Sarah to tell her, or do you want to?"

"I want to. It's mine to do." Jill was surprised at her own response. It would be so much easier to let Sarah and Michelle tell Alex.

"When will you do it?"

"There's not enough time left today. I can't just drop this on her and rush out."

"Of course."

"She's not going to handle it well, you know?"

"I know."

"How about Wednesday?"

"Wednesday is good."

"Will you and Sarah be there?"

"If you want us there, we will be there."

"Yes, please."

"You got it."

❧ ❧ ❧ ❧

"Am I being ambushed?" Alex said with a smile when the three walked into her office. Her smile quickly faded when she noted their somber looks. "This can't be good."

"Alex, we need to talk to you," Sarah said, speaking for the group.

"Okay." Alex looked from face to face, trying to figure out what was going on, but all she could tell was something was seriously wrong.

"I need to talk to you." Jill's voice was barely louder than a whisper.

"Okay." Alex put down her pen and rose from her desk. Jill was fidgeting with her hair, never a good sign. "What's the matter?"

"I think we should sit down," Michelle said.

"Okay," Alex said for the third time. She put her hand on Jill's back and guided her toward the sitting area. The material on her back was thin. The sweater, once a warm and vibrant blue, was threadbare and faded.

"What's this all about?" Alex looked at Jill and then Sarah and Michelle. Jill was looking down at her well-worn jeans.

"Jill, do you want to do this, or do you want me to?" Michelle asked.

"No, it's mine to do." Jill continued to stare at her knees but said nothing more.

"Would somebody say something?" Alex said loudly, the tension getting to her.

Jill responded in a quiet voice, "Alex, I have to tell you this all at once, or I won't be able to do it. You have to promise not to say anything or ask any questions until I'm done. Promise?"

"I promise. Please, just look at me."

"I can't." Jill continued looking down, her hair hiding much of her face.

Jill's answer stabbed into Alex's chest. She started to protest, but stopped herself when she saw the look on Michelle's face. "Okay, I'm listening. I promise I won't interrupt."

Jill began slowly, seemingly searching for the right words. She spoke in monotone, as she confessed to her lies and the misinformation concerning her various injuries. Several times she stopped and took a deep breath before continuing. In limited detail, she explained how these injuries actually happened. She gave only the facts, never once mentioning how she felt when these things occurred. Alex sat speechless. Jill didn't look up or change her robotic delivery. Eventually, Alex hung her head and stared at the pattern the threads made in her jeans. She tightened her hands into fists; her fingernails dug into her palms. Michelle had tears running down her cheeks, and Sarah sat with her jaw clenched. After several minutes, Jill stopped talking. No one spoke or moved for what seemed like an eternity.

"I'm done," Jill said, breaking the silence. "Alex, you can say something now."

Sarah and Michelle slid to the edges of their chairs, both focused on Alex. Alex looked up; her eyes blazed and her nose flared. She took a deep breath and bolted to her feet. Jill flinched and hunkered further into the corner of the couch.

Alex began to swear, most of her thoughts so jumbled that the tirade made little sense. The only thing clear was her desire to hurt Jill's husband and to get Jill and the girls out of harm's way.

Michelle got up and sat next to Jill while Sarah approached Alex.

"Alex, enough." Sarah grabbed her friend's arm. Alex looked at Sarah's hand as if it were a mosquito trying to take her blood and swatted it away. "This is not helping."

"And why in the hell did you know before I did?"

"We figured it out," Sarah said, raising her voice. "Michelle asked Jill on Monday, and she admitted it. Jill wanted to tell you herself."

"Really great! What kind of friends are you, anyway? How long ago did you figure it out?" The veins in Alex's neck pulsed as she spoke.

Alex towered over Sarah, but that didn't stop Sarah from standing toe-to-toe with her. Sarah squared her shoulders and put her hands defiantly on her hips. "You're starting to piss me off, Alex. Get over yourself already. This isn't about you. It's about Jill."

Michelle got up from the couch and stood next to Sarah. There was sharpness in Michelle's voice when she spoke. "You know I love you, but you're being a jerk. She just told you about getting the shit kicked out of her. Are you going to sit here feeling sorry for yourself, or are you going to suck it up and make sure she's okay?" Alex glared at Michelle, her face flushed. "Because if you're not, then you might as well get the hell out of here and let us take care of her. I know you're in pain, but it's nothing compared to what she's dealing with. What she needs more than anything is your unconditional love. What she doesn't need is some asshole making her feel worse." Michelle stopped and took a breath before she finished. "So Alex, are you going to give her the unconditional love she needs, or am I going to personally escort your ass out of here?"

Alex's face dropped. The anger in her eyes flickered out, replaced by pain. It was an effort to stand upright, the life completely sucked from her. She'd gone from a raging bull to a defeated child in a couple seconds.

Sarah patted Alex's arm and gave her an encouraging smile. With a subtle flick of her eyes, Sarah communicated that Alex should go to Jill. Alex nodded and gave her friend a slight smile.

Alex hesitantly sat down beside Jill and said softly, "Jill, I'm sorry. I didn't mean to frighten you. The thought of someone hurting you makes me crazy. I'm not angry at you. I hope you understand that." Jill did not respond, so Alex continued. "I'm feeling so helpless right now. I don't know what to do, and I don't know what to say. You need to know I'm here for you. We all are. You've got friends now who can help. You're not alone anymore, Jill."

Alex looked across the room at her friends, her eyes pleading for help. Michelle nodded her head toward Jill, encouraging Alex to go on. Alex gave her a weak smile and turned back toward the silent Jill.

"I need you to throw me a lifeline because I'm drowning here. I'm afraid you're fading away into that distant place, and I'm scared to death that you won't come back. Please don't shut me out."

Seeing Jill so shattered and still not speaking was taking its toll on Alex. Jill looked small in the corner of the couch. Her worn out clothes, which at times made her look carefree and casual, only served to make her look like the battered woman that she was. Alex was losing the battle to keep her tears at bay. In frustration Alex used her forearm to swipe at the tear rolling down her face and saw Jill flinch at the movement. Jill's reaction caused Alex to lose her resolve, and the floodgates opened.

❧ ❧ ❧ ❧ ❧

Jill looked up for the first time and saw Alex struggling to breathe, the tears rolling freely down her face. Jill reached out and laid her hand on Alex's cheek. With her thumb, she brushed away a tear. Their eyes met for the first time. The pain was evident in Alex's eyes, but it was the compassion that broke through to Jill. Alex's eyes told her what her words could not. With no further hesitation, Jill moved closer to Alex and rested her head against Alex's chest. Alex protectively wrapped her arms around Jill and pulled her tightly against her body.

They sat like this for several minutes, neither speaking. Words were unnecessary. The closeness gave them both the comfort they needed. Michelle gestured to Sarah, and they quietly left the room. In Alex's arms, Jill felt safe and cared for for the first time in years. The numbness she felt earlier was beginning to wear off. The first wave of pain hit her, more intense than she could imagine. Years of pent up emotions bubbled to the surface, threatening to overwhelm her. Her body began to shake, and try as she might, she couldn't control it. She realized it was a losing battle and she finally succumbed to the tears that started slowly and soon turned to sobs. Alex was her anchor and held her tightly while she cried. She was a compactly wound spring from the years of fear. Alex said nothing; instead, she let Jill have the release she so desperately needed. Eventually, she cried herself out and lay limp in Alex's arms.

"Are you okay?" Alex asked.

"I think so."

"You and the girls can stay in my apartment. I can stay with Sarah and Michelle."

"I can't, Alex."

"No, it's fine. It has two bedrooms. I know it'll take a while to get on your feet. You can stay there for free for as long as you need."

"You don't understand. I can't." Jill felt Alex's body tense.

"Oh, I get it. You can't possibly leave him. Is that what you're saying?" Alex didn't even try to hide the sarcasm in her voice.

Jill disengaged from Alex and sat back against the arm of the couch. Alex's eyes held a mixture of hurt and anger. "It's not like that. It's complicated. You don't understand."

"I understand perfectly. You love him; how could you possibly leave him? Blah, blah, blah." Alex moved away from Jill and crossed her arms over her chest.

"Please don't, Alex. I can't…" Jill said, her voice trailing off; her exhaustion was evident.

The angry look in Alex's warm eyes was too much for Jill. She knew she needed to get out of here, before another wave of defeat overwhelmed her. Jill started to stand, but Alex reached out and took her hand. Jill looked into Alex's eyes and saw the warmth returning. The fear that gripped her released and she collapsed against Alex.

"We need to talk about this."

"I know, but I can't right now. I feel wrung out. I don't have anything left. I just want to spend the rest of the time we have tonight, talking like we always do. Whenever I'm with you, I walk away feeling energized. I need that now, more than ever. I know it's not fair to you, and I'm sorry."

Jill saw the battle raging behind Alex's eyes. Finally, Alex took a deep breath and drew Jill into her arms. "It's okay, Jill. Right now, it's about you and what you need."

Jill felt herself relax and melt into Alex.

※※※※

They were laughing so hard, they almost didn't hear the knock on the door. "I think someone's here," Jill said. She wasn't sure how long they'd been sitting side by side on the couch, like lowriders. Their shoulders touched and their feet shared a footstool. And most important to Jill, their tears had been replaced by laughter.

"Good, reinforcements!" Alex said. Jill laughed, as Alex continued muttering and shaking her head.

There was another louder knock, and Alex yelled, "Come in."

Sarah and Michelle entered. Jill smiled at the look of confusion on their faces, sure that they did not expect to hear laughter coming from inside.

"I'm sure they'll see it my way. I've never seen someone with such lousy taste," Alex said.

Jill slapped her on the shoulder and scowled. "I like you. Do you still think I have such bad taste?"

"Oh God, what does that say about me?" Alex said in fake horror.

"What are you two talking about?" Michelle said, relief apparent on her face.

"Starsky or Hutch?" Alex said.

Michelle and Sarah looked at the two on the couch, then at each other. The look of confusion sent Alex and Jill into another round of giggles.

"What have you two been smoking?" Sarah asked.

"Just answer the question," Jill said.

"What question?"

"Starsky or Hutch?" Jill repeated.

"Starsky or Hutch, what?" Michelle asked.

"Choose," Alex said. "Boy, you two are slow on the uptake."

"Starsky," they both said in unison.

Jill groaned and Alex raised her hands signifying a touchdown. "Hello. He's a little man. Who else did you think the little ankle biters would choose?" Sarah and Michelle faked a glare, but were happy to be the brunt of the joke if it kept the mood light.

"Wait, not so fast. You can't claim victory on one question." Jill turned toward Sarah and Michelle. "Facts of Life. Jo or Blair?"

"Blair," Sarah said at the same time Michelle said, "Jo."

"Split decision, my turn. The Bionic Woman or the Six Million Dollar Man?" Alex said.

"No fair, you can't use that one," Jill said.

"Why?" Alex feigned innocence.

Before Jill could answer, Sarah joined in. "Asking lesbians. I think Jill's right. You should lose a point for trying to cheat, Alex."

Before Alex could come up with another pairing, Jenna and Trina burst into the room. Their hair was still wet, and the distinct smell of chlorine clung to them. They leapt into Jill and Alex's laps, wrapping their tiny arms around their shoulders.

"Hey, I thought you two were supposed to stay in Sarah's office until we came and got you," Michelle said.

"Too much fun in here," Trina said, looking at Michelle, as if the answer was obvious.

The tension on Alex's face was apparent to the adults in the room, but the girls seemed oblivious to it and continued to chatter happily about their swimming exploits. It was nearly time for them to leave in order to get home before Steve became suspicious. As the minutes ticked by, Jill felt the tension in the room rise. Jill looked toward Michelle, hopefully.

Michelle took her cue and said, "Hey girls, it's about time to go home." Their faces dropped, and the happiness from a moment ago was gone. "Do you want to help us get the van?"

"Yeah," they said, jumping up and running to Michelle.

"Did you forget something?" Jill asked.

They looked confused for a second, then ran back to the couch and gave Alex a good-bye hug. Alex fought back tears. She started to say something to them but her voice cracked, so she stopped speaking. The girls were busy finding their coats and bags, and seemed not to notice. Jill and Alex got up from the couch and joined the group.

"Looks like we're ready to get the van," Michelle said.

"Thank you for everything" Jill gave her a weak smile.

Michelle hugged Jill tightly. "That's what friends are for. You'll get through this; everyone will. We're all here for you." When they let go, Michelle stepped back and bumped into Sarah.

Michelle and Alex exchanged a glance when Sarah walked up to Jill and awkwardly put her arms out. Jill stepped into Sarah's embrace, and the awkwardness faded.

"Are you going to be okay?" Sarah asked while

she hugged Jill.

"Yes. And you'll take care of Alex?"

"I will. We both will."

"She's going to want to do something stupid. Promise you won't let her."

"We'll keep her in line." Sarah squeezed Jill tighter.

❧❧❧❧

They were alone again and had only a few minutes left. Jill felt better than she had in years. Letting her secret out and having someone to share her story with was cathartic. She had hope and no longer felt so alone. The tears had been cleansing. They released much of the tension built up for years. She would be happy if it weren't for the look of anguish on Alex's face. It was almost as if she had transferred some of her pain, and it was now weighing heavily on Alex. Jill was unsure what to do but knew Alex deserved her effort.

"Alex," she said softly, taking her hand. "I know this is hard on you. I'm sorry I'm causing you so much pain. But you need to know, you've made such a difference in my life. Because of you, I know things will get better. Please just bear with me and try not to worry."

"Hey, no problem; that should be easy."

She ignored the tears welling in Alex's eyes, knowing she was trying to hide them. They held one another for some time, neither wanting to let go.

"I'll see you Friday at the laundromat," Alex said hopefully.

"It's a date." Jill winked at Alex, turned, and left the room before either started crying again.

❧❧❧❧

Alex was sitting in her office in the dark when Sarah walked in, carrying a six-pack. The only light came from the computer monitor on her desk. Despite the dim lighting, Alex couldn't hide the fact she had been crying. Her eyes were swollen and bloodshot, and a couple tears still clung to her cheeks.

Sarah sat in the chair opposite Alex, twisted the caps off two bottles, and handed one to Alex before she spoke. "Michelle wouldn't let me ride along. She sent me across the street to pick this up."

"You think we'll get in trouble for drinking at our workplace?" Alex asked.

"Screw 'em. I hear the owners are a couple bitches anyway, so who cares if we lose our jobs. Drink up."

Alex tipped her head back and took a long drink from her bottle, but said nothing.

"How ya holding up?" Sarah said.

"I've been better."

"I can understand that. What can we do?"

"I want to hunt him down and kick the shit out of him."

"As much as I agree with you, I promised Jill to keep you out of trouble. You can't do anything stupid, as much as you may want to. It would only make the situation worse."

"I know, but she won't leave him. I offered her and the girls my place, and she said no. All she would tell me was that it was complicated, and she didn't have it in her to talk about it." Alex started to put the beer to her lips, but stopped. "I swear, 'it's complicated' may be the most loaded phrase ever."

"Isn't it typical in these situations? The victim keeps returning to their abuser over and over. I think it's some kind of sick cycle."

"It doesn't feel that way to me. I've never once heard her say anything positive about him. Hell, she barely talks about him." Alex ran her hand through her hair. "I think if he fell off the face of the earth tomorrow, she'd be happy. You're my best friend, so tell me the truth. Am I deluding myself?"

"I'm confused, too. She doesn't seem to fit the typical pattern, but then again, what do I know? I'm certainly not an expert on domestic violence. I don't want to believe she loves him so much that she can't live without him. None of it makes any sense." Sarah paused for several seconds before continuing. "What about you? How are you going to deal with it? Can you handle being friends with her?"

"What are my choices?"

"You could walk away before you get in any deeper."

"Do you really think I'd do that?" Alex snapped.

"No. I was just being selfish."

"You really want me to walk away from her?"

"For your sake, yes. For her sake, no."

"You care about her, too. You don't want me to walk away." Alex said it as a statement, not a question.

"No, I don't. I just know this is going to rip you apart like nothing in your life ever has. We've been friends for a long time and been through a lot together, but this is tough. I know you, Alex. This is going to take a toll. Every time she is out of your sight, you'll worry. Not just worry, you're going to be a mess. Even now, you're wondering if he's noticing anything different about her or doing anything to her."

"How did you know?" Alex was surprised that her friend was so astute.

"Because. I'm doing the same thing, and I'm not even in love with her."

"Can I have another one?" Alex held up her empty beer bottle, ignoring Sarah's comment about being in love with Jill.

The door opened and closed quietly.

"I hope you two saved one for me," Michelle said. She squeezed into the chair next to Sarah and took the bottle offered to her.

"Is she okay?" Alex asked.

"She's good. She's a tough woman. She's more concerned about you. That's all she talked about the whole ride home. She made me promise to take care of you."

"But who's going to take care of her? I feel so fucking helpless."

"I don't have the answer, but I believe there is one. It may take longer than we'd like, but this won't end badly." Michelle spoke with such conviction that Alex believed her.

❧ ❧ ❧ ❧

There were dark circles under Alex's eyes, and her normally perfectly spiked hair was flat in spots and had clumps fused together in other spots. Her athletic face was pale, making her look gaunt. Jill knew she was trying to be upbeat, but the strain was obvious.

The annoying wash machine clanked next to them, and Alex kept distractedly glancing over at it. The laundromat seemed extra busy today, and when one of the children shrieked, Alex visibly jumped. Jill wished they had a quieter place to talk, but the setting had never bothered them before.

"I was going to get you a pretty purple one, but I settled on this one." Alex held up a non-descript black flip phone. "I know it's old school, but I figured it would be easier to hide."

"It's perfect." Jill smiled and took the phone. She ran her hand over the smooth surface. "You know you didn't have to do this."

"Yes, I did. It's for me, as much as for you. This way I'll know you can always get in touch with me whenever you need me. I programmed Sarah and Michelle's cell numbers in, too."

"Thank you." Jill smiled and put the phone into her purse. Alex managed a slight smile.

"Why do you look so damned good?" Alex asked. "I'm sorry. That was rude. It's just that you look like you've been at the spa, and I'm sure I look like I've been on a three-day bender."

"I'm sorry, Alex." Jill's heart ached for Alex. "I've slept well the last couple of nights, best in years."

Alex started to speak, but stopped and nodded instead.

"Go ahead and say it, Alex. I see it on your face. You're thinking it must be nice being so refreshed, after I've unloaded all my burden on you."

"No," Alex said forcefully. "Well, yes, I was thinking it must be nice to sleep, but I have never thought of you as a burden. And I never will."

"Thank you. I hope you know how much I appreciate you." Jill was rewarded with a genuine smile from Alex. "For the first time in forever, I have hope, and you are the one that has given that to me."

Several times, Jill tried to change the subject and

talk about lighter topics, but Alex kept bringing the conversation back. Jill finally relented and agreed to fill in some of the details. Steve had hit her for the first time six months after their wedding. Jill couldn't remember the catalyst for the first attack. She believed it was an isolated incident until he backhanded her about two months later. That time she remembered it was because she couldn't find the remote. She tried to convince Alex that she was not in serious danger. Normally, it was something simple, a shove, a backhand or a single punch, nothing that caused too much damage. When pressed, she finally admitted that a couple times a year it was more serious, but she refused to give Alex any details.

"So, when was the last big one?" Alex locked eyes with Jill.

Jill looked away, wanting this conversation to be over. She debated whether she should refuse to answer, but knew that wasn't fair. She looked back at Alex, and sighed. "Ironically, it happened the same day that I met you. Funny how one of my best days in years was also one of the worst."

Alex looked up and to the right before looking back at Jill. "That was nearly four months ago, which means an attack is on the horizon. Jill, we have to do something before it happens again."

"You'll drive yourself nuts thinking like that." Jill put her hand on top of Alex's. "One day at a time is how I have to approach things."

"But you and the girls can have my apartment. I can stay with Sarah and Michelle."

Jill struggled, seeing the hope in Alex's eyes, knowing she would soon extinguish it. "I can't talk about this anymore. Let's just enjoy our lunch and talk about something else."

Alex tried to compel her to say more, but Jill remained firm. She could see the strain on Alex's face, but could do nothing to ease it.

The lunch ended too soon. Jill wondered how many partings it would take before the look of panic would no longer cross Alex's face. She knew the answer was probably never, and she felt sad. *How long could she continue to put Alex through this?* It was too upsetting to think about, so she quickly put the thought out of her mind.

Chapter Nine

Jill watched impatiently as Jenna and Trina half-heartedly picked up the toys littering the living room floor. Everything needed to be cleaned up before they left for swimming, or Steve would be furious when he got home. Jill snapped at the girls, and then she felt bad. "I'm sorry, girls. I'm not myself this afternoon."

"It's because we won't see Alex anymore, isn't it?" Jenna said.

Jill's mouth dropped open. "How did you know that?"

"You're happy now since we met Alex, but we can't let anyone know about her. When swimming is over tonight, it'll go back to the way it was before. You won't be as happy."

Out of the mouths of babes, she thought. "You're a pretty smart girl." She smiled and ruffled Jenna's hair. "But you know what? We have each other, so we'll still be happy."

"I'll miss her. She's fun and makes us laugh. We don't have much to laugh about here."

Jill's heart broke, and she fought back tears. *Jenna was too young to have to think about these things.* "Sweetie, you don't have to worry, we'll have fun. It'll be okay."

"She loves us. She especially loves you. She doesn't want you to be hurt anymore," Jenna said in a matter-of-fact way.

"Did she tell you that?" Jill felt her anger rising; it wasn't right for Alex to involve the girls.

"No, she didn't tell me," Jenna said, putting a hand on her hip. "Her face did. Ever since that day you were both crying in her office, she looks at you so sad. She knows he hurts you, doesn't she?"

Jill wrestled with how to respond, but settled on the truth. "Yes, she knows."

"Is she going to stop him?" Jenna asked hopefully.

If only it were that simple, Jill thought but said, "Don't you worry about that, Little Miss, it's time for swimming."

⁂

The conversation with Jenna reinforced what Jill knew she had to do. Swimming was ending tonight, which meant their extra time together would be over. It had been nearly a month since she told Alex about Steve, and the revelation was taking its toll. Every Monday Alex looked awful. Weekends were for relaxing, but Alex looked as if she'd been tortured. It probably felt that way to her, as she waited and wondered if Jill was okay. The pain and fear in Alex's eyes broke Jill's heart. When they hugged good-bye on Fridays at the laundromat, Alex struggled to let her go, as did Jill. It wasn't fair that she put Alex through so much.

Jill ducked into the bathroom and locked herself in a stall. She was not ready to face Alex, so she sat down and wrestled with her thoughts. As much as she hated to do what she was about to do there were no other options. Her stomach was in knots. She didn't think she would throw up, since she hadn't eaten in the last twenty-four hours. She sat in the bathroom for nearly fifteen minutes, trying to work up her courage.

Jill knocked on Alex's office door before entering. Jill missed the easy smile and playful banter that used to greet her; instead, Alex studied her, seemingly looking for any new injuries. She couldn't blame Alex for her reaction, but it still bothered her.

It wasn't lost on Jill that Alex wore a light blue denim shirt, which was one of Jill's favorites. Dressed all in denim, she looked rugged and strong. "Nice shirt."

Alex blushed and didn't respond directly to Jill's comment. "Where've you been? I was starting to worry."

"Just freshening up," Jill lied. "Come sit on the couch with me."

They engaged in small talk, but it seemed forced and unnatural. They discussed the weather, swimming, and the local news. They talked as if they were strangers sitting next to each other on the bus.

"So, shall we talk about the elephant in the room?" Jill was tired of their uncomfortable attempt at conversation.

"What do you mean?"

"You know damn well what I mean, Alexandria."

"Ouch. You know, if Sarah said something like that to me, I'd slap her silly." Alex's eyes widened and the color drained from her face. "Oh God, I'm sorry. I didn't...You know I...Jill, I'm so sorry." Alex stumbled over her words, a look of horror on her face.

"Relax, Alex. I didn't take you literally. Besides, I would seriously doubt it. My money would be on Sarah if you ever tried." Jill laughed. Alex pretended outrage, but the smile that lit her eyes and quiver at the corner of her mouth gave her away.

"God, I'm going to miss you," Jill said.

"What's that supposed to mean?"

"Oh Alex, I'm sorry. I didn't mean to tell you that way."

"Tell me what?" Alex's voice was higher and louder than usual. She stood abruptly and walked across the room to her desk.

"Please come back. We need to talk about this."

Alex didn't join Jill on the couch; instead, she defiantly sat on the corner of her desk. Jill talked to her from across the room and spoke for several minutes. Alex did not respond and at times appeared not to be listening. Jill laid out the argument she had been developing over the last couple of weeks. Tonight was the last day of swimming, which meant they would be back to seeing each other a few stolen hours a week. The only guarantee was Friday at the laundromat.

Jill pointed out that Alex was a wreck on the days they didn't see each other, and she lived in constant fear for Jill's safety. Jill painted the picture of the negative impact she was having on Alex's life, avoiding entirely the positive impact Alex had on hers.

Jill finished with a bombshell. "That's why this has to be the last time we ever see each other. I go back to my life, and you go on with yours."

The only indication Alex heard what Jill said was her flushed face. She showed no emotion, and her eyes were unreadable. She fiddled with a pen cap for several seconds before responding. "You've obviously got it all figured out. Thanks for consulting me."

"I'm sorry, but I knew what you'd say."

"Really? Do you think, maybe, I deserve the right to speak for myself?"

"You do."

Alex launched into her rebuttal. She spoke in a calm voice, laying out a logical argument for why Jill should accept Alex's offer to help. Jill had heard all these arguments before, so she was able to steel herself against them. She knew it would be unfair to Alex if she showed any signs of wavering.

Alex must have sensed she was not getting through to Jill, because she stopped mid-sentence. Jill's heart ached as she watched Alex crumble. She slumped against her desk, looking like a discarded ragdoll. Her eyes filled with tears and her voice cracked when she spoke. "Please, Jill. Please don't do this."

Alex switched tactics, and dropped her logical appeal, instead laying her heart wide open. She talked about all the times they spent together, and the fun they had. She talked about their connection, and all their intimate talks. Ironically, it was the most difficult for Jill when Alex talked about their Fridays at the laundromat. Jill concentrated on Alex's chin, making it look as if she was still looking at her, but stopped listening to her words. She knew she could not handle hearing any more stories without breaking. When Jill failed to respond, Alex begged Jill to reconsider.

Seeing Alex so vulnerable was breaking Jill's heart, but she couldn't let Alex know. She sat staring at Alex, showing nothing on her face. The years of practice with Steve was serving her well. Early in their relationship, she found a way to withdraw into herself. It was how she survived all these years. She felt guilty using this technique on Alex, but she knew no other way. Alex had stopped talking and was staring at her, awaiting a response. Everything she would like to say to Alex flashed across her mind, but she choked the words down.

"I was hoping to get the chance to say good-bye to Sarah and Michelle. Are they here today?"

Alex's face fell. "Did you hear a word I just said?"

"Yeah, but it doesn't change anything." Jill fought the urge to bolt from the room. The pain on Alex's face was unbearable and threatened to break through her façade. "So, where are they?" She kept her tone light and cheerful.

Jill expected Alex to protest, but instead she was met with a stunned look. "They left for Florida last night. They're checking out that gym we hope to acquire."

Just two weeks before, Alex told her the truth about who owned the gym. Alex used the information to persuade her that she had the financial means to help her and the girls out. Jill laughed when Alex explained the name Sal-Rexah was a combination of her and Sarah's names, not an Arab sheik. Jill agreed with Michelle; it was a horrible name.

"I thought you were in charge of the new acquisitions?"

"I am, but they knew I didn't want to be away from you." Alex paused and looked at Jill, as if she were awaiting a response. When Jill remained quiet, Alex continued. "They hate the heat and humidity, but pretended they were dying to take a mini-vacation to Florida. They did it for me, and for you. They knew it would destroy me to be away from you."

Jill fought her emotions. It was terrible seeing Alex so vulnerable when she knew she would have to

slam her down. The realization that she would not see
Sarah and Michelle again threatened to break her. She
tapped into her strength and withdrew deeper into
herself. "That's a shame. Oh well, tell them good-bye
for me."

"So that's it? These last few months have meant
nothing to you?"

"Come on, Alex, we had some fun. Now it's
over." Jill shrugged. She was surprised at how well she
was pulling off nonchalance, but felt horrible seeing
the look on Alex's face. *And the Oscar goes to,* she
thought.

"Why are you doing this, Jill? I don't understand.
I've never begged anyone for anything in my life, but
I would get down on my knees right now if it would
get through to you." Alex no longer swiped away her
tears, instead letting them pour down her cheeks.

Each word hit Jill like a bullet, but like the
warrior she was, it never showed. She remained stoic,
looking almost disinterested as Alex poured her heart
out.

"Please, Jill, don't." The look of anguish on
Alex's face was heartbreaking. "I feel so damned
helpless. My heart is breaking. If you walk away from
me, I'm not sure I will ever recover."

Jill couldn't stay in the room with Alex much
longer without shattering. She needed to find a way
to end the conversation soon. From deep inside, Jill
worked up the courage to give Alex the last shove she
needed. She put steel in her eyes and venom in her
voice, and she delivered the blow.

"I can't deal with it anymore, Alex. It's bad
enough, the way you look at me when we first see each
other. It's worse when I go to leave. You get that pa-

thetic sad look on your face, trying to make me feel guilty for going back to my husband." Jill hoped she could deliver the final lie. She was convinced it was the best thing she could do for Alex. "I could never leave him; I love him. He loves me. I just need to learn to be a better wife and hanging out with you and your friends isn't helping."

Jill had heard that people's mouths fell open when they were stunned, but had never seen it until now. When Alex closed her mouth, her body seemed to deflate. Her shoulders slumped inward and Jill swore she shrank at least four inches. Jill had seen her own eyes in the mirror for many years, so she recognized the look of defeat in Alex's. The warm brown eyes she'd come to love were filled with a deep sadness. Alex looked into Jill's eyes for several seconds, before she stood. Without a word, she turned and left her own office.

Jill wanted to drop to her knees and throw up the bile that churned in her stomach. She looked around the office, trying to memorize every detail of the place that had given her so much comfort. She went to where Alex's coat was hanging and pulled it from the hook. She hugged the coat, putting her face into the lining, trying to get one last trace of Alex's scent. She replaced the coat and robotically walked to the door.

෬෬෬෬

Two hours later, Alex sat in her office with the lights out and a beer in her hand. She swiped at her cellphone several times, unsure whether she should make the call. Finally, she made her decision and hit the call button.

"Hey Alex," the voice on the other end said.

"I hate caller ID," she responded.

"What's up?" Sarah said, ignoring her complaint.

"Is Michelle there too?"

"No, I dumped her at the pool and picked up some hot Latin babe. Of course she's here, where else would she be?"

"I need to talk to you guys, can you put me on speaker?"

"Will do, can you hear us?"

"Yeah."

"Are you okay?" Michelle asked.

"No, I don't think so." Alex launched into her story of what happened with Jill earlier in the evening.

"The poor thing," Michelle said when Alex finished.

"What?" Alex said thinking she misunderstood.

"I feel so bad for her," Michelle answered.

"For her, what about me?"

"Yeah, what about Alex?" Sarah piped in.

Michelle snorted. "Don't tell me you two are that stupid." Alex greeted her with silence. "Never mind, I guess you are. You actually believed her?"

"She was pretty convincing. You should have been here. I've never seen her like that. She didn't give a damn how I felt. She was so cold, so distant."

"And so shut down," Michelle said. "Alex, she was trying to save you the only way she knew how, by pushing you away. She sees how hard this is on you and can't stand to hurt you anymore. She threw herself under the bus for you. My guess is she is a wreck right now. She's all alone again, or at least she thinks she is. We're not giving up on her and you're not letting her walk away like this."

Steve noticed Jill's preoccupation while she prepared dinner. She overcooked his hamburger and served it to him without apology. He intentionally made a sudden gesture, but she never flinched.

"You know I like my burgers medium rare."

"Sorry, I forgot," Jill said without conviction. He was stunned when she didn't offer to cook him a new one.

"This shit is inedible," he said loudly.

"We're out of burgers. I guess you'll just have to eat it."

He stared at her, not believing what he heard. "What did you just say?"

"I said, we are out of burgers. You will just have to eat it." She said it slowly, as if talking to a small child.

He raised his hand as if to hit her and she looked right through him. She stopped showing emotions long ago or at least the hurt, but he could always see the fear. Tonight, there was no fear because she was only a shell. He backhanded her across the left cheek. Her head snapped back, but she made no sound and had no reaction. He raised his hand again; not even a flinch.

"What the fuck is the matter with you?" When she didn't answer, he half-heartedly smacked her again. Her eyes were empty, and she said nothing. Part of him wanted to beat a reaction out of her, but he was afraid he might kill her without ever seeing one.

"I asked you a goddamned question." He slammed his fist down on the table. She didn't respond. *Had he finally broken her*, he thought, more scared than he cared to admit. He picked up the plate and threw it across the kitchen. The plate shattered, sending food and glass shards sailing in all directions.

Jill picked up her burger and took another bite. She chewed slowly and licked her lips after she swallowed. "I think it's pretty tasty."

He shoved her plate off the table. "Get me a fucking sandwich and clean up this mess."

Obediently, she stood and went to the refrigerator. Her movement was robotic as she constructed the sandwich and brought it to him. Without a word, she knelt and started picking up pieces of glass from the floor. He wanted to get away from her; her reaction was making him uncomfortable.

"You're making too damned much noise." He stood, picked up his sandwich, and glared down at her. She continued to slowly gather the broken plates and food littering the floor. He kicked the pile she'd just made. "I'm going to watch television. This kitchen better be spotless when I come back."

꙳꙳꙳꙳

Later, after he went to bed, she laid on the couch thinking about the incident. She had baited him. It was almost as if she wanted him to hit her. In a sick way, she welcomed his fists. She hurt so badly inside that she hoped the physical pain would take some of it away. Her strategy was unsuccessful. His slaps did nothing to alleviate the pain that gripped her heart.

She laid in the dark. The pain slowly ebbed and in its place was emptiness. The depth of her despair scared her. Despite everything, she always had a will to go on, but tonight was different. She lay, not moving, and not caring. There were no tears; there was nothing. She thought of the girls, but even their faces could not rally her. She replayed the scene with Alex over in her mind, but it seemed surreal. Sleep escaped her, so she lay staring at the ceiling. Finally, she closed her eyes, trying to force sleep to come. All at once, Alex's eyes, full of hurt, crashed into her mind. The image caused her stomach to lurch and the pain cascaded over her. At least she was feeling something. Her eyes filled with tears, which silently rolled down the sides of her face, stopping when they reached her pillow. Mentally and physically exhausted, she cried herself to sleep.

Chapter Ten

Logan International Airport was extremely busy, which made it difficult to find two small women. Alex stepped back, leaned against the side of the coffee kiosk, and scanned the crowd. She had insisted on picking them up even though it was easier to take a cab. They had been gone for only ten days, but to Alex, it felt like an eternity.

When they had talked last night, Sarah and Michelle were more than ready to be home. Alex enjoyed business travel and had closed all their previous deals. She liked meeting new people and seeing new places, whereas Sarah was content being at the gym every day. Maybe Alex would feel the same way, if she had someone to come home to. Alex pushed those thoughts out of her mind and studied the people pouring out of the gate.

Alex pulled out her cellphone to see if Sarah had texted her, when she felt something behind her. Before she could react, Sarah jumped onto her back. Alex pretended to stagger and grabbed the kiosk as if to steady herself. "Shit, how many pina coladas did you drink down there? You must have put on ten pounds."

Alex spotted Michelle, who shook her head and rolled her eyes. They had been playing this game for years. Michelle warned them that one of these days, Alex's knees or back would give out and they would both end up in a heap on the ground. She made it clear she would keep walking and act as if she didn't know either of them.

Still hanging from her back, Sarah reached up and ruffled Alex's hair. "Ya missed me, didn't ya, partner?"

"I couldn't eat, I couldn't sleep."

"Could you poop?"

"Enough. Sarah, get off her. Everyone is staring at the lesbians gone wild," Michelle said.

Once Sarah slid from her back, Alex turned to Michelle and gave her a big hug, lifting her off her feet. "I missed you too," Alex said in a loud voice, causing other travelers to look their way. Sarah and Alex laughed while Michelle scowled.

"You two can carry the luggage. That'll keep your hands busy so you'll keep them to yourselves. I swear you guys act like school children sometimes."

Alex stashed the luggage in the trunk and slid behind the wheel. The parking lot was jammed so their progress was slow. Alex had the radio tuned to an oldies station and was humming along to the music.

"Note to selves," Sarah said to Michelle. "Never come to the airport on a Friday. This is nuts."

"At least our chauffeur seems to be chipper. Hey Alex, I take it you talked to Jill," Michelle said.

"Not really." Alex's face dropped.

"How can you not really talk to her?" Sarah asked.

"I told you I've been calling and leaving her messages and she changes her outgoing message every day, letting me know she's okay. So even though we haven't spoken, in a roundabout way, we're still in touch."

"So why are you in such a good mood?"

"You guys are home. What more could I want?"

"Good try, suck up. What else has you in such a good mood?" Sarah asked.

"I was driving here and feeling sorry for myself. I was quite pathetic, actually. Then it dawned on me, it's Friday."

"Looking forward to the weekend?"

"No, once I drop you two off, I'm going to the laundromat."

"Woo hoo, washing undies always gets me jazzed too," Sarah teased.

≈≈≈≈

Alex paused outside the laundromat and looked in the window. Her heart skipped a beat when she saw Jill sitting alone in the corner, reading a book. Her hair was pulled back in a ponytail, her face gaunt, and dark circles underscored her eyes. She wore an oversized sweatshirt that made her look small, almost fragile. Any doubts Alex had about going inside vanished. Jill didn't look good; she obviously wasn't handling their time apart any better than Alex.

Jill didn't look up when Alex approached. Alex cleared her throat, but Jill continued to be lost in her book. "Is this seat taken?" Alex asked.

It took Jill a moment to register someone was speaking to her and another moment to recognize the familiar voice. She looked up and smiled. Alex noted that she looked extremely tired, but there was warmth in her eyes. Alex was relieved, afraid she would see the icy vacant look that still haunted her. The warmth was all the encouragement Alex needed; she smiled back.

"I've missed you so much," Alex said.

"Me too. I'm sorry, I thought…"

"Shh, it's okay. You don't have to apologize. I know why you did it, and we don't have to talk about it. I just want to be here, in our favorite haunt, spending time with you." Alex picked up Jill's hand and held it between hers.

Jill rose to her feet and stood looking directly into Alex's eyes. A giant smile spread across Alex's face and her eyes welcomed Jill, who stepped into Alex's embrace.

Chapter Eleven

Present Day

Since Jill showed up on Alex's doorstep, bloodied and bruised, Alex was on autopilot. When Jill opened her robe, as if Alex would take advantage of her too, Alex was mortified, and all she could manage to say was, "God, no."

Alex quickly covered Jill with a blanket, searching for something more to say, but words escaped her. Alex's heart ached when she thought of the trauma Jill endured for so long. Her thoughts threatened to overwhelm her, so she pushed them aside. Now was not the time to worry about her own feelings; Jill needed her.

Alex sat on the bed and faced Jill. She gently stroked Jill's hair, but said nothing. After a while, Jill closed her eyes and her breathing became steady. Alex stood slowly in order not to disturb her and was almost to the bedroom door.

"Where are you going?" Jill spoke her first words since arriving. Panic was evident in her voice.

"I was getting cold. My t-shirt and underwear aren't very warm. I'm just going to the laundry room to throw on some sweats, but I'll be back in a minute. Okay?"

Jill nodded, but didn't speak.

When Alex returned, Jill's eyes were wide open and she no longer looked like she might fall asleep. Alex rolled an office chair in front of her and positioned it next to the bed, close to Jill.

"I'm sorry, Alex," Jill said. She repeated it again, this time tears running down her cheeks.

"You don't have anything to be sorry about."

"Yes, I do. For thinking...for acting like you would hurt me."

"It's okay. I understand."

"No, it's not. It's not all right and it's not un-derstandable." Jill sat up forcefully. The movement caused her to grimace, but she remained sitting up-right.

Alex didn't know how to respond, so she re-mained silent.

"You didn't deserve for me to act like that. You've been my friend. My rock. You're the only thing I can count on in my screwed-up life. I've never trusted anyone like I do you. I was an idiot and I hurt you. You deserve better."

"Jill, you've been brutalized tonight. Hell, you've been brutalized more than just tonight. The trauma is enough to make you react in ways you wouldn't normally. Your apology is more than enough for me."

"You're too good to me," Jill said with a slight smile.

"Somebody needs to be." Alex returned the smile.

"You're not mad at me?"

"Of course not."

Jill visibly relaxed and laid her head back on the pillow, her eyes heavy. "I'm so tired, Alex. I hurt ev-erywhere. I know you want answers. I know we need to talk about what happened, but I don't have the strength right now. Can I ask you for another favor? I think this will be favor number two thousand and ten."

"Anything." Alex gently brushed Jill's hair out of her eyes.

"Can we just get some sleep and talk in the morning?" She pulled back the covers and gestured for Alex to join her.

"Are you sure you don't want me to leave you alone? I can sleep on the couch."

Fear flashed in Jill's eyes and she shook her head no.

"Hey, hey, it's okay. I won't leave you by yourself if you don't want me to." Alex's heart ached as she climbed into bed beside Jill. She wanted to comfort Jill and make her feel safe, but was afraid to touch her. Instead, she lay silently in the dark, listening to Jill breathe. Jill inched closer to Alex, until her head rested on Alex's shoulder. Alex stiffened.

"Alex?" Jill said softly.

"Yes."

"Could I get favor number two thousand and eleven?"

"Sure, why not," Alex said, a smile in her voice.

"Would you," she started and stopped. "I'm in so much pain, Alex. It's never been this bad. You always make me feel better. I need that right now more than I've ever needed anything. Would you...would you mind just holding me?"

"No, I mean yes. No, I mean no. I mean no, I wouldn't mind holding you. I would love to. Damn, Jill, in a moment like this, did you have to give me a brainteaser?"

Jill rewarded her with a laugh. "I have to keep

you on your toes."

"Great, just what I need." Carefully, Alex slid one arm under Jill and gently drew Jill to her. Jill lay with her head on Alex's shoulder, while Alex stroked her hair. The closeness was what they both needed. The pain in Alex's chest receded and she felt Jill's body relax. Tears washed down both of their faces. Jill snuggled closer and her body began to shake, wracked by the sobs that could finally escape.

"It's okay, Jill, just let it go. I'm right here and I won't let anyone hurt you. You're safe." Alex held Jill as tightly as she could, careful not to squeeze too hard and aggravate Jill's injuries. Alex wanted to draw Jill's entire body inside her chest where her heart could shelter Jill forever, but she knew it was impossible. Alex kissed the top of her head and continued to whisper encouragement, until Jill finally drifted off to sleep. Alex was slow to fall asleep herself, worried that Jill might awaken and be frightened. She didn't want to be sleeping if Jill needed her. She watched Jill for some time before she kissed the top of Jill's head and closed her own eyes.

❦ ❦ ❦ ❦

Jill heard her name called and tried to determine the origin. When she opened her eyes, she was looking into Alex's warm brown eyes. Jill smiled and said good morning. Alex returned the smile and the greeting.

"It's nine o'clock," Alex said. "I hated to wake you, but I knew we had to come up with a game plan. Did you sleep well?"

"Like a baby." Jill stretched and rolled onto her back. She giggled and said, "I guess sleeping with a lesbian does that for you, huh?"

"Aren't you the comic genius this morning? If I knew you were this clever, I would have slept with you a long time ago."

"Promises, promises." It felt good to banter with Alex; if only the circumstances were different. The truth of the situation flooded back when she moved and the pain gripped her. She pushed it aside, wanting to feel happy awhile longer.

They lay in bed talking about nothing in particular, simply enjoying each other's company. Jill rolled over and laid her head on Alex's chest. Unconsciously, Alex ran her fingers through Jill's hair.

Jill knew this moment couldn't last, but she wanted to savor it for a little longer. She knew Alex would have a million questions, rightfully so. Alex was being a trooper, giving her space by not bringing it up, but she knew eventually Alex would give her the familiar spiel of why she and the girls should move into Alex's apartment. And she knew she would have to see the defeat on Alex's face when she said no.

It felt good lying next to Alex. At this point, Steve would be furious, so it didn't matter if she went home now or two hours from now. The girls were safe at their grandma's house until tonight, so she wasn't worried about them. Jill closed her eyes and enjoyed the sensation of Alex's fingers running through her hair.

"That feels nice." Jill sighed. "Can we make a deal?"

"Depends on what it is," Alex said playfully.

"We ignore the situation until ten o'clock, and then we get up, go into the living room, and talk about it."

"That sounds good to me, but we can stay in

here and talk about it at ten o'clock."

"No, this feels too nice. I want to remember it just like this."

"I understand." Alex squeezed Jill.

❧❧❧❧

Alex watched Jill get out of bed, and her mood was shattered. Jill could barely move and she winced when she tried to stand. Alex's breath caught when she saw the bruising and swelling that distorted her face in the morning light. Alex was comforted that Jill's eyes weren't lifeless, like they were the night before.

"I know I look hideous," Jill said when she caught Alex staring at her.

Without thinking, Alex responded, "No, I still think you're pretty."

"Alex, I do believe you just called me purty." Jill smiled.

"I didn't mean it that way. You are, but that's not what I meant." Alex started to go on, but noticed the amused look in Jill's eyes. "You're just screwing with me, aren't you?"

"Uh huh." Jill winked at Alex.

Alex tried to glower, but she couldn't hide the twinkle in her eye. "Come on, smartass, let's go get your clothes."

Alex took Jill to the laundry room to retrieve her clothes. While Jill dressed, Alex went to the kitchen. She put a couple breakfast sandwiches in the microwave and started a pot of coffee. Jill was sitting on the couch, dressed in her own sweat pants and one of Alex's sweatshirts when Alex carried in the tray. She set the tray on the coffee table and sat down next to Jill.

❧❧❧❧

While they ate their breakfast, Jill filled Alex in on the events of the previous evening. Jill left the laundromat walking on a cloud, since she'd reconciled with Alex. She arrived home at around four o'clock and went to pick up the girls from Mrs. Harrison. They weren't there. Steve had already picked them up. He'd taken them to his mother's house for the night, under the pretense of spending some quality time together. Jill knew this spelled trouble, but had no choice but to go home.

When he returned from his mother's, she could tell immediately he was in a mood. Apparently, he'd gotten into some kind of trouble at work. He was angry and couldn't wait to take it out on Jill.

Jill was anxious all night, trying hard not to do anything to upset him. It was part of his game. The more nervous he made her, the more he enjoyed himself. He was a predator hiding in the bushes, waiting to pounce on his prey. Her nerves were raw by the end of the evening, every sound and movement causing her to tense. She was almost relieved when he finally hit her, since waiting was psychological torture.

He left her lying in a heap on the floor, as he always did after a beating, and went to bed. Jill didn't know how long she laid there because she was in and out of consciousness, but finally she woke shivering uncontrollably. In order to find some comfort, she thought of what Alex would do and say, if she were there. Suddenly, it wasn't enough just to imagine Alex there, she needed her there. Jill put on her shoes and snuck from the house. When she got to the street, she ran, taking sides streets, hoping he hadn't heard her leave. The whole time, she was afraid he would come after her and stop her before she got to Alex's apartment. Luck was on her side. He either didn't hear her or couldn't catch up to her.

Alex pressed her for what he'd done to her, but she refused to give any details. She told Alex it wouldn't do either of them any good. Jill certainly didn't need to relive it, and Alex didn't need the images running through her head. She knew the pictures Alex already had in her head was enough to haunt her for months.

In order to end Alex's questioning, Jill reminded her they needed to deal with the problem at hand. Jill needed to come up with a plausible explanation for where she had been when she returned home.

"Don't you think it would be better to talk about what we can do so you don't have to return home?" Alex said in a measured voice.

Jill noticed the change in Alex and saw her internal struggle. She knew Alex was frustrated and was doing everything in her power not to lose her cool. Alex had every right to yell and scream and tell her to get the hell out of her house, but she knew Alex wouldn't.

"Not today, Alex."

"I fail to understand why you would go back there." Alex fought to keep herself controlled. Despite her best efforts, her forehead was deeply creased.

"It's complicated." Jill delivered her usual line. She was sure her answer was like nails on a chalkboard to Alex. It certainly would be to her, if she were in Alex's shoes.

Alex's face reddened. She got to her feet and piled the dishes on a tray. "I guess that's the end of the conversation then." Alex picked up the tray and started toward the kitchen.

"Alex, don't walk away from me."

Alex turned, the frustration evident on her face. "What do you want from me?"

"I want you to understand."

"How the hell can I understand when you won't explain anything?" Alex's voice remained at a normal volume, but the vein in her neck throbbed.

"You're not being fair. Can't you just believe in me?"

"I can't believe you just said that to me. This conversation is over, Jill." Alex turned to leave the room.

"Alex, please, come back. I can't deal with you being upset with me. Not right now, not today." Jill sighed. "Who am I kidding? Not ever."

Alex stopped with her back towards Jill. Her shoulders rose and fell several times before she turned and set the tray back on the table. She sat down on the couch across from Jill and perched on the edge of the seat cushion. She rested her elbows on her legs, clasped her hands in front of her, and rested her chin on her hands. She looked at Jill for several beats before speaking.

"I don't know what more I can say. What is it you want from me?"

"I don't want the conversation to be over. I want you to talk to me. Tell me what you're thinking, what you're feeling."

"Do you really want to know?"

"Of course I do."

Alex paused and looked at Jill, but she couldn't maintain eye contact; instead, her eyes dropped to the floor, and she began to speak in a quiet voice.

"Okay, I'll tell you how I feel. I've never felt so helpless in my entire life. You may never understand how painful it is for me to see you like this and not be able to do anything. Then I feel guilty because you're the one that's lived it for all these years, and I've only known for the last month or so. It's tearing me apart. I don't know how long I can take it. There are days I think I am going to break, and then I get mad at myself because you need me to be strong for you. And I try. I try so hard to do whatever I can to make your life better. Then I see I'm not because you stay, and even now you're going to walk out of here and go back to it."

Jill opened her mouth to speak. Alex, still staring at the floor, didn't notice, and continued. "The images play over and over and over in my head. I close my eyes at night and I see you slammed against a wall. I shut my eyes in the shower and I see you being thrown to the floor and lying there in a heap. I don't even want to tell you the other things I see. The movie plays in an endless loop in my head, scene after scene of you being hurt. And all I can do is stand there and watch. Last night was the first night I slept well. I didn't have the images in my mind because you were there in my arms, safe."

Alex dropped her head into her hand, and rested her forehead against her palm. Her hand covered part of her face so Jill could no longer see her eyes, but the anguish in her voice left no doubt as to her feelings.

"I look at you now and my heart breaks. I want to wrap you in my arms and never let you leave here, but I know I can't. I have to let you walk out that fucking door knowing that this will happen to you again. And knowing that maybe one day you won't be so lucky, and you won't get up and come to me because you can't. And I'll call and call, and you won't answer and you won't call me back. And several days later I'll find out you're gone. That you died alone in the dark, frightened and cold. Knowing your last moment was filled with pain and I wasn't there to offer you comfort, no one will be. And for the rest of my life, I'll have to live with the knowledge that I failed you. I let you walk out of here, and I did nothing. I…"

Alex tried to continue, but her voice cracked. Jill stared in stunned silence. Alex, the one who had been her rock, sat across from her, broken. Without hesitation, Jill went to Alex and knelt in front of her. Jill put her hands on Alex's knees and looked up, but Alex kept her face covered. Silently, Alex cried, the tears wetting the front of her shirt. Jill moved next to Alex on the couch. She wrapped both arms around Alex's shoulders and hugged her.

Twisting like that immediately sent pain shooting through her body, but she didn't let go of Alex. All she wanted to do was offer comfort, so she pushed her own pain out of her mind. When she breathed too deeply, the pain was exacerbated, so she took in smaller breaths. She felt sweat beading on her forehead, but she continued to hold Alex.

"Jill, are you okay?"

"I'm fine," Jill lied.

The truth of the situation hit Alex and she jumped up, causing Jill to twist back to a normal sitting position. The pain ebbed from her face. "My God, Jill, you're white as a sheet. Twisting like that must have hurt like hell." Alex touched Jill's forehead with the tips of her fingers.

"I'm all right." Until now, Jill hadn't understood the depths of the agony she was putting Alex through. How helpless Alex must feel. "I'm so sorry, Alex. I knew it was hard for you, but I never realized just how hard. I was selfish."

"No, I'm the one being selfish. You've been focused on surviving. Makes it hard to think about anything else. I know it hasn't been on purpose."

"It doesn't matter if it's on purpose. This has to end!"

"Not again, Jill. Please don't."

Jill looked confused and then comprehension dawned. "No, Alex, that's not what I meant. It's time I tell you the whole truth."

"That would be nice." Relief washed over Alex's face. "But first you need to get comfortable. You still don't look so good." Alex gathered pillows and began constructing a pillow nest against one arm of the couch. Jill put her hand on Alex's arm, stopping her from her mission.

"Would you be my pillow, instead?" Jill laughed when she saw the puzzled look on Alex's face.

"Let me show you." Jill motioned for Alex to sit and put her back against the arm of the couch. She had Alex stretch her legs out in front of her, down the length of the couch. Jill sat between Alex's legs and rested her back against Alex's chest. "Feel free to put your arms around me." Jill melted into the comfort of Alex's embrace.

"Okay, much better. Now I'll answer whatever questions you have. With one exception. I won't tell you the details of what he does to me."

"I really only have one question. Why won't you leave him and bring the girls to live with you here?"

"They're not mine."

The girls were not Jill's children. They belonged to Steve's sister, Stephanie. Stephanie's drug problem began when she was thirteen and progressed from marijuana to cocaine. She got pregnant at seventeen and said she didn't know who the father was. At the age of eighteen, she gave birth to Jenna. Initially it looked like her pregnancy turned Stephanie's life around. She went into treatment and came out clean. During treatment, she completed her GED and enrolled in college to become a nurse. She met Mark when he was finishing his final year of medical school. Mark got a job at the local hospital in the emergency room. He knew about Stephanie's past, and despite his career, he was willing to take a chance on her and asked her to marry him. They planned to marry once she graduated, but in her last semester in college, it happened.

Shortly after Steve and Jill were married, the police called and said they had Stephanie in custody. The cops stopped her one evening and asked if they could search her vehicle. She allowed them and they found two bricks of cocaine under her seat. Apparently, they received an anonymous tip that she was dealing drugs. Stephanie swore they were not hers, but the Public Defender was unable to do much with her defense. She was convicted of felony possession with the intent to deliver and sentenced to prison. Jenna came to live with Steve and Jill. While she was in prison, she discovered she was pregnant. Trina was born and brought to them, as well.

The hospital encouraged Mark to resign; he did. He could have helped in her defense, but wanted nothing to do with Stephanie or Trina. He disappeared one night and never told anyone where he was going. After he left, Stephanie stopped caring and dropped her appeal.

Steve forbade Jill from visiting Stephanie. Shortly after her sentencing, Jill went to visit her anyway, but somehow Steve found out. He beat her senselessly and made it clear she shouldn't disobey him again. Jill adored Stephanie and it tore her apart to abandon her, but could not afford to put herself or the girls at risk. When Jill told this part of the story, she had to stop several times before she could go on. Her betrayal of Stephanie haunted her, and she couldn't forgive herself for it.

Steve was the sole guardian, so Jill had no legal rights to the girls. If she left Steve, she would have to leave them too. Steve subtly and sometimes not so subtly made it clear the girls would not be safe with him. He had her trapped and forced to choose between saving herself or staying and protecting the girls. She chose the girls and had been living with that choice for nearly five years.

Jill finished the story and Alex remained silent. Even though Jill could not see Alex's face, she was able to read her reactions by the protective way her arms gently engulfed Jill as she spoke. Jill could tell that Alex was crying and trying to hide it. Jill put her arms over the top of Alex's and squeezed, trying her best to comfort Alex. "It's okay, Alex, you don't always have to be the strong one."

"Why didn't you tell me sooner?"

"He warned me if I told anyone, or if anyone found out, he would kill the girls. He'd make sure I would be there to watch."

"Oh God, Jill." Alex held Jill tighter, but could

find no other words.

"He said killing me would be too good for me, so he would let me live. He wanted me to remember the images of the girls dying for the rest of my life, knowing it was all my fault."

"No wonder you stayed."

"Yep, it was almost like he knew when I was trying to find a way out. Because he would tell me in vivid detail how he would kill them, and what he would do to them before they died." Jill shivered and held on to Alex's arms.

"You're an incredible woman, Jill, a brave woman."

"Thank you," Jill said and hugged Alex's arms again. Alex's words meant more to her than Alex would ever know. In that one sentence, Alex affirmed and empowered her. Society looked down on women in her situation and treated them like lepers, but sometimes circumstances forced women to remain in a bad situation. It was clear that Alex saw how much strength it took for her to endure and respected her for it.

"I hate that son of a bitch even more, but I know that does nothing to make the situation any better. I understand why you've made the choices you have, but it's time to find another way. Please let me help you before you end up seriously hurt or possibly worse."

"Can I tell you something awful?"

"You can tell me anything."

"I've resigned myself to how this is going to end. Either he'll end up killing me or I'll kill him, but either way the girls will be safe. I just want them to be old enough, so they will be okay. Because the bottom line is, my life is over either way. I know in my heart I won't survive until they're old enough to be on their own. I don't believe he will be able to keep his hands off them when they become pretty teenagers, so if he hasn't killed me by then I will take his life. Do you think I'm an awful person?"

"No Jill, I don't. I think you are an incredible person who has sacrificed everything for the sake of two little girls who aren't even yours. Here you claimed I was the superhero, when all along it was you."

"Do I get to wear the little bracelets and belt? I always thought they were so stylish," Jill said, trying to lighten the heaviness.

Alex smiled and pretended to size Jill up. "I'm thinking you could pull off the outfit. Linda Carter doesn't have anything on you."

Jill reached up and put her hand on Alex's forehead. "Nope, no fever. I thought that maybe you were delirious with fever if you think I could come close to measuring up to her. Wait, she must be about seventy by now, so maybe it would give me a fighting chance. I doubt it, though."

"You could have given her a run for her money even in her heyday."

"Love is truly blind," Jill said without thinking. When she realized what she said, she quickly changed the subject. "Unfortunately, I don't have the invisible plane so I can fly back into the apartment without Steve seeing me."

At the mention of Steve, it brought them back to the immediate problem. "You've given me hope, Alex, but for today we need to figure out how to explain where I've been. It's almost noon, and he is going to be furious."

They weighed several options, but soon found a hole in their plans. "I've got it," Alex said after they had been sitting in silence for several minutes. She grabbed her cell phone and called Sarah and Michelle.

"Jill and I need you to come right away," Alex said into the phone. "Yes, she's okay...Have Michelle dress like a straight housewife." Jill turned and looked at Alex, bewildered. "I don't know how a straight housewife dresses, but Michelle will...See you soon," Alex said, ending the call.

"What the hell was that all about?" Jill asked.

Jill continued to lie in Alex's arms, while Alex filled her in on the plan.

Chapter Twelve

Steve stomped to the door, thinking, *it had better be the bitch.* He would teach her a lesson. She thought last night was bad; she hadn't seen anything yet. This time she would suffer. He flung open the door, expecting to see Jill.

A small dark-haired woman stood ready to knock again, Jill behind her. With a charming smile, the woman spoke.

"Mr. Bishop, I am so sorry. I owe you a huge apology. I just hope you can find it in your heart to forgive me. Forgive us all, well, that is, me and George. There isn't really anything to forgive your lovely wife for."

Steve stood looking at her, trying to figure out what was happening. He looked past the woman into Jill's eyes. He only sensed discomfort, not the terror he would expect in this situation. Before he could respond, the small woman pressed on.

"Me and my husband, George, feel just terrible. He asked me to give you his sincere apologies. He couldn't come because he had to work. He thought about calling off so he could come with us, but you know with the economy and all he shouldn't turn down work. Seeing it's Saturday and all, it's overtime too."

The woman rambled in a fast, nervous voice. Her charm was infectious, but he still didn't know what she was talking about. He started to speak, but she did not pause long enough for him to break into the conversation.

"Oh dear, I'm doing it again. George says I sometimes go on and forget to tell people what my point is. I'm afraid that's what I've been doing, isn't it, sweetie? Let me start over. I'm Michelle. I'm bringing your wife back, that's why I'm so sorry. Oh darn, doing it again. I'm not sorry for bringing your wife. I'm sorry that I had her in the first place. Well no, I'm not sorry we had her because if we didn't have her lord knows what would have happened to her. I am sorry that we made you worry. Oh gosh, no wonder you're standing there so quiet, you must be speechless seeing her all torn up like this. Do you mind if I bring her in, so I can explain?"

Steve stepped away from the door and invited Michelle in. He eyed Jill suspiciously when she entered, but she kept her eyes on the ground.

≈≈≈≈

Jill was impressed with how easily Michelle controlled the situation. She'd maneuvered it so they ended up sitting on the couch, while Steve sat in the chair across from them. While Michelle talked, she kept patting Jill's hand, authenticating her character, while at the same time offering Jill reassurance.

"Now let's see, where was I?"

"You were telling about finding my wife," Steve offered.

"Of course, yes. Well, me and George, or is it George and I? No matter, we were out walking our dog, Otis. That's his name, the dog that is. He's a golden retriever, a beautiful dog, but he doesn't seem to be

as bright as they claim his breed should be. I always
thought they were supposed to be really smart. Isn't
that what you've heard?" Michelle said to Steve.

"I have heard that," Steve answered, a look of
confusion on his face.

"Oops, doing it again. I'm sure you're more interested in hearing about what happened to your poor
wife, not talking about dogs. It's just you're so easy
to talk to, I keep getting sidetracked." Michelle gave
Steve a wink. Steve beamed at the compliment. "Well,
we drove to the park because Otis really enjoys it there.
Silly dog, we have plenty of sidewalks around our
house, but he prefers to go to the park. I keep telling
him, Otis that is, when we have kids, meaning George
and me, then he's going to have to get used to the
neighborhood sidewalks. But for now, he's kinda like
our baby, so we take him into the park. Anyway, we
were walking Otis, and George pointed to this person
staggering through the park. We were both disgusted,
thinking it was a drunk or worse yet, a drugged-out
teenager. You know some of the drugs these kids take
today; it's surprising it doesn't kill them. You know
that's why we can't even get our Sudafed anymore,
without being strip-searched. I'm exaggerating, but
you know what I mean."

"I do," Steve answered.

"Anyway, this staggering person falls down
right there in the park. Well, George and I talk it over.
It was too cold to leave them in the park, even if it was
some drunkard. Thank the Lord we went to check it
out. I shudder to think what could have happened to
your lovely wife if we hadn't."

Michelle turned to Jill. When they made eye contact, Michelle reached out and touched Jill's battered

face. Unexpectedly, tears welled up in Michelle's eyes. She waved her hand in front of her face and quickly incorporated her reaction into her story.

"Look at this, I tell you. The thought of seeing the poor dear go down in the park like that chokes me up. Oh, I'm so sorry. It must be choking you up, not knowing what happened. Well, let me tell you. George, he's so chivalrous, he insists on going and checking the situation out. You men, always such knights in shining armor. He gets there and yells for me to come quick. I get there and that's when I see Jill for the first time. The dear was a mess, all torn up. I have to tell you, I've seen it in the movies and on TV where someone sees something and they rush into the bushes to, you know..." Michelle lowered her voice and said, "Puke. That's what I felt like doing when I saw her, but I didn't. I just felt like it, the poor thing. She was not completely in her right mind, probably in shock. I sat down next to her and tried to offer her some comfort."

As if reenacting the scene, Michelle put her arm around Jill.

"So, I've got my arm around the poor thing and she's shivering. I'm not sure if it was from the cold or from being scared, probably a combination of both. I tried to get out of her what happened, but all she could tell us was it was a couple teenagers who jumped her. That's all she'd say. We wanted to take her to the police or the hospital, but she got skittish, kinda like a newborn colt, and refused to go. We pressed a little, but could tell it was upsetting the darling thing, so we stopped."

"I'm sorry, I keep hugging on you." Michelle let go of Jill. "I just can't help it, picturing you in the park like that." She turned back to Steve. "That's when my man took over. He gets all gallant and says we need to take care of this girl. But the sweet man, he gets this torn look on his face. He's worried those hoodlums may still be in the area and is afraid to leave either of us alone without him. Then you wouldn't believe what he does. He bends down and scoops Jill up in his arms and starts carrying her. We get about halfway to the car and he's a huffing and a puffing. Sweat is pouring off him, and I ain't seen him that shade of red, ever. When we can see the car, I convince him Otis and I can run and get it. I tell him he can watch us the whole way. I would have sent him, but I was afraid he was gonna have a heart attack. And don't you go telling him I told you that, Steve."

"I wouldn't dream of it," Steve answered with a smile. Jill looked down at her hands, struggling not to laugh at Michelle's performance.

"So, in the car, I sit with Jill in the back. George'll never let me drive, says it's the man's job. Anyway, I try to talk to Jill on the way to our house. I wanted to see what more she could tell me. She never mentioned she had a husband, which is a shocker seeing how handsome you are. In fairness to her, I think she was in shock or maybe even had a concussion. Even with a concussion, I'm not sure I would forget a looker like you." Michelle winked at Steve again.

"This is the part I'm embarrassed to tell, but George says I have to take responsibility and apologize to you. We get Jill back to our house and get her cleaned up and she's still in bad shape. She was hurting, so I figured I needed to do something for her." Michelle put her hand on Jill's knee. "The poor thing looked miserable, so I rummaged around in our medicine cabinet and found some of George's back medicine.

He uses it for when he throws his back out. I thought I'd just cut to the chase and give her two of 'em. I don't think it was even fifteen minutes and she was zonked out, sound asleep. George gave me one of his looks, the one that says he thinks I've been up to mischief. He asks me what I gave her and I tell him I gave her two of his back pills. I thought he was gonna blow a gasket. I guess those pills are powerful and the doctor only has him take one at a time. He's a far side bigger than her too. I promise you, I watched her like a hawk all night. I kept putting a mirror under her nose to make sure she was still breathing. Did you know that actually works?"

Steve had an amused grin on his face and replied, "I've never tried it."

"Well, if you ever give someone too many meds, I'm telling you it works. So, you see, it's all my fault. George had nothing to do with it, but the poor sweet man was beside himself over the whole thing. Anyway, she didn't wake up until eleven this morning. She was frantic and kept calling out your name. She wanted to come home in the worst way. I hope you know we meant no harm."

"I understand."

"It just touched my heart." Michelle patted her chest and somehow made her voice crack. "She was calling out your name and when I found out about you, I was heart sick. All I could think was how beside yourself with worry you must be. I am so sorry, you poor dear. George and I never meant to put you through such hell. I hope you can find it in your heart to forgive us."

"Yes, it was a sleepless night," Steve said, looking sorrowful.

"Oh lord, I feel just terrible." Michelle looked to the sky and shook her head.

"No need. I've forgotten my manners. I should be thanking you for saving my wife," Steve said, laying on the charm.

"Oh, you are such a forgiving man. Thank you. George and I were just glad to be of help. We still couldn't convince her to go to the police, but maybe you can."

"I'll do my best."

"I should get out of your hair. Despite all the sleep she got, I think she could use more." Michelle put her hand on Jill's and held it. "I'm sure you'll take good care of her."

"You bet I will." Steve shot a look at Jill, and it sent chills up her spine.

Jill got to her feet when Michelle stood to leave. Steve walked with Michelle to the door while Jill stayed standing by the couch. Michelle was about to reach for the doorknob, but stopped and turned back.

"Oh Jill, come here. I have to give you a hug good-bye. A crisis like this always creates a bond; it's like you're family." Michelle made her way back toward Jill and embraced her.

"Honey, I hope you're okay. Me, George, and Alex will be thinking of you, oops, I mean Otis. Alex was our last dog, God rest her soul. We love you and will be keeping you in our prayers." Jill smiled, receiving Michelle's message.

Before Jill let go, she whispered in Michelle's ear, "Take care of Alex."

After the door closed, Steve eyed Jill suspiciously, but he said nothing when she changed into her pajamas and laid down on the couch.

Chapter Thirteen

Alex checked her cell phone again, for what must have been the hundredth time. It was after 8:30, and Jill still hadn't called. Alex had convinced Jill to let the gym's computer expert set up video surveillance equipment in order to obtain evidence against Steve. Jill was supposed to let her know when Steve left for work, so they could get started.

The later it got, Alex became more concerned that Steve decided to stay home, or worse. Alex tried to push the thoughts out of her mind, but the wait was making her edgy. Her need to see Jill, to make sure she was okay intensified with each passing minute. She'd gotten out of bed at 5:30am, not that she'd slept much during the night. She'd showered, dressed, and tried to keep herself busy. The apartment walls felt like they were closing in around her. She needed to get out before she paced a hole in the carpet.

Alex circled the block for the second time, when her phone rang.

"Jill," she said, relief flooding over her.

"Alex, are you okay?"

"I am now."

"He's been gone for over half an hour, so it should be safe. How soon can you come?"

"If you buzz me in, now."

"Where are you?"

"Parking outside your apartment."

"Stalker." Jill laughed. "Be extra quiet when you come upstairs. Trina went to play with Mrs. Harrison, but if she hears your voice, she'll be back in a flash."

Alex normally let Jill initiate physical contact, but she didn't wait this time. As soon as Jill opened the door, Alex wrapped Jill in her arms and held on tight. Tears of relief rolled down Alex's cheeks. She didn't realize how tightly wound she'd been the last two days of not being able to see Jill.

"Sweetie, it's okay." Jill touched Alex's face and looked into her eyes. "I'm fine."

"Sorry, I don't know where that came from." Alex was embarrassed. She promised herself she would act cool for Jill's sake. She looked at Jill closely for the first time. The swelling in her face had subsided, but the bruises had turned a dark purple.

Alex reached out and lightly touched Jill's cheek. "Do they hurt?"

"Not too bad. Now that you're here, not at all."

"What about the rest of you?"

"The rest of me will take a while, but I'll be fine. We don't have time to waste on my ailments; we need to get started."

"I'll call in the cavalry."

⁂

Sarah and Michelle were in tow when Tanya arrived to set up the video equipment. They each carried a small box and Tanya had what looked like a small tool kit in her other hand.

"Let me put on my shoes, so I can help you get

the rest," Jill said when they entered.

Tanya cackled. Jill nervously looked from Tanya to Alex, her eyes pleading for help. Sarah and Michelle stifled a laugh. Alex realized she'd forgotten to warn Jill about the colorful Tanya.

"Video surveillance equipment is really small so it's not detected. By Tanya's reaction, I'm thinking this is all the equipment she needs," Alex said.

Tanya continued to giggle while she unpacked the boxes. She piled the equipment on the table, muttering to herself the whole time. She ran her hand through her thick mop of hair and it stayed standing on end where her hand had been. She peered over her tiny glasses and scowled at the project in front of her. Alex always thought she was the female equivalent of Albert Einstein, more concerned with her intellectual pursuits than her appearance. Social graces also escaped her and she snapped orders at the others in the room. Alex put her arm around Jill, who was standing off to one side looking shell-shocked. Alex winked at her and led her from the room.

"I'm sorry, I forgot to warn you that Tanya is a little eccentric," Alex said when they were out of earshot of the others.

"A little? I'm already nervous about this equip-ment. I swear if she lets loose with another one of her high-pitched shrieks, you're going to have to peel me from the ceiling."

"She only does that when she's really excited about something."

"Well then, this equipment must be making her positively giddy. She's done it three times since she started." As if on cue, they heard a screech coming from the other room, and Jill flinched.

"We better get back in there and rescue Sarah and Michelle," Alex said.

Tanya had sorted the equipment into several piles and was explaining the inner workings to Sarah and Michelle. Their eyes were unfocused, but they continued to nod and make interested grunts. Tanya did not seem to notice and happily continued her monolog.

"Look, Jill's back. You can ask her about the set-up," Sarah said, throwing Jill under the bus.

Tanya launched into an explanation as to which camera should go where. It was evident that Jill did not understand much of what she said by the way she kept nodding with a smile plastered on her face. Once Tanya finished, Jill said, "That sounds really good, but I don't want any in the bedroom."

"Your decision." Tanya swept a pile into an empty box. She frantically rearranged the items on the table, making sure they were equidistance apart. She was talking about the rest of the cameras when Alex interrupted.

"Jill, they need to go everywhere. It defeats the purpose if the cameras miss anything."

Alex began picking the equipment back out of the box. Jill put her hand on Alex's hand. "No, I don't want them everywhere."

Alex momentarily glanced up from her task. "Jill, we already talked about this. What's the problem?"

"No, we didn't." Jill had an edge to her voice, which made Alex stop and look up from what she was doing. She saw Jill shoot a look at Michelle, and wondered what she was missing.

"Alex, I think you should let Jill make her own choices," Michelle interjected.

"Huh?" Alex looked from Jill to Michelle.

"Put those pieces back in the box. We won't need them," Michelle said.

"Why not?" All at once, Alex's eyes darkened and her face flushed. "Oh God, you still have sex with him."

"Alex, stop," Michelle said.

Tanya looked up from the table, oblivious to the tension in the room. "Hey Alex, she doesn't want us recording, you know." Tanya made a circle with one hand and thrust her finger in and out several times. Sarah let out an audible gasp and hurried around the table to position herself between Tanya and Alex. Tanya leaned over the wires in front of her and started whistling, unaware of Alex's growing anger.

"You do, don't you?" Alex said, ignoring Tanya. Her sole focus was on Jill.

"That's enough, Alex. This isn't the time or the place," Sarah said and walked toward her. The vein in Alex's forehead throbbed, and Tanya's whistling was like a dentist drill boring into her skull.

"Why can't she just answer my question?" Alex glared at Sarah. Their eyes locked, and they stood staring one another down. A loud voice interrupted their battle of wills.

"Do you really want to know? Fine," Jill said, raising her voice. Michelle took a step toward her and reached out to take her arm, but she was too late to stop her. "The answer is no, I don't, but he still does." Jill stormed from the room.

Alex felt like she'd been punched in the stomach. She stood staring at the spot Jill vacated when she left the room.

"Hey, where did she go?" Tanya looked up from

the equipment she'd been working on. "I need to get started setting these babies up."

"Go and clean up your mess, Alex. We'll help Tanya," Michelle said, the anger evident in her voice.

"I'm sorry. I wasn't..." Her words trailed off when she looked into Michelle's fiery eyes.

"We're not the ones you should be apologizing to." Michelle jerked her head toward the door. Alex dropped her eyes to the ground as she walked out.

Alex found Jill in her bedroom and knocked on the doorframe. She didn't cross the threshold until Jill invited her in. Jill's eyes held a mixture of hurt and anger when Alex approached her.

"I'm so sorry, Jill. I don't even know what else to say for myself. Please forgive me."

"Why did you have to push? I never wanted to say any of those things to you. I never wanted you to think about them." Alex stepped forward and reached for Jill's arm. "No, Alex, don't touch me."

Alex flinched and took two steps back. Jill's rebuke cut through her. She wanted to run from the room, but she stayed.

"I understand," Alex said quietly. "I'll go. I'm sure Sarah and Michelle will stay until Tanya is done."

"I didn't mean it that way. It's just so humiliating. It's not that I don't want you to touch me. I just don't understand why you would want to. I feel so filthy." Jill picked up a t-shirt from her dresser and rubbed it hard down her arm. She made a couple more passes over her arm before Alex stepped forward.

"Please stop." Alex gently took Jill's hand in order to prevent her from rubbing her skin raw. With her other hand, Alex brushed the hair out of Jill's eyes. "I think you're incredible."

Alex could see that her words had penetrated Jill's armor. Jill no longer looked around the room frantically; now she just looked weary. Alex wanted to pull Jill to her, but held back, wanting to make sure Jill was ready to let her in.

"I never wanted you to know the details. I can't talk about it with you. I can't talk about it with anyone."

Alex looked into Jill's lifeless eyes and hated herself for causing it. At times like this, the depth of Jill's pain was apparent. Jill made it so easy to forget with her sweet smile and normally trusting eyes, but the reality crashed down on Alex.

"I won't make you talk about it again, unless you're ready. I'm so sorry, Jill. You've been through so much. I hope you know you're the most courageous woman I've ever known."

"Why is it that you always make me feel better?" She put her hand over Alex's hand that was resting on her face and closed her eyes.

"I'm afraid that I don't deserve any credit here. Did you forget I'm the one that upset you in the first place?"

Without opening her eyes, Jill leaned into Alex and rested her head against Alex's shoulder. Alex wrapped her arms around Jill and drew her closer.

"You've brought me more comfort than I ever thought possible. I wish you knew how good it feels being in your arms."

Alex's breath caught, Jill's words going straight to her heart. "If it feels half as good as it feels having you in my arms, then it's pretty amazing." Jill let out a contented sigh and relaxed against Alex's body. "I just wish I could shelter you in my arms forever."

"Don't you know how much shelter you've already given me? For the first time in years, I believe I might get out of here alive."

"How do you expect me to be able to walk out of here without you, after you say something like that?" A tear escaped and ran down her cheek.

"Oh sweetie, I'm sorry. I didn't mean it that way. I wish there was another solution, but you understand there's not, don't you?"

"I don't like it, but I understand." Alex held Jill tighter. "Promise me you won't worry about me. The only thing I want you thinking about is staying safe."

"How can I not worry about you?"

"No." Alex's voice was full of panic. "Promise me that you'll only focus on staying safe."

"Alex, relax." Jill ran her hand up and down Alex's back. "I'll be fine."

"Don't you understand? If anything happened to you, I would never get over it."

Jill pressed against Alex. "I think I'm starting to understand how much of a sacrifice it's been for you. And yet, here you are, still standing beside me."

"Always. But please promise me you won't think about me and just do everything you can to stay safe."

"I promise you that I'll keep my ultimate goal first and foremost in my mind."

"Your safety?"

"No, to get out of here, so I can be sheltered in your arms forever," Jill answered. "I need you to be strong for me. I need you to be my rock for a little longer. Can you do that for me?"

"You've had to face this all alone for years. Let me carry some of your burden, some of your pain."

"You don't have to carry it. Just hold me a little

longer because when you do, it just melts away."

"It would be an honor." Alex drew Jill tightly against her.

When they separated several minutes later, Alex said, "You know, I'm sorry for earlier."

"Shh." Jill put her finger against Alex's lips. "Don't say any more."

"But do you forgive me?"

"There's nothing to forgive. Now let's get out there and rescue Sarah and Michelle, or they may never forgive us."

Alex smiled and her eyes twinkled. Jill returned Alex's smile and took her hand. Without another word, Jill led Alex back into the living room to join their friends.

⚜⚜⚜⚜

Jill made another pass through the apartment, making sure there were no signs of Tanya's handiwork. Satisfied, she turned to Michelle and handed her a tiny piece of wire. Michelle put it into the small bag of trash she carried.

Alex turned off the vacuum and started to wind up the cord before Jill stopped her. "No, let me do that. I always do a figure eight pattern. He might notice it's different."

"Damn, Jill," Sarah said. "How can you live like this?" Michelle shot Sarah a dirty look, but Sarah pretended not to notice.

"Hopefully I won't have to much longer." Suddenly, she wanted to feel Alex near her before they left, so she slid up beside her. Alex naturally draped her arm over Jill's shoulder.

"I suppose we better get out of here to be on the safe side," Michelle said.

"Unfortunately, you're right," Jill agreed. Alex pulled her closer. Jill wondered if Alex even realized she had done it.

"Why don't you meet us outside?" Sarah said to Alex.

"That's okay, you two can go ahead and go."

"Alex, I think it's better if we wait for you." Michelle picked up another small piece of wire off a nearby table.

"Michelle's right, you should go with them." A pained look crossed Alex's face. Jill turned to Sarah and Michelle. "No offense, but can I have a few minutes alone with Alex?"

"No offense taken," Michelle answered. "Can I get a hug before we go?"

"Of course." Jill took a step forward and opened her arms. After a round of hugs and words of encouragement, Sarah and Michelle left to wait for Alex outside.

Alex stood stoically with her hands shoved in her pockets. Jill turned from the door and their eyes met. Jill reached up and touched Alex's face, hoping to erase the worry lines on Alex's forehead.

"Thank you for everything."

"How can I leave you?" Alex's voice cracked.

"You have to, sweetie."

Alex shook her head; the pain was etched on her face. "But I don't want to."

"I know you don't, and I love you for that. But as much as I'd like to take your hand and let you escort me out of here, I can't."

"What if I put my arm around you and escort

you out instead?" Alex tried her hardest to give Jill a playful smirk, but she was only partially successful.

"As tempting as that is, I can't."

Alex gently cupped Jill's cheek. "I'm going to do what you've asked me to, but are you aware that this is the hardest thing I've ever had to do?"

"I'm sorry."

"No, don't apologize." Alex looked into Jill's eyes, trying to let her gaze say what her words couldn't. "Please tell me to go. I don't think I can if you don't."

"Come here first." Jill opened her arms. A look of relief washed over Alex's face.

They clung to each other for some time, before Jill said, "Okay Alex, please go."

"Be safe." Alex lightly touched Jill's face. Without another word, she turned and quickly left.

Once the door clicked behind Alex, Jill put her hands on the door and rested her cheek against it. She could hold back her tears no longer.

⚶⚶⚶⚶

"How ya holding up, partner?" Sarah asked when Alex emerged from Jill's building. Michelle immediately went to Alex and put her arm around her.

"It's not fair," Alex said, turning and looking back at the building. "She's up there all alone."

"She's stronger than you think," Michelle said.

"I know, but it's still not right. Here I am with you guys to prop me up, and she has to face everything by herself."

"She's probably stronger than all three of us combined," Sarah said.

"She's got a point." Michelle squeezed Alex's

arm. "She's still standing after everything. Hopefully it won't be much longer before she'll be here with us."

"And you've got a lot of work to do to make it happen," Sarah said.

"In other words, suck it up and get my ass moving."

"You said it; I didn't," Sarah said. "Just keep your eye on the prize. Soon she'll be yours."

"That's not what this is all about." Alex shot Sarah a look.

"Well then, I guess it'll just be an added perk."

Alex started to retort, but instead turned and walked toward her car. She was emotionally drained and didn't have the strength to be angry with Sarah.

"Wait, Alex." Michelle caught up to her. "Sarah didn't mean to upset you."

Alex spun around, her eyes full of hurt. "Do you guys really think that little of me? Do you think I would ever dream of taking advantage of her?"

"Who said anything about you taking advantage of her?" Sarah said, joining them.

"That's what it would be. She needs me to help her, not to put the moves on her. What kind of animal do you think I am?"

"Judging by the way she looks at you, the way she lights up whenever you're around, I'd say she wants both," Sarah said.

"No, she doesn't. She needs a friend she can trust, not one that's trying to get into her pants," Alex snapped.

"What happened to the Alex that was asking us not to clip her wings and support her in her feelings for Jill?" Michelle asked. She lightly put her hand on Alex's arm and smiled. "Nothing has changed. If anything, your feelings for her are a thousand times deeper."

"Don't you get it? Everything has changed. I didn't know what he was doing to her then."

"What does that have to do with anything?" Sarah's frustration was evident. "Sometimes you don't make any sense."

"Before she was just a woman." Alex longed for her friends to understand. "A straight woman, which complicated things, but still there was a possibility. That door slammed shut when I found out what she's going through."

"I'm thinking the door was kicked wide open," Sarah said.

"No, Sarah," Michelle said. "I think I'm beginning to see what Alex is trying to tell us."

"Well then, maybe you can explain it to me, because I'm sure the hell not getting it."

Alex put her hand on Sarah's shoulder and looked her in the eye. "She's vulnerable after everything she's been through. She trusts me. I won't use her trust and vulnerability for my own gain."

"Tell me you're not in love with her," Sarah said.

"That's not the point." Alex paused and looked up as if thinking before continuing. "Or maybe that is the point. I love her too much to do that to her."

"So, you're going to free her from the hell she's in, and then set her free from you?" Sarah said incredulously.

"Yes." Alex's voice was no louder than a whisper. The pain in her chest made it impossible for her to speak the word any louder.

Sarah started to respond, but Michelle cut her off. "Come on, Sarah. I think Alex has had enough for one day." Michelle went to Alex and hugged her. "Let's just focus on getting her safe. Then you can deal with the rest later."

"Thank you." Alex squeezed Michelle tightly. When she let go of Michelle, she playfully messed up Sarah's hair. "Michelle will explain it to you, partner."

As Alex walked away, she heard Michelle say, "Let her go. She needs to be alone right now."

Chapter Fourteen

A lex was deep in thought, preparing a final offer on the Florida deal. After their visit, Sarah and Michelle were enthusiastic about the gym's potential and felt the owner was ready to sell. Alex's concentration was broken by a loud scream coming from Tanya's next-door office. Alex slammed her pen down on the desk and stood up. Since Jill had shown up on her doorstep, nearly a month ago, so badly beaten, Alex had been on edge, and Tanya's bellowing was not helping.

She burst into Tanya's office. "What in the hell are you shrieking about?"

Tanya's face was ashen and her eyes wide. "I wasn't trying to eavesdrop. I was just testing the equipment, but..." Her voice trailed off and she turned toward her computer screen.

For the first time since entering the office, Alex heard the loud sounds coming from the speakers and noticed the movement on the screen. She felt her chest tighten as the truth of the situation dawned on her. "Oh God, no," she said, reaching for the flat screen monitor. She put one hand behind it and cradled it like a child, tears immediately welling in her eyes. She saw his fist rise, but closed her eyes before she saw the impact. The sound was enough to set her in motion. She ran from Tanya's office.

"Alex, wait. Help! Sarah!" Tanya screamed. "Sarah!"

Sarah and several of the girls from the gym raced around the corner.

"What in God's name is going on?" Sarah said.

"He's beating her and Alex saw it. She went to her office and I don't know what she's going to do."

"Oh shit. Tanya, listen to me. I need your help. First, call the police and send them to Jill's house. Then call Michelle and tell her what's going on. I'll take care of Alex. Did you get that?"

"Call the police, then Michelle," Tanya repeated then ran to do as asked.

Sarah looked at the three women beside her. "I'm going into Alex's office. One of you get the van and bring it around front. The other two stay out here and whatever you do, don't let her leave without me."

Sarah entered the room cautiously. The carnage surprised her. Alex was pulling open her last desk drawer. The contents of the other three drawers were spilled all over the floor.

"What in the world are you doing?" Sarah asked.

"I can't find my fucking car keys."

"Alex, stop it. Remember, Michelle borrowed your car this week." When Alex stopped and looked directly at her, Sarah continued as if she were giving instructions to a small child. "Tanya called the police and they should be on their way. The van should be out front as we speak, plus I have three of our girls as backup. We are going to go there now; just don't do anything stupid."

"Thank you," Alex said as she ran past Sarah toward the door.

"It's okay, girls, let's go," Sarah yelled from behind Alex.

❧❧❧❧

The van hadn't come to a stop before Alex opened the door and jumped out. Sarah was right behind her.

"It doesn't look like the cops are here, yet," Sarah said. "But I think I hear sirens in the distance. Don't you think we should wait?"

Alex continued running toward the building, ignoring Sarah's question.

"Hurry up, girls," Sarah yelled to the others in the van. "Alex isn't going to wait for the police, and we don't want her going in there alone."

They burst into the entryway, and Alex began frantically punching the buttons next to the security door.

"Hello," an elderly voice said.

"Mrs. Harrison? It's Alex. Would you—"

"Thank God. I'll buzz you in."

A buzzer sounded and Alex pushed through the heavy door. The girls from the gym followed close behind her. Sarah brought up the rear. They raced up the four flights of stairs, only slightly winded when they reached the top. Alex ran to the door and turned the knob. It was locked. She ran back down the hall, passing Sarah along the way. She stopped at the halfway point and turned back. Alex sprinted down the corridor and launched her body at the closed door. She heard the door groan, but it did not give way. The impact propelled her backward, causing her to lose her balance, and she landed awkwardly on the floor. Pain seared through her shoulder, but she ignored it and scrambled to her feet. She took several steps back, ready for another assault on the door when Mrs. Harrison stepped into her path.

"I think this may help." She held up a key. Jenna and Trina huddled next to Mrs. Harrison, their innocent faces tear-stained and pale.

"Thank you, Mrs. Harrison. Please take the girls back inside." Alex took the key. She couldn't raise her injured right arm high enough to reach the top lock. Every time she tried, the excruciating pain in her shoulder drove her arm back to her side. She switched the key to her left hand, but she was struggling to get the key into the keyhole. The adrenaline coursing through her body coupled with trying to use her non-dominate hand was making the task difficult. Sarah coaxed the key from her and unlocked the door.

⁂

Steve was shocked when the door flew open, and in rushed four big women and their Chihuahua counterpart. He tried to take them all in and make sense of what was happening. Before he could say anything, the first woman through the door shouted, "Get the fuck away from her, now."

He temporarily forgot Jill and left her lying in a heap between the couch and the coffee table. She instinctively curled into a ball and covered her head with her arms. He came around the coffee table and snaked between the two lazy boy chairs, keeping one of the chairs between him and the women. Three of the women were still standing just inside the door, but the aggressive woman was already inside, standing across from him on the other side of the chair. Her eyes were filled with hate, and she glared at him.

"Who in the hell are you and what are you doing in my fucking house?" Out of the corner of his eye, he saw the Chihuahua scramble to Jill and kneel next to her. He turned fully to where Jill lay bruised and bloodied. "Get away from my wife, you bitch."

In that moment, as quick as lightning, the other woman moved, positioning herself between him and the two women on the floor. Rage boiled inside of him, but he was smart enough to realize he wouldn't be able to throw this woman around as easily as he could Jill. He carefully slid behind one of the chairs, placing it between himself and the angry woman. Once behind the barrier, he stopped to assess the situation, planning his next move.

❧ ❧ ❧ ❧

More than anything, Alex wanted to be where Sarah was, tending to Jill, but she knew she needed to hold her ground, or it would put Jill and Sarah in danger. She clenched her jaw tightly shut, fighting the urge to rush Steve, knowing it would only make matters worse. She refrained from saying all the angry words that swirled in her mind. Instead, she stood stoically and glared.

Alex glanced behind her, and saw Sarah push the coffee table away from the couch, in order to give them more room to maneuver. Sarah and Jill were at their most vulnerable, as long as they remained on the floor, but there was no way that Alex would let Steve get to them. Sarah whispered to Jill, but Alex could not make out her words. Jill nodded in response. One of their reinforcements made her way to Sarah and

Jill, and practically lifted Jill to her feet. The other two women from the gym flanked Alex.

Alex looked back at Steve, hatred burning in her eyes. His eyes darted back and forth between Alex and Jill. He looked to be calculating his next move, but for now he remained behind the chair. His knuckles were white as he gripped it.

Alex felt a hand lightly touch her back and heard a voice say softly in her ear, "Alex, let me take your place. Jill needs you."

Alex felt a sharp pain in her chest when she heard Jill's name spoken. She stepped aside and let the other woman fill the gap. She felt Steve's eyes boring into her as she made her way to Jill.

When Alex reached Jill, she lovingly put her hand against Jill's cheek. Alex looked into Jill's eyes, and saw that the terror had begun to subside. Alex opened her arms and Jill fell into them and started to cry. Alex's heart broke as she held Jill and felt her body shake from the sobs that escaped her. She ran her hand down the back of Jill's head, smoothing her hair and talking to her softly, reassuring her that no one was going to hurt her anymore. She felt Jill's body stiffen when Steve started to yell again.

"Jill, who the fuck are these people? That bitch better take her hands off you this second or I am going to kill you both."

Alex tried to shield Jill from seeing him, but realized that this only served to frighten her. Jill was used to tracking his every move, and not being able to see him was increasing her panic. Alex shifted so Jill could keep an eye on him. Jill pushed her hair back and locked eyes with him.

"You fucking bitch. Don't ever look me in the

eye."

Jill remained silent, but continued to stare.

"I'm warning you, bitch, you will pay for this."
Jill continued looking at him, until Steve looked away.

At that moment, the police burst into the room.

❧ ❧ ❧ ❧

After the initial chaos subsided, the police began
separating them. Two burly officers went to handcuff
Steve, but he resisted, insisting he was innocent.
He accused Alex and her group of being a gang of
thieves who invaded his home and attacked his wife.
He turned to Jill and gave her a quick piercing look
before turning on the charm for the police.

"Honey, tell them what these horrible women
did to you. We can't have people like this on the street
when we have two little girls to think about. You
know what could happen to them?" Alex picked up
his meaning, even if the police didn't.

Sarah grabbed Alex before she could rush Steve,
which slowed her momentum enough for the police to
position themselves between the two.

"You stupid motherfucker, you will never hurt
any of them again, ever. Even if I have to kill you myself." Alex's face was crimson and the veins in her
forehead stood out.

"Jesus!" Sarah pulled harder on Alex's arm.
"Alex, for God's sake, knock it off. You're surrounded by police, threatening to kill someone, not a good
idea."

"Did you hear that?" Steve angrily pointed his
finger at Alex. "I told you they're violent. She just
threatened me. Arrest her."

"Alex, look at Jill. All of this is scaring the shit out of her. Is that what you want?" Sarah grabbed Alex by the shoulders.

Brought back to the moment, Alex looked behind her and saw Jill cowering against the entertainment center. Alex immediately forgot Steve and moved toward Jill. One of the police officers started to intervene, but the woman in charge put her hand on his arm and shook her head. Jill was looking at the ground with hunched shoulders, her hair covering much of her face. Alex stopped an arm's length away. She wanted to touch her, but knew it was the worst thing to do when Jill was this frightened.

"Jill, are you okay? I didn't mean to scare you. I'm sorry." Jill looked out from behind her hair. When Alex smiled at her, Jill's shoulders relaxed, and she pushed her hair behind her ear. As soon as they made eye contact, Alex stepped forward and put her arm around Jill.

"Arrest that woman. Get her away from my wife." Steve strained against the officers that were holding him back. Jill nestled against Alex's side, and Alex draped her arm protectively over Jill's shoulder.

"Get your filthy hands off my wife." The spittle flew from his mouth as he raged. He glared at the female officer across the room who seemed to be in charge. "You pieces of shit need to do something."

The officer nodded to the burly cops flanking Steve. They tightened their grip on him and escorted him out of the apartment, while he shouted obscenities.

The woman approached Jill and Alex and introduced herself as Detective Barrett. She asked Jill to have a seat on the couch, so they could talk about what happened. Alex started to follow, but Detective

Barrett stopped her, saying she needed to question Jill alone. She instructed Alex and the rest of the women to go with the two remaining officers into the kitchen for questioning. The officers assigned to that detail turned to leave, but Alex didn't follow. She stood defiantly in the middle of the room with her hands on her hips. Sarah tried to reason with her, to no avail. The two officers turned back, showing signs of impatience.

"Detective, please. Alex is just upset, but she'll go if Jill asks her to. Please don't let a bad situation get any worse," Sarah pleaded.

The two officers were standing in front of Alex, looking as if they might try to overpower her. One officer was reaching for the handcuffs clipped to her belt, while the other officer moved around behind Alex.

"Hey guys, let her come over here for a second," Detective Barrett said. The two yielded to her authority and let Alex pass.

"I know you're worried about your friend, but I won't let anything happen to her. We just need to do our job." Alex stood her ground, having no intention of leaving the room.

Detective Barrett looked at Jill and said, "Honey, could you help me out here? I don't think she'll listen to anyone but you. We certainly don't need any more problems today."

"Come here." Jill reached for Alex's hand. Alex immediately took it and knelt on one knee in front of the couch. Jill smiled and reached out, touching the side of Alex's head. "Alex, I'll be okay. Honest. I need for you to cooperate with the police and that means going with them into the other room."

"Are you sure you're gonna be all right?"

"I'll be okay, Alex. Would you please do this for me?" Jill squeezed Alex's hand.

"You know I'd do anything for you."

"I know." Jill blinked back tears.

"But now you're crying."

"I'm fine. I'm just a little overwhelmed."

"It's been one hell of a day."

"No, it's not that. I don't know if I'll ever get used to having someone who cares about me the way you do."

"You will if I have anything to say about it." Alex grinned. Jill smiled and squeezed Alex's hand. "I suppose I better get into the other room before they drag me out of here." Alex rose to her feet, kissed Jill on the top of the head, and turned to follow the officers.

"Thank you," Sarah mouthed to Detective Barrett.

❧❧❧❧

The questioning seemed to go on forever. What happened? Who are they? How did they know the victim? How did they know to call the police? Could they provide these tapes to the police?

Alex tensed when they questioned her concerning the nature of her relationship with Jill. "What relevance does the nature of our relationship have to do with anything?"

"Just standard protocol," the officer responded.

"So, what are you saying? If we were in a lesbian relationship, then she deserved the beating?" Alex asked.

"That is not what we are saying, ma'am," the young female cop replied. "We just need to get the facts of the case."

"Well, the facts are the son of a bitch has been beating the shit out of her for years and it's time someone did something about it."

"That's why we're here," the more seasoned officer interjected. "We want to do something about it, but we need your help. The more information you can give us, the more solid our case. I understand you're upset, I really do, but we aren't the enemies."

"Sorry, I don't want to mess up your investigation. I'll answer your questions."

"I apologize, but I have to ask you this question. Are you and Jill involved in a lesbian relationship?"

"No, we're just friends."

"Are you in love with her?"

Alex looked down at her hands and picked at her fingernails. Almost inaudibly, Alex answered, "Yes."

"In light of your last answer, I have to ask you again. Were you involved in a lesbian relationship with the victim?"

"No, I wasn't. We're just friends. She doesn't know how I feel about her."

"I don't want to argue with you, ma'am, but it's pretty apparent how you feel about her. Are you sure she doesn't know?"

"I don't know. All I know is that I've never told her."

There was a knock on the door and Detective Barrett entered. The two officers immediately jumped to their feet, awaiting their orders.

"Jill needs a break and I think a little time with her friends would do her some good. She's with a

Michelle who showed up a while ago, says she's with you?"

"Yes, she's with us." Alex smiled.

Michelle was sitting next to Jill on the couch when they walked into the room. Jill looked worse than she had before, her face was starting to show signs of bruising, and there was dried blood on her lips and under her nose. Alex sought solace in Jill's eyes, but instead got an uneasy feeling in the pit of her stomach. Jill was remote; Alex hoped she could reach her.

"I want to give you a big hug, but I'm afraid it would just hurt you." Alex looked down at Jill, who was slumped on the couch.

"Be my pillow," Jill answered. Her eyes showed signs of life and a slight sparkle when she smiled at Alex.

"It would be my pleasure." Alex returned Jill's smile. Alex lowered herself to the couch and rested her back against the arm. Jill scooted between her legs and rested her back against Alex's chest. Alex raised her legs on each side of Jill, creating a nest around her. She wrapped her arms loosely around Jill, rounding out the cocoon she was trying to create. Jill sighed and her body relaxed against Alex. Michelle materialized out of nowhere with a blanket and covered Jill. Within minutes, Jill was breathing rhythmically, fast asleep.

Detective Barrett looked around when she entered the room. She went over to the three women from the gym, who were standing off to the side having an animated conversation. She said something to the women, who nodded as she spoke. She made her way over to the couch and looked down at Sarah and Michelle, who were huddled next to the couch, looking like miniature guard dogs.

Jill laid in Alex's arms, sound asleep. The peace that only sleep can bring replaced the pain on her face. Alex watched her sleep, but looked up when Detective Barrett spoke.

"Alex, I'm going to need to ask you a few questions."

"Okay." Alex looked helplessly at the sleeping Jill.

"I shouldn't interview you in front of the victim, but I'm going to be a bit unorthodox." Detective Barrett looked at Jill with compassion. "I don't have the heart to disturb her. Besides, I doubt she'll hear anything anyway."

"Thanks, Detective," Alex said.

Detective Barrett released the other witnesses and allowed Sarah and Michelle to wait in the kitchen while she interviewed Alex. Once everyone cleared out, Detective Barrett sat down across from Alex and pulled out a notepad.

"I have to start by asking you what happened to your shoulder. I notice you've been favoring your right arm considerably."

Alex was embarrassed and blushed. She told the detective about her unsuccessful attempt at breaking in the door. She ended by saying, "It always looked so easy on TV. The cops are always busting down doors."

Detective Barrett smiled. "On TV, the doors aren't made of reinforced steel. You're lucky you didn't really hurt yourself."

"I think maybe I did. I can barely lift my arm." Alex winced as she demonstrated for Detective Barrett.

"Sounds like a separated shoulder. You should probably get it checked out." Detective Barrett looked at Jill and continued. "Maybe it's a good thing that you need medical attention. I'd really like her to go to the hospital, but she refused earlier."

"I'll get her there," Alex assured Detective Barrett.

"That would be great. Now that that mystery is solved, I have some questions about Mr. and Mrs. Bishop's relationship."

Alex felt a shiver run through her. "Could you please just call her Jill? He lost the right to have his name attached to her the first time he laid a hand on her."

"Fair enough, I can do that. So, when did you first find out that Mr. Bishop was being physically aggressive with Jill?"

Alex relayed the entire story to the detective, starting with how they met. The detective interrupted a few times with clarifying questions, but for the most part let Alex talk without interruption.

"Why didn't you call the police when Jill showed up on your doorstep in such a state? Didn't you want to protect her?"

"More than anything." Alex looked at Jill, who continued to sleep peacefully in her arms. She had been fighting her guilt since the police arrived, and Detective Barrett's questions did nothing to alleviate it. "Maybe I should have. I did the wrong thing, didn't I?"

"I'm not here to judge. I just need to understand what happened."

"I can't understand why it happened so soon." Alex was distraught and shook her head as if to clear her mind.

"What do you mean, 'so soon'?"

"I thought I had more time to work things out. I thought she would be relatively safe. He usually left her alone for a couple months after a vicious attack like the last one. I think instinctively he knew her body couldn't take it." Alex cradled Jill, feeling the anguish of not protecting her.

"Alex, it's not your fault. Apparently, he came home for lunch and found her cell phone sitting on the table."

"Shit. She called me this morning, but I had a meeting to go to, so I told her that I'd call her at lunch. Her body hadn't healed completely. Even though she would never admit it, she was still moving gingerly."

"I'm sure she'll be fine. You guys got here quickly."

"But it took us at least ten minutes."

"Yes, a relatively short time. According to Mrs.—Jill, the serious attacks could go on for well over an hour. So, he was just warming—" Detective Barrett stopped mid-sentence. Alex stared back at her with a look of horror on her face. "You didn't know that, did you?"

"No, she wouldn't tell me any of the details." Alex breathed deeply, trying to still her anger. "But how could her body take such a prolonged attack?"

"Alex, I've already said too much, but rest assured you got here fast enough."

"So, the asshole circled her like prey, toying with her. Imagine the terror she lived with, never knowing if he would come back for more."

"It's okay, Alex. She always knew when it was over," Detective Barrett answered. "I need to continue with your questioning."

Alex ignored Detective Barrett. "How could she

have? What, did he come back three times before he lost interest? Or did…" Alex's voice trailed off and her face turned bright red. Her eyes narrowed and she fought to control her breathing. "Oh, fuck." Alex ran her hand through her hair and fought against the churning in her stomach.

"Alex," Detective Barrett said, obviously realizing her mistake.

"What you're telling me is beating the hell out of her is his idea of foreplay." Her anger was replaced by compassion when she looked at Jill. Alex lightly touched Jill's cheek. "I'm so sorry. I should have done more. I should have protected you."

"Are you ready to answer the rest of my questions?" Detective Barrett's posture stiffened.

Alex noted the Detective's tone and paused before answering. "I know you probably said more than you intended, but I want you to know I appreciate it. This situation sucks, and I wish none of us were here right now." Alex looked down at Jill before continuing. "I'm scared to death for her, but it gives me solace that you're the officer on her case. Maybe you haven't done things completely by the book, but you've treated us like people. Thank you."

"You're welcome, but I do need to ask you some more questions." Detective Barrett's tone was softer and her shoulders relaxed.

"Okay, ask away."

"I have to ask you about the nature of your relationship with Jill."

"We're friends, but I'm sure the other officers told you I'm in love with her." Alex unconsciously took Jill's hand. "I didn't mean for it to happen. I made the fatal lesbian mistake."

"Which is?"

"I fell in love with a straight woman."

"How did Jill handle your feelings for her?"

"She doesn't know."

"I mean no disrespect, but do you seriously believe that? Every one of us were able to ascertain how you felt about her in, oh, about the first thirty seconds on the scene. So how is it that you think she doesn't know?"

"Well, she knows I love her, but we've never talked about anything more. You have to remember she's been living in hell. She's been trying to survive, so I'm thinking a romantic relationship is the farthest thing from her mind. I've become her closest friend, the person she relies on, so that's the light she sees my love in."

"Okay." Detective Barrett nodded. "Let's move on to what you've been doing the last three weeks since the day Jill was beaten. Jill mentioned you've hired two attorneys."

"Yes, I retained Samantha Sanchez to work on guardianship for the girls and Jacob Marshall for Stephanie's appeal."

"It's my understanding that Mr. Bishop has sole guardianship of the children," Detective Barrett said.

"Yes, that's the problem," Alex answered. "I'm hoping his arrest will help with the case."

"What about the appeal for Stephanie, what is the status?"

"I talked to Mr. Marshall yesterday. He's been working with Chief Evans and is telling me we have a good chance. I'm hoping the case gets stronger once you get Steve's fingerprints."

"Why would Mr. Bishop's fingerprints matter?"

"Stephanie still maintains her innocence on the drug charges. Apparently, there were fingerprints on the bags of cocaine, but none were hers."

"I see, but Jill told me Stephanie didn't fight the charges and pled guilty."

"That's true, but only because she gave up. She was devastated when her fiancé ran out on her after her arrest. She'd cleaned up her life, and when he didn't believe her, it put her into a tailspin. After her arrest, she found out she was pregnant, but he wanted nothing to do with the baby. She was devastated and folded."

"How do you know these things?"

"I've been visiting Stephanie in jail the last three weeks. She's a great girl, but life hasn't dealt her a fair hand."

"You say you're hoping Mr. Bishop's fingerprints might help the case. Alex, don't you think it's a pretty big stretch to accuse him of framing his own sister?"

"Not at all."

"What motive would he have?"

"To shut Stephanie up and trap Jill. It served both his purposes."

"What did he want to shut Stephanie up about?" Detective Barrett's eyes narrowed.

Alex looked at Jill and smoothed her hair, listening for her rhythmic breathing before answering. "Jill doesn't know this yet, Detective. She had enough on her plate just trying to survive. I didn't want to burden her with anything else, especially something that would only rip her apart."

"So, what is it that Stephanie told you?"

A pained look crossed Alex's face. "Jenna is Steve's."

"So, Stephanie was caring for his child?"

"Their child."

"What...?" Detective Barrett's eyes got bigger, the picture suddenly becoming clearer. "You mean, he had a baby with his sister?"

"Yes. Apparently, Jill isn't the first woman he raped."

Chapter Fifteen

Alex helped Jill from the car with her left hand. Jill winced when she stood and steadied herself against Alex. The spring air was crisp, but held a hint of warmer weather. Alex inhaled deeply, enjoying the freshness, trying to get the smell of hospital from her nose. They walked slowly up the sidewalk, looking like two soldiers returning from battle. Jill still wore her bloodstained clothes, and Alex sported a sling on her right arm. Sarah and Michelle trailed after them, carrying Jill's suitcase and a bag of Chinese carryout. Even though they showed no physical evidence of the day, their faces told the story. It was rare to see either looking tired, but tonight, they looked exhausted. Their normally youthful faces were hardened with concern.

When they got inside, Alex looked at the flight of stairs with trepidation. They looked steeper than she remembered. Sarah and Michelle scurried around them and hit the stairs first. Alex took Jill's hand as they made their slow ascent. By the time they reached Alex's apartment, Michelle had stashed Jill's suitcase in the guest bedroom, and Sarah had put the food into the refrigerator.

"Are you sure you don't need us to stay and help out?" Michelle asked.

"No, thanks," Alex said. "I think a quiet evening

is in order."

"What? You're saying that you can't have a quiet evening with us around," Sarah said.

"I'm sorry, but the word quiet and Sarah should never be used in the same sentence," Alex shot back.

Michelle ignored the banter and approached Jill, who stood quietly just inside the door. "Are you going to be okay, honey?"

Jill smiled slightly. "I'll be fine."

"I'm sure Gimpy over there will take good care of you." Michelle motioned toward Alex.

Jill's smile widened as she looked at Alex. "She always does."

Alex joined them, putting her arm protectively around Jill. "I promise I'll look after her. Thank you for everything. Don't tell Sarah, but I'm not sure what I'd do without you two."

"Your secret is safe with me," Michelle said while Sarah stood next to her pretending not to listen.

After a round of hugs and more reassurances that Jill would be okay, Sarah and Michelle disappeared down the stairs.

※ ※ ※ ※

Alex locked the door then turned to Jill. "How ya doing?"

Jill started to answer, but stopped when she made eye contact with Alex. Jill's breath caught when she saw the compassion and concern in Alex's warm brown eyes. No one ever looked at her with so much genuine caring. Somehow answering with a one-word response seemed inadequate.

"Are you all right?" Alex asked.

"I am." Jill wanted to say more, but she was having

trouble finding the words. More than anything, she wanted Alex to hold her and take away the lingering pain.

"But…" Alex said. "What is it you aren't saying?"

"How come you read me so well?" Jill smiled. "I just really need a hug."

Alex pretended to look at her watch and then got a panicked look on her face. "Oh no, the doctor's gonna be pissed at me. I was supposed to give you your next dose of hugs ten minutes ago."

Jill laughed and stepped into Alex's one-armed embrace. Jill felt the bone-weary fatigue lift as she drew energy from Alex. They held one another for several minutes, neither wanting to let go.

"Are you upset with me?" Jill asked when she saw the angry look on Alex's face when they parted.

"God, no. I was just thinking about that son of a bitch and what he's done to you."

"No, Alex, I'm okay now. I don't want to think about him, and I don't want you to either. I want to enjoy being here with you."

"I just don't get it." Alex shook her head. "How could he throw it all away? You're beautiful, intelligent, caring, funny. You're an incredible woman that any man would be lucky to have."

"What about any woman?" Jill smirked.

"Um, well, yeah, any…well, yeah, woman too." Alex stumbled over her words. Her face flushed and she quickly looked away from Jill. "I'm starving. You better get your shower so we can have some dinner." Before Jill could say anything, Alex hurried toward the kitchen.

Jill grinned as she watched Alex leave the room. She wondered when Alex would accept what Jill had known for several months; they were falling in love. No, falling was the wrong word. They'd already fallen.

❧ ❧ ❧ ❧

"Something smells good," Jill said as she entered the room. Her hair was still wet, and she'd pulled it back off her face. She was dressed in one of Alex's sweatshirts and a pair of Alex's pajama bottoms. She knew she looked small and frail in the oversized clothes, but she didn't mind because she found them comforting.

"Sarah and Michelle brought a bunch of your clothes. They put the suitcase in your bedroom," Alex said.

"I know, I just like wearing yours. Is that okay?"

"It's fine by me. You wear them well." Alex grinned and motioned to the table. "Come sit down. I don't want our food to get cold. I've been slaving over a hot microwave the whole time you were in the shower."

"What a chef." Jill's smile faded after she sat down.

"What's the matter?" Alex set down two steaming bowls of hot and sour soup, and pushed one toward Jill.

"I was just thinking about the girls." She stirred the soup and blew on it, watching the steam cascade off it.

"Sorry, I might have heated that up a little too much. I guess I need to brush up on my microwave skills." The microwave dinged, and Alex turned back to get the main course. "When we talked to the girls, they seemed fine. I think spending the night with their grandma will be good for them and you."

"You're right, no more sadness." She was

starving, but the soup was still too hot, so she blew on it again. Tentatively, she took a bite, savoring the spiciness of the dish. "I just can't believe how hungry I am. You'd think after everything that's happened, I would've lost my appetite."

"Or maybe now that it's finally over, you've found it." Alex carried a large bowl of shrimp fried rice to the table and sat down.

"Is it really over?"

"What do you mean?" Alex stopped mid scoop and stared at Jill.

"What happens now?" Earlier, when she was in the shower, a new fear haunted her. What if Alex couldn't or wouldn't let herself cross any lines? What would that do to their friendship? Would the Lone Ranger's job be done and if so, did that mean Alex would ride off into the sunset? The thought terrified her and made it difficult for her to breathe.

"Right now, we eat." Alex piled a large scoop of fried rice onto Jill's plate, and started to scoop out another before Jill put her hand out and shook her head. "Then we get you back on your feet, so you can have your life back."

"And you'll be there?" Jill looked up from her food, hopefully.

"Every step of the way. Being in business, I'm used to dealing with courts and lawyers, so I can help you navigate the system. It'll be easy." Jill's face dropped, when she realized Alex was strictly focused on the professional, not the personal.

"What about afterward?" Jill pushed her food around her plate, no longer hungry.

"You'll probably be so busy I'll rarely see you." Alex's words cut into Jill; she seemed so reserved and distant. They had shared so much over the last several months, but now the conversation seemed strained. *No, strained was the wrong word. Superficial!*

"I guess this gives you your life back too." Jill knew she was baiting Alex, but didn't care if she could get a reaction out of her.

"No sense of thinking about that now." Alex blew on her soup before taking a bite. "We've got a lot to get done."

"You're right." Jill decided to let the conversation drop. "Want to fill me in on the game plan? I know Detective Barrett was giving you the rundown."

"We try to push the courts to move as quickly as possible." Alex jumped up from the table, and brought back the bag the carryout came in.

"No problem. That should be really easy."

"Do I detect sarcasm?" Alex smiled. She tipped the bag and let the packets of hot mustard and soy sauce fall out. "I already talked to both attorneys and they have assured me they're on it."

"When did you do that?" Jill grabbed a couple of the packets and unsuccessfully tried to rip one open.

"While they were checking you over in the ER." She took the packet from Jill, put it between her teeth, and ripped it open before handing it back.

"Thanks." Jill stifled a smile at the familiarity of Alex's gesture, knowing Alex would be embarrassed if she pointed it out.

"I swear I could have run a marathon with as many tests as they ran on you."

"I'm sorry."

"No, no...I'm teasing. I'm happy they were so thorough. I think someone's tired."

"Don't you really mean someone's cranky and

overly sensitive?"

"You said it, not me." Alex grinned.

"Fine." Jill feigned anger. She felt herself relax, now that their familiar banter had returned. She loaded her spoon with rice, suddenly hungry again. "You might as well fill me in on everything you've been keeping from me the last few weeks."

"Let's finish eating first. I'd hate to spoil such a lovely meal and conversation with unpleasantness," Alex said with a smirk.

"You're a shit."

❦❦❦

After they'd finished dinner, they quickly cleaned up and moved to the living room, where they could stretch out on the couch. Jill was exhausted, but didn't want to wait until morning for Alex to fill her in on how the legal proceedings were going.

"I want to see Stephanie," Jill said. Even though Alex was smiling, Jill couldn't read her eyes. "What are you thinking?"

Alex glanced up at the ceiling, before her eyes settled back on Jill. "You amaze me. After all I just told you, that's the first thing you say."

"She's been through so much. She's been so alone, abandoned by all of us. I can't begin to imagine how she must feel. She probably hates me, but I have to see her."

"I can guarantee you Stephanie doesn't hate you. She's been much safer than you've been."

"But I had my freedom."

"Did you?"

Jill looked at Alex and fought back tears. When the conversation began, she promised herself and Alex she wouldn't cry. She unconsciously moved nearer to Alex on the couch, needing to feel safe. "I do now, thanks to you. The Lone Ranger does it again. You're not going to ride off into the sunset, are you?"

"No, not yet." Before Jill could respond, Alex changed the subject. "We're going to have a busy day tomorrow. Don't you want to get some sleep?"

"No."

Alex waited for Jill to elaborate, but she didn't. "You have to be drained. We probably should have saved this conversation until morning."

"I'm afraid if I go to sleep that this will all be a dream." Jill squeezed Alex's hand and continued. "And when I wake up, I'll be back there again with him."

"The nightmare's over." Alex protectively put her arm around Jill.

"This is just the beginning of the good dream," Jill said, laying her head against Alex's chest.

"The beginning of the rest of your life."

"You sound like a greeting card." Jill laughed. She snuggled in closer to Alex, enjoying the safety of Alex's embrace. Tonight, she wasn't going to analyze what it meant or question herself as to why she always felt so good when Alex was there with her. Tonight, she wanted to forget and enjoy the moment.

"Rough crowd, I go for inspirational and I get laughed at." Alex unsuccessfully tried to add a whine to her voice.

"Your acting has a lot to be desired too."

"Geez, I can't do anything right."

"I wouldn't say that," Jill said sleepily. "You definitely give good hugs."

Chapter Sixteen

"Alex, why didn't you wake me up sooner?" Jill said, glancing at the clock. She wondered how long Alex had been up, since she appeared showered and ready to go. "It's already ten-thirty. I need to get ready if I'm going to be presentable. We can't all pop out of the shower and look good in five minutes, like you can."

"You'll be fine; besides, you don't have to do anything special to look good."

"Right, I'm sure this torn up face will look really nice in public." Jill self-consciously touched her cheek.

"I thought you needed sleep more than anything else." Alex sat down on the corner of the bed.

"That was sweet of you, but I have no idea what I am going to wear." Jill threw back the covers and went to her suitcase. She tossed several items aside as she rummaged through it.

"What are you doing?"

"I'm going to look like a homeless person. We'll have to stop by the apartment, so I can get my good sweater."

"It's wool. You'll spontaneously combust if you wear it in this weather. Besides, Michelle has it covered. I'm surprised she's not here yet."

"Was she stopping by the apartment to pick up more clothes?" Jill picked through her suitcase again, as if something new would appear.

"No, she went shopping to pick up a few things for you. She should be here any time."

"You guys can't keep doing this." Jill put her hands on her hips and narrowed her eyes at Alex.

"What?"

"You're always taking care of me. Doing things for me. I feel like such a burden." Jill straightened the clothes in her suitcase and zipped it.

"You're not a burden. You're one of the best things that's ever happened to me."

"Sure, I've made your life so much better." Jill snorted. "You've done so much for me and I have nothing to offer you. Yep, I can see why you want me around."

"Please stop." A pained look crossed Alex's face.

Jill smiled and touched Alex's cheek. "I'm sorry. Sometimes I don't think you realize how good you make me feel or how much I appreciate everything you guys have done for me."

"We know. Trust me, you've told us enough." Alex pretended exasperation, but her eyes twinkled. "Now, you better get yourself into the shower before I get blamed for you not being ready on time."

"Don't worry, you'll get blamed anyway." Jill winked at Alex before she turned away.

❧❧❧❧

Michelle rushed in, her arms full of bags, and began rambling as soon as she crossed the threshold. Alex tried to help with the packages, but Michelle slapped her hand away. Alex stepped aside, knowing not to argue when Michelle was on a mission. She followed behind Michelle, but when they got to the guest room, Michelle shooed her away.

From the living room, Alex heard bags rattling and Michelle muttering. After several minutes, Michelle emerged in a frenzy, went to the bathroom, knocked, and disappeared inside. Alex wandered into the bedroom to peek at Michelle's purchases. There were clothes spread out everywhere. Jill would love what Michelle bought, but be mortified by how much she'd spent.

Alex heard the bathroom door open and knew she should escape before Michelle caught her gaping. She didn't move quickly enough, and Michelle hurried into the room and nearly crashed into her. Alex put her hand out to steady Michelle and noticed the look on her face.

"Whoa, are you okay?" Alex asked.

"Huh? Oh, yeah," Michelle answered as she picked up a skirt from the bed.

Alex studied Michelle while she held up a shirt to the skirt she was holding. She was pale and her eyes were watery. Her movements seemed unfocused and frantic as she picked up several shirts and tossed them back with hardly a glance. "You don't look so good," Alex finally said.

"I didn't realize. I never thought about how bad it was. I've seen her face, but I never thought about her body." Michelle stopped and looked at Alex. "Oh God, Alex, he's messed her up."

"I know," Alex said quietly. "I felt the same way when I saw it too. You're actually doing better than I did. I puked."

"If I wasn't on a mission, I probably would." Michelle went back to sorting through the clothes. "Do you think it's stupid that I want to give her a choice?"

Alex was puzzled by Michelle's question, not sure what it meant or where it came from. "I don't think I understand the question."

"You know me." Michelle stopped what she was doing and looked directly at Alex. "I normally just take charge, and if it were you or Sarah, I would just pick the outfit and tell you, 'wear this'."

"Yep, I've been the victim—I mean the benefactor of that." Alex smiled. "I guess I'm not understanding why you'd be different with Jill."

"With Jill, it doesn't seem right." Michelle blinked back tears, again. "She's had no control of her life for a long time, so in some small way I want to give her back control. Is that ridiculous?"

"No, I think that is one of the sweetest things you've ever said." Alex didn't think she could possibly love Michelle any more than she already did, but in that moment she did.

"Stop looking at me like that." Michelle blinked back tears and waved her arm at Alex. "You need to get your butt out of here. She'll be out of the bathroom soon, and we have work to do. Scram."

"Okay, okay. It's pretty bad when I can't even go where I want in my own home."

"Quit your whining and go."

⚜ ⚜ ⚜ ⚜

Alex was pacing around the living room under the pretense of straightening up when Michelle emerged from the bedroom.

"Whatever you do, get it right," Michelle said under her breath.

"What am I supposed to get right?"

Michelle started to respond, but when the bedroom door opened, she stopped.

Jill timidly walked into the room. She was dressed in a long, flowing skirt. It was patchwork with several textured fabrics, all various shades of brown. She wore a simple lightweight tan sweater that complimented the skirt. Her hair was down and fell to her shoulders. Michelle must have trimmed the ends because Jill's hair no longer looked stringy. Her bruises were still visible, but her make-up went a long way to mask the worst of them. Alex felt her breath catch and her chest tighten. She'd never seen Jill in anything but worn out, ill-fitting clothes.

"Jill, you look amazing." Alex took a step toward her.

"I'd look better without this messed up face." Jill nervously reached for her hair.

"You still look beautiful." Alex found Jill attractive since the day she met her, so she was shocked how much more amazing Jill looked today.

"I think it's the clothes." Jill smoothed her skirt and adjusted her sweater before looking up. Her eyes found Alex's, but Alex quickly looked away, not wanting Jill to see the fire burning in her eyes.

"It's not just the clothes; you are beautiful." Alex swallowed hard, fighting back her emotions. Her intense eyes softened and became shiny with unshed tears.

"No Alex, don't look so sad and please don't cry. If you start, I will too and I don't have time to fix my make-up."

"Alex is right," Michelle said. "You look incredible."

Jill smiled. "I think you guys are miracle workers."

"How's that?" Michelle asked.

"Look at me, I'm all torn up." Jill pointed at her face. "But I can't remember a time I felt more beautiful."

"I'm just happy I could help. Oh, Jill…" Michelle stopped. "No, you told Alex not to, so I won't either. I'm going to get out of your way, so I don't make you late."

When Jill went to get her purse from the bedroom, Michelle whispered to Alex, "You got it right."

"See, I told you I had it in me, and you didn't believe it."

"Not after all the disastrous blind dates. I was pretty sure caveman was the best I could expect from you."

"I guess you haven't done a very good job of picking my dates, or maybe you would have seen this side of me before."

❧❧❧❧

They'd been at the courthouse for over two hours, meeting with lawyers and family services. Everyone was pulling Jill in various directions, all having their own agenda. She knew she'd handled herself well, answering the same question several times, without losing her patience or becoming frustrated. But now she felt the tension rising as they sat in a little visitors' room inside the courthouse.

"How you holding up?" Alex asked.

Jill took a deep breath before answering. "I'm hanging in there. Thanks for being here with me."

"There's nowhere else I'd want to be."

"I'm sure you could think of somewhere."

"Well maybe. This doesn't quite have the ambiance of the laundromat." Alex swept her arm toward the dingy, marred walls. She pointed at a faded painting with a three-sided frame. "But the artwork here is better."

Jill laughed and felt herself relax as they talked. Alex always had a way of putting her at ease, and today was no exception. The butterflies still danced in her stomach, but she knew they wouldn't go away until she finally saw Stephanie face-to-face. She was prepared for it to be awkward; she only hoped there would be no anger. She'd had enough anger from the Bishop family to last her a lifetime. Her stomach clenched when she heard the door click.

Alex smiled and squeezed her hand. The door opened slowly and Stephanie stepped into the room. Stephanie stopped just inside the door and let it close behind her. Her once long hair was cut in a short bob. It was still a rich auburn, shiny without a trace of gray. She'd always been thin, but her thinness had changed. She was now lean, her body toned like an athlete. Despite being in prison, she looked healthy. She glanced at Jill and quickly looked away. She made eye contact with Alex and smiled.

"Hey," Alex said and stepped toward Stephanie.

"You had me worried sick," Stephanie said while moving toward Alex. Stephanie wrapped both arms around her and squeezed tightly. Alex winced at the pressure on her right shoulder. Stephanie stepped back. "Sorry. I heard you were in a sling, where is it?"

"She's refusing to wear it," Jill said.

At the same time, they rolled their eyes and said, "Figures."

They both laughed and the tension in the room evaporated. Stephanie approached Jill and opened her arms. Jill stepped into the embrace, fighting a flood of emotions. When they separated minutes later, both had tears rolling down their cheeks, as did Alex.

"Hey now, you stop that." Stephanie playfully slapped Alex on her good shoulder. "You're supposed to keep us from falling apart."

"Right," Alex said with a big smile. "I'll get right on it."

"I suppose we should give her a break." Stephanie turned to Jill. "She's been under a lot of stress too. She worries about you constantly, you know?"

"I know. She's going to get an ulcer if she doesn't knock it off."

"Hello, I'm still in the room. Can we stop talking about me like I'm not here?"

"Did you hear something?" Stephanie asked.

"I think it was just the wind." Jill laughed.

With the uncomfortable part of the meeting over, the conversation became light-hearted. The years since they'd last seen each other melted away as they talked. They talked and laughed for some time before Stephanie's expression turned serious.

"So, tell me what happened yesterday," Stephanie said.

"Do you really want to hear about that? I'm sure we have plenty more catching up to do," Jill said.

"I'm so sorry. I'm being insensitive. Of course you don't want to talk about it."

"No need to apologize. I'm sure I'll have to repeat it many times before this is all over, so why not start with someone I feel safe with?"

Jill and Alex gave a recap of the events, while

Stephanie listened without comment. She grimaced at times and her eyes filled with tears, but she said nothing. By the time they finished, Stephanie was visibly shaken.

"Why don't you hate me?" Stephanie blurted out.

"What?" Jill asked.

"You should hate me," Stephanie met Jill's eyes, but had to look away. "There's not a day that goes by that I don't think of you and hate myself. I knew what a beast he was and I didn't tell you."

"No, you couldn't have known what he would do." Jill took Stephanie's hand and squeezed it.

"He was never right after our dad left us. Something changed in him. I've never seen such rage in such a young boy. It was like he hated me and our mom. I think he blamed us for Dad leaving." Stephanie looked sad and hesitated before she continued. "I did know. I let you walk into a life of hell because I was a coward. I should have warned you. I should have told you to run, but I liked you and didn't want you to leave. It was my selfishness that caused all this." Stephanie tentatively reached out and touched the bruise on Jill's face, the pain etched on her own face.

"Every day I think of you and feel guilty," Jill said. "Alex assured me you didn't hate me, but I was sure you must. I left you in here all by yourself."

"No, never. You've sacrificed yourself for my girls. No, that's not right. They are our girls."

Stephanie's words filled her heart. She was terrified that she would get shut out of the girls' lives. Her fear ran so deep that she hadn't even spoken to Alex about it, in fear that saying it would make it happen.

"You don't know how much I needed to hear that. I was afraid you might not want me around you or the girls."

"You've given your life for us. How could I not? I love you, Jill."

"I love you too, Stephanie." Their tears flowed freely and they hugged. They were both laughing and crying when they let go.

With their fears alleviated, the conversation turned to lighter subjects and they laughed together like old friends. A knock on the door startled them. Samantha Sanchez, Jill's attorney, stepped into the room. "I hate to break up the reunion, but the judge is going to hear arguments on your case in half an hour. I wanted us to get on the same page before we walk into the courtroom. Can I come back in five minutes, so we can discuss a few things?"

"Of course," Jill said.

"The girls and their grandmother are here already," Samantha said.

"They're here?" The color drained from Stephanie's face.

"They're talking with family services now, but I'm going to ask the judge to allow you some time with them."

"Thank you," Stephanie said softly.

"I'll be back in five," Samantha said before she left the room.

"Are you okay?" Jill asked.

"I'm gonna see my girls." Stephanie's hands were shaking when she reached up to brush away a tear. "I haven't seen Trina since she was two days old."

"It'll be okay." Jill took her hand.

"Do you think Jenna will remember me?"

"I'm sure she will. We talked about you all the time when Steve wasn't around. It's going to be okay."

Alex and Jill continued to offer encouragement. The color eventually returned to Stephanie's face, and she stopped shaking.

"Jill, I have one more thing I need to say before Ms. Sanchez comes back." Stephanie glanced at Alex before she continued. "You've found yourself a good one. Don't let her do something stupid and try to slip away."

"So, you know about the Lone Ranger thing?"

Stephanie nodded.

"I'm keeping a close eye on her, so she doesn't try to ride off into the sunset once we get through this," Jill said.

"Hopefully, I'm out of here soon, so I can help you keep an eye on her too."

"Hello, once again, I want to remind you, I am in the room," Alex piped up.

Stephanie and Jill both looked around, but avoided looking in Alex's direction.

"Must be the wind again," Stephanie said.

"Must be," Jill replied with a wink.

⚜ ⚜ ⚜ ⚜

"I can't believe you have to wait forty-five days," Alex said once they were back in the car. "What the hell kind of justice is that?"

"It's all right," Jill said. "Ms. Sanchez said it was the best we could hope for. Look at it from the court's perspective."

Alex scrunched up her face, looked into the air, and pretended to be thinking. "Nope, still not getting it."

Jill laughed. "Alex, they don't know me. I'm relieved that they're cautious when it comes to the safety of children, even if it affects me."

"But you were the one getting the shit kicked out of you to protect them. Shouldn't that count for something?"

"You heard the judge. I got plus and minus points for that. It's obvious he questioned my judgment and thought I had other options."

"That's bullshit. You did what you had to do."

"I know, but it's okay, really, it is. To be honest, I think it's the best thing for me. I have a lot to accomplish, so knowing they'll be safe with their grandma takes a load off my mind. I can focus all my energy on getting back on my feet."

"In other words, chill out, Alex," Alex said, smiling.

"Pretty perceptive of you." Jill smiled back.

Samantha Sanchez had been pleased with the results of the court proceedings and encouraged Jill to look at it as an opportunity. The judge granted her visitations, and Steve's mother assured her that she was more than welcome at her home any time. Jill was also ordered to see a counselor twice a week during that time in order to determine her fitness. She was to find a job, so she could support herself and the girls. Jill was right; she would be busy, so Alex reluctantly agreed that maybe the judge knew what he was doing.

"Enough court talk," Jill said. "Where are you going to take me for dinner?"

"Where do you want to go?"

"Well, I'm all dressed up, so it seems a shame to waste such a nice outfit."

"I've got the perfect place, but it's a forty-five-minute drive."

"I'm game. Let's do it."

Alex smiled and started the car. Jill slumped in her seat and let her body relax. Her eyes felt heavy, but she fought to keep them open. Alex turned on the radio, tuning it to a soft rock station. "Why don't you go ahead and close your eyes? It's pretty comfortable when you put the seat back a little."

"Are you sure? I should keep you company while you drive."

"I'm fine, but you look exhausted."

"I am tired." Jill looked into Alex's eyes. They looked at one another for several seconds without a word. Their eyes said more than words could. Alex was the first to look away. She put the car in reverse and pulled from her parking space. Jill put her hand on Alex's thigh and Alex rested her hand on top of Jill's hand.

"Thanks, Alex."

Alex lightly squeezed her hand and responded, "You're welcome, sweetie. Get some sleep, okay?"

Jill was asleep before they made it out of the parking lot.

❧❧❧❧❧

It was nearly ten o'clock when they returned to Alex's apartment. Despite being tired, Jill was buoyant. The evening had been perfect, a five-star restaurant, with an exotic menu, an extensive wine list, and plenty of ambiance. They laughed and talked the entire meal, avoiding any unpleasant topics. Many times during the evening, Jill imagined that this was what her life with Alex could be. She found it incredibly comforting, never once being alarmed by what the thought implied. For her, it felt like a natural progression in their relationship. She'd caught herself looking at Alex's lips when she talked, wondering what it would be like if Alex kissed her.

When Alex turned from the door after engaging the deadbolt, she nearly bumped into Jill, who'd not moved far from the entrance. "What's that look for?" Jill asked with a playful smile. She felt the heat and welcomed the passion she saw burning in Alex's eyes. Jill took a step toward Alex.

Alex unconsciously took a step back and bumped into the door, drawing more attention to her retreat. Her face turned a deep red and she stammered, "Um, I was thinking how nice it is to have you here." She looked at Jill like she'd seen a ghost, before she bumbled on, "I mean, obviously the circumstances aren't nice."

"Are you okay?" Jill took another step toward Alex, but this time Alex had nowhere else to retreat so she was forced to stand inches from Jill.

"Yes, I'm just tired. It's been a long day." A curtain came down over her blazing eyes, leaving them dull and distant. A cold chill descended like an unwelcome fog, replacing the heat from moments earlier.

"Alex?" Jill said with a question in her voice. She shivered unconsciously, her mind racing. Had the last five years warped her reality so badly that she could no longer read anyone other than Steve, or had her own desires caused her to imagine something from Alex that wasn't there? Her breath caught and fear replaced her warm feelings.

"I'll be fine. It's just been one hell of a day. Why don't I put our leftovers in the fridge and get us a drink?" Alex slipped from her trapped position against the door and headed toward the kitchen.

"Okay." Jill stared at the spot where Alex had disappeared from to go into the kitchen. Jill acutely felt Alex's absence, even though she was in the next room. It was more than Alex's physical exit; it was the emotional withdrawal that left Jill shaken.

Jill felt completely alone. She struggled to breathe as the physical pain and the emotional turmoil of the last couple of days caught up with her. The tears didn't come; she was too numb. Her limbs felt heavy and holding herself upright was proving to be difficult. She should follow Alex, but found she didn't have the strength to put one foot in front of the other. She slumped against the door, still fighting for breath, wondering if this is what a panic attack felt like. As she struggled, her body slowly slid down the length of the door until she was lying in a heap against it. Her breaths were coming out in short gasps as she struggled to take in enough oxygen. Her vision began to blur, and she felt like she was walking down a dark tunnel. She struggled to push aside the blackness, but felt herself losing the battle.

❧ ❧ ❧ ❧

Alex put the leftovers into the refrigerator, and then leaned against it, trying to clear her head. *What was she going to do?* She hoped Jill hadn't picked up how flustered she was when they were standing so close, but she didn't know how she couldn't have when Alex acted like such a bumbling fool.

Several times over dinner an uncontrollable urge to kiss Jill came over her, causing warning bells to go off. She had fought her natural inclination to withdraw, not wanting to spoil Jill's evening. Jill had been radiant, joking with the waitstaff, doing so with more animation than she'd ever shown in public. Her appearance, or at least her new clothes, seemed to give her greater confidence.

How was she going to handle having Jill so close? At the restaurant, a table and a room full of people separated them, but now there was nothing between them. She took several deep breaths, hoping her heart rate would come down. She couldn't stay in the kitchen forever, or Jill would come looking for her. She took one final deep breath before busying herself with getting their drinks.

She walked into the room, carrying two glasses of wine, when she saw Jill slumped against the door. She set the glasses on the table and ran across the room, forgetting her earlier concerns.

"Oh my God, Jill what's wrong?" Alex dropped to her knees. Jill was in a fetal position, with her left shoulder pressed against the door. Her breaths were rapid and shallow and tears streamed down her face. Jill's eyes were unfocused and she trembled slightly.

"Jill, you're scaring me." Alex fought to keep the panic from her voice. "Jill, I need you to tell me what's wrong." Alex gently put her hand on Jill's arm and talked to her softly, offering comfort.

With Alex's touch, Jill curled into a tighter ball, but her breathing noticeably slowed. Alex continued to talk to her softly, but Jill's eyes remained distant. Alex reached up, put her hand on Jill's cheek, and immediately realized her mistake. Before Alex could correct her error, Jill abruptly pushed away from the door and dropped into a full fetal position. Her breathing became more rapid and her body began to shake. Alex looked around the room helplessly, wondering if she should call someone for help. Knowing Jill, she wouldn't want anyone to see her like this and would be upset enough that Alex witnessed it.

Without thinking, Alex knelt down and lifted Jill off the floor. A searing pain shot from her injured shoulder down her right side to her hip, but somehow, she managed to keep her grip on Jill. The adrenaline coursing through her body must have helped, but she knew she couldn't hold Jill this way for long. Jill didn't fight against Alex, which was fortunate since her damaged shoulder would not hold up against a struggle.

"Jill, I'm going to carry you to the couch." Alex hoped her words would register somewhere in Jill's subconscious mind. Alex carried Jill across the room, but stopped short before setting her down. Jill seemed to be relaxing in her arms and the distressed look on her face had nearly disappeared. Alex looked around helplessly, knowing she couldn't hold her much longer with only one arm. Alex made her decision, turned so her back was to the couch, and let herself fall backward. She couldn't use her right arm to cushion the fall, so she landed hard on the sofa cushions. Jill's body drove into hers, knocking the wind out of Alex.

Jill's shaking subsided and her breathing evened out. Alex continued to hold her, slightly rocking back and forth on the couch.

"You're safe, sweetie, I won't let anyone hurt you," Alex said softly. "Please, come back to me. I'm scared and don't know what to do." Alex continued talking to her softly and gently rubbing her arm. Jill relaxed further and laid her head against Alex's chest, her breathing almost normal now. Alex desperately wanted to see her eyes, but couldn't from the angle she laid. Alex wondered if it were safe for Jill to stay in this state for long, or if she should call an ambulance. She continued to talk softly as she struggled with her decision. She was so wrapped up in her own thoughts that she almost missed the nearly inaudible sound of Jill's voice.

"Alex?" Jill said, her voice low.

"Jill?" Alex wanted to say more, but her words stuck in her throat. She wanted to scream, cry, or jump up from the couch, but knew any of those actions would only panic Jill.

"Alex, what's going on?" She turned and looked into Alex's frightened eyes.

"Thank God, you're back," Alex unconsciously hugged Jill closer to her. "What happened?"

"I'm not sure I know." Jill tried to sit upright.

"Here, let me help you," Alex slid from under Jill and stood up from the couch. Alex nervously looked around, suddenly aware of how Jill could easily misinterpret Alex's intentions. Alex went to sit on the other end of the couch, but the panic in Jill's eyes stopped her.

"Where are you going?" Jill's voice was panicked, too.

"Um...I was giving you some space. I thought that's what you needed."

"I need you." The fear was still evident in Jill's eyes.

"Okay, I'm right here. I'm not going anywhere."

Alex sat down next to Jill on the couch. Jill closed the gap between them, so they sat shoulder to shoulder. She took Alex's hand and squeezed; Alex returned the pressure. They sat like this for several minutes, neither speaking, both lost in their own thoughts.

"Am I going crazy?" Jill asked, finally breaking the silence.

"No, I think whatever just happened was a culmination of all the stress you've been under for so long."

"But why now, when it's finally over?"

"I'm not sure; maybe it's post-traumatic stress or something like that." Alex hoped to alleviate Jill's fears.

"Oh God, no, that's like a disorder or syndrome or something," Jill pulled away from Alex. "You're already sick of all the drama I've brought to your life. This is the final straw, isn't it?"

"What?" Alex said incredulously. She turned to Jill with a perplexed look, trying to figure out where Jill's assumptions came from.

"That's how this all started. I'm starting to remember."

"You're going to have to clue me in because I never said you had too much drama, and I certainly never said I didn't want you around." Alex held out her hand, and Jill took it and moved against her again.

"We were standing by the door, and you were acting weird." Jill looked to the ceiling, trying to remember. "Then you said you were glad I was here."

"Exactly, I never said anything about not wanting you around."

"No, but then you hurried away and I watched you disappear. Then everything started happening."

"What happened?" Alex spoke softly, hoping Jill would continue.

"All of a sudden, I felt like I couldn't breathe and everything felt heavy and I couldn't move."

"Go on." Alex lightly rubbed Jill's arm, offering encouragement.

"I remember wondering if I was having a panic attack, but I couldn't cut through the fog. I couldn't stop myself from thinking you were just being nice and didn't want me around with all the drama."

"Jill, that's so not true."

"I tried to fight it, I did, but I couldn't overcome it. I just stood there thinking you wanted me gone, and that I should just leave, but I couldn't move. The last thing I remember is sliding down the door, and then everything got weird. In my mind, I was back with Steve and he was doing things to me, but every now and then, I'd hear your voice. I tried to call out to you, but you didn't hear. Then you'd disappear, and he'd be there again."

"Sounds like you were having a flashback. After all you have been through, I doubt it's uncommon." Alex hoped her words were reassuring to Jill. "I was talking to you the whole time, trying to get you to come back, so on some level you were hearing me."

"How did I get to the couch?"

"I carried you."

"I felt it, Alex." Jill's voice cracked. "I was in this really dark place and he was there, he grabbed my face."

"Unfortunately, that was me. I'm sorry. I was trying to get your attention."

"You didn't do anything wrong. You were trying to help." Jill shivered and hugged herself. "Then he threw me across the room and I curled into a ball."

"After I touched you, you actually pushed away from the door and curled into a ball. I should have known better than to touch you when you were like that."

"You couldn't have known." Jill's shoulders hunched and she drew into herself further. "Then it was really dark and he was coming toward me. I was shivering so hard. I was so scared, but then I heard you say my name. All of a sudden, I felt safe and warm. I bet that's when you were holding me in your arms. After that, the images of him started to flicker and disappeared. I don't know how long I was caught in between, but all of a sudden, I knew you were there. That's when I called out to you."

"Are you okay now?"

"I think so." Jill closed her eyes and leaned into Alex. "I'm wiped out, though. I feel like I just ran a marathon."

"Your heart was racing, so it wouldn't surprise me if your body feels like you did."

Jill suddenly stiffened and said in a louder voice than she'd been talking, "What if it happens again? I could be out in public. I can't be dropping to the ground in the middle of the grocery store."

"Relax. You'll be fine. I'll be right here with you all weekend."

"Now you have to babysit me, great," Jill said with obvious frustration. "You have to be getting sick of this."

"Jill, it's only been twenty-four hours."

"The son-of-a-bitch held me hostage for over five years, so I don't want to allow him to steal another minute of my life."

"Give yourself a break."

"I want to move on with the rest of my life."

"And you will, but it may take a while to heal."

"Damn it, I want to be better, now."

"That's the spirit. With that spunk and a good counselor, you'll be just fine."

"And you?" Jill said, her voice almost a whisper.

"I'll be fine too."

"That's not what I meant. I need spunk, a good counselor, and you."

Alex hesitated. "Better yet, you have me, Sarah, and Michelle." Alex knew Jill hadn't missed her dancing around the question, but she suspected that Jill wouldn't push it any further tonight.

"I'm pretty lucky then."

"So am I," Alex said, happy to be back on firmer ground.

Chapter Seventeen

I'm not crazy," Jill said when she walked into Alex's office.

Alex looked up and smiled. Jill was dressed in a pair of blue jeans and a white button-down shirt. Alex's eyes opened wider at how good Jill looked in the casual outfit. She silently cursed Michelle, who knew Alex found blue jeans and a white button-down shirt the sexiest outfit a woman could wear.

"Are you sure about that?" Alex teased. She hoped her playful comeback would distract Jill from noticing Alex's reaction to her.

"Well, I may be crazy about something," Jill said flirtatiously. "But the counselor says I'm not certifiable." Jill crossed the room to the couch and sat down. She patted the seat next to her, indicating Alex should join her.

"That's a relief. So, I don't have to worry about a Janet Leigh moment when I'm in the shower?" Alex's eyes danced playfully, happy to see Jill seemingly feeling better. Jill had been tentative the entire weekend, which Alex knew was fear she would have another episode.

"You should be safe, but I can't guarantee there won't be a Glenn Close elevator moment." Jill's eyes showed a mixture of playfulness and intensity.

Alex fidgeted with the papers on her desk and

felt her heart race. She couldn't keep letting Jill catch her so off balance, so she casually sauntered over to the sitting area, taking a seat across from Jill. "Thank God I don't have a pet rabbit."

Jill laughed. "So, the counselor thinks I had an acute stress reaction or something like that."

"So, it won't happen again?"

"She can't say for sure, but it's a good sign I didn't have another one this weekend. I guess it isn't uncommon when someone comes through something extremely stressful. I can't remember the technical term, but it's kinda like the mind needing a release." Jill kicked off her shoes and brought her feet under her on the couch.

"Like a flashback?"

"Exactly."

"I'm just happy the appointment went so well." She considered giving Jill a celebratory hug but thought better of it. Alex was afraid of the confident woman in front of her.

"I'm going to be okay, Alex. No, not just okay, I'm going to be better than okay."

"Did you have any doubts?"

"Some. I asked my counselor if I was going to have permanent emotional scars to match the physical ones."

"And?"

"She looked me right in the eye, and without missing a beat said, 'only if you let it.'"

"Really? Isn't that blaming the victim?" Alex felt herself bristling at the insensitivity of the counselor.

"Not at all. It's empowering. Whatever happens now is up to me. She said I can let it keep me down, or I can choose otherwise. I can refuse to let that son-of-a-bitch victimize me any longer, and give him the ultimate fuck you by creating an incredible life for myself."

"She said that?"

"Well, not in quite those words." Jill grinned. "She was a little more professional."

"I would hope so." Alex laughed. "So, it's that simple?"

"No, she said I'll struggle, but that's to be expected. I have some pretty deep emotional scars that I'm gonna have to work through. The damage he did is going to take a while to undo."

"But the scars will heal?"

"They will, but they will always be a part of me. I'm one of the lucky ones. I had amazing parents that didn't leave any scars, which is unusual. And so many women endure abuse for years and years. I won't lie, the last five years have been hell, but I won't let him win." There was conviction burning in Jill's eyes.

"I have no doubt you'll succeed."

"With you in my corner, I have no doubts either. My counselor thinks I can work through counseling fairly quickly."

"I thought counseling was supposed to be long and drawn out."

"You've been watching too much TV." Jill laughed.

"Seriously, why did she say that?"

"I would have been out the door in a heartbeat if it weren't for the girls. In hindsight, I probably never even loved him. I met him shortly after my parents died. I was so lost and felt so alone." Jill's voice cracked. "He preyed on me when I was at my most vulnerable."

Jill's words hit Alex like a punch in the gut. Alex

was no better than Steve, preying on Jill when she was at her most defenseless. Just like then, Jill couldn't possibly make a rational emotional decision when her life was in so much turmoil. Alex felt a resolve wash over her. She crossed her arms over her chest and sat back against the back of the couch. She needed to keep her distance from Jill while she was so vulnerable.

"Sounds like you got lucky getting a good counselor." Her eyes lost their warmth, and her tone turned professional. Alex saw the confusion and hurt on Jill's face, and her chest ached. She wanted to smile or run to Jill and wrap her arms around her, but she did neither. Instead, she sat staring at Jill, waiting for her to respond.

"Yep, good thing I have a good one," Jill said in an overly perky voice. "I should probably let you get back to work. I'm going to go change my clothes. Then I think I'll try out the gym, if that's okay with you." Jill stood and picked up her shoes from the floor.

"Sure, that's fine."

"I'll catch you later." Jill walked out of the room, carrying her shoes.

Alex sat staring at the spot Jill vacated. She could still see her beautiful brown eyes, so full of hope and the way her shirt loosely hung over her curves. She was so lost in thought that she didn't register that someone else entered the room.

❧ ❧ ❧ ❧ ❧

"Do they pay you just to sit and stare into space?" Sarah said. When Alex didn't respond, she spoke louder, "Alex, wake the hell up!"

"Huh?"

"I know that look," Sarah said with a grin. "I saw your little hottie in the hall."

"Jill?"

"Yes, Jill, who else is there?" Sarah flopped onto the couch. "Just this once I have to say that you were right and I was wrong."

"This is a first." Alex was finally engaged in the conversation. "What is it that I was right about?"

"When I first met Jill, I thought she was average at best, but damn, she's a knockout. She looks good in that outfit."

"You have Michelle to thank, or should I say blame, for that."

Sarah laughed. "Did she tell Jill that white button-down shirts drive you crazy?"

"God, I hope not, but she bought the clothes for her. I think she's just trying to torture me."

"Or maybe she hopes you'll pull your head out of your ass and ask the girl out."

"Damn it, can't you guys just leave well enough alone?" Alex got up from the couch and returned to her desk. "It's never going to happen, so just let it go." She mindlessly shuffled papers, signaling the conversation was over.

"I don't know what the hell your problem is, but this gallant act is getting old." Sarah rose from the couch, stood in front of Alex's desk, and glared down at her. "Stop being such a fucking martyr and ask her out already."

"I can't." Alex continued moving the papers from one pile to another.

"Why not?"

"She just told me that Steve preyed on her when she was vulnerable and that she never really loved him."

"So, what does that have to do with anything?"

"She's vulnerable again." Alex looked up from her papers.

"Oh, for fuck's sake, are you trying to compare the two situations?"

"Yes, they're the same. She was vulnerable then and she's vulnerable now, and I will not take advantage of her."

"Really? Did you forget he is a manipulative psychopath? Admittedly, you might be a little crazy, but you're not a psychopath. Plus, you love her."

"That doesn't matter. She's at a weak point, so I can't be like him and play on that."

"Are you serious? No, don't answer that. I can see in your eyes that you are." Sarah shook her head. "May I remind you that he drew her in, so he could control and hurt her? I know damn well that you'd rather throw yourself in front of a moving train than hurt her. So, there are some differences here, Alex."

"Okay, I'll give you that. But the fact remains she is emotionally raw and I won't prey on that."

"I think she'd be pissed if she knew you were trying to protect her from you." Sarah locked eyes with Alex. "Don't you see the way she looks at you? Whenever you're near, she relaxes so much it looks like she just had a massage. I can guarantee she doesn't see you as a predator."

"I'm sure she didn't see him that way either."

"I give up." Sarah threw her hands in the air. "Maybe Michelle can talk some sense into you because right now I just want to slap it into you." Sarah turned and left before Alex could respond.

Alex put her head in her hands, suddenly feeling

exhausted. She was relieved that Jill was finally safe, but she didn't know how long she could continue to live under the same roof. She ached constantly, and being so close to Jill only made it worse. She would get temporary relief when they hugged or sat close, but it only made her long for Jill more when they were apart. The more time she spent with Jill, the harder it was going to be to walk away. Jill would be devastated, losing Alex's friendship, but Alex didn't think she could watch Jill meet a man and fall in love, without it ripping her heart out.

❧ ❧ ❧ ❧

Alex tried to concentrate on her work, but found it impossible. She kept seeing the hurt in Jill's eyes, and it caused her chest to ache. She'd vowed never to let anyone hurt Jill again, so how could she justify being the one to hurt her now? Even though they hadn't fought, the wedge she felt between them was making it impossible for her to think of anything else. She needed to reestablish their connection if she wanted the pressure in her chest to subside. Maybe she would casually wander into the gym and check how Jill was doing.

Alex stopped along the way to talk with some of the regulars at the gym. She felt better, knowing she would soon see Jill. She joked with a couple of the women who flirted mercilessly with her. She was laughing with them when she entered the main room, but her laugh caught in her throat.

She immediately spotted Jill across the room, talking to a large, muscular man. Alex's heart lurched when she saw the man hand Jill a piece of paper.

Jill smiled broadly and hugged him. Alex couldn't breathe and suddenly felt like she might vomit. The women with her were still talking and laughing, but Alex didn't hear a word they said.

"Um, sorry ladies, I just remembered I need to make a call." She spun around quickly, needing to escape. One of the women grabbed her, and she fought the urge to shake off the woman's grasp. Instead, she plastered on a smile and turned around.

"Alex, someone's calling you," the woman said, pointing in Jill's direction. "Are you okay?"

"Sorry, I was just thinking about that call," Alex lied. She knew Jill must have witnessed the woman alerting her, so it would be too obvious if she hurried out of the room. Alex took a deep breath and looked in Jill's direction. Jill was waving at her and smiling; the man had shifted so Alex could see more of his face. He was handsome, Alex noted with revulsion. He must be new at the gym because Alex didn't recognize him. Slowly, Alex made her way across the room, hoping she could get through the encounter without showing her feelings, or worse, throwing up on his shoes.

When she got to the pair, the man turned fully to her with a big smile on his face. His bright blue eyes twinkled when he looked at her. "Alex!"

Alex stopped, startled, then a huge smile lit her face. "Jim, what the hell happened to your hair? I didn't even recognize you."

Jim grabbed Alex and wrapped her in a bear hug. "The wife finally convinced me that a balding middle-aged man shouldn't have shoulder length hair." He laughed an easy laugh, and Alex joined him. She was suddenly lighthearted as the tightness in her chest released.

"Nancy was right. You look positively dapper."

"It would mean more coming from this pretty lady," Jim said, smiling at Jill.

"I'm telling Nancy you're flirting with all the girls again." Jim just winked, so Alex continued. "I see you've met my friend Jill," She wondered what Jill and Jim were talking about, but didn't know how to broach the subject without being intrusive.

"Alex, I'm so excited. Jim's wife just started a new business and is looking for a graphic designer."

"Unfortunately, it doesn't pay a lot, but I know Nancy will be interested in a friend of yours, Alex."

Alex finally looked at Jill and saw the hope dancing in her sparkling brown eyes. Without a thought, Jill jumped into Alex's arms. Alex spun her around, both laughing. Alex loved seeing Jill so full of life, her excitement contagious.

Alex set Jill down and said, "That's great, Jill. You'll love Nancy. She's even more charming than this guy."

"Hey now, I wouldn't go that far," Jim said with a big smile.

⚜ ⚜ ⚜ ⚜

"You seem to be feeling better," Jill said, looking across the table at Alex. It was almost nine o'clock and they were finally sitting down to eat dinner. Alex worked late on the Florida deal and although she'd told Jill to go ahead and eat, Jill waited.

"How could I not be after your good news?"

"You're not mad at me." Jill's voice tentative. Alex wanted to take Jill's hand to alleviate her fears but resisted. Touching Jill was becoming too familiar, and Alex knew she needed to break the habit. Letting go of Jill was going to be hard, and Alex discovered just how hard after her reaction to seeing Jill talking with Jim.

"Of course not. Why would I be?" Alex immediately regretted her words. She didn't want to open a conversation that Jill could question her about her feelings.

"You seemed upset earlier."

"Did I?" Alex hoped Jill wouldn't notice that she'd answered Jill's question with a question.

"Yes. Why won't you tell me what's wrong?"

Alex looked away, unable to take the pain she caused in Jill's beautiful brown eyes. Alex knew they couldn't go on like this; living in such close quarters with Jill was too much for her. The more she pulled back, the more stress she was putting on Jill, who had enough to worry about without Alex adding to it.

"I was just wondering when you think I should go stay with Sarah and Michelle?" Alex blurted out.

"Never." Jill's face dropped. "Unless you want to get away from me that badly."

"It's not like that. You need to get ready for the girls to move in. I was thinking maybe the end of the month."

"I'll go; you don't have to." There was steel in Jill's voice. "I'll move back to the apartment."

"No," Alex said in horror. "There are too many bad memories there. I don't want to put you through that."

"But you don't mind putting me through you moving out? I can't figure you out, Alex. You say you want to keep me safe and protect me, but then you're the one that is hur..." Jill's voice trailed.

"Go ahead and say it."

"No, I didn't mean it. Please, Alex, just forget I said anything."

"No, go ahead and say what you were going to; don't be shy. I'm the one hurting you. Isn't that what you wanted to say?"

Jill opened her mouth to speak but said nothing. Tears rolled down her face and without warning, she dropped her fork on her plate, abruptly stood up, and hurried from the room.

"Fuck," Alex said to the empty room. She set down her fork and put her head in her hands. Her appetite was suddenly gone. She hated herself for taking away Jill's euphoria. Alex sat for several minutes, staring at her plate but not seeing it. An internal battle raged; should she go to Jill or should she leave her alone? She remembered Jill's panic attack and decided she should check on her.

Alex walked down the hall toward the bedrooms and immediately noticed that Jill hadn't closed her door. Even though she was upset, she hadn't tried to close Alex out, which was a positive sign. Alex stopped at the open door. Jill was lying on her bed with her back to the door. Softly, Alex knocked on the doorframe, but Jill didn't answer. She knocked harder.

"Jill, may I come in?" Alex asked when Jill still didn't respond.

"It's your house." Jill didn't turn to face Alex.

"But this is your space, so I won't come in unless you invite me in."

"What, are you a vampire or something?" After a couple seconds, Jill let out a small giggle. "I suppose that was a bit overdramatic, huh?"

"Maybe just a little," Alex said, holding her

thumb and forefinger a couple centimeters apart.

"Please, come in." Jill rolled over and faced the door.

Alex's heart broke at seeing the tears streaming down Jill's face. "Why do I keep hurting you?" Alex spoke before she could edit herself.

"I was wondering the same thing." Jill gave Alex a slight smile.

"I don't mean to."

"Come lie down with me," Jill reached out for Alex's hand.

Alex thought of resisting, but her longing to comfort Jill overshadowed her own needs. She tentatively sat on the edge of the bed and took Jill's hand.

"No, come lie down."

Alex laid down next to Jill. Her body was stiff, and she uncomfortably stared at the ceiling. Jill sidled up to her and rested her head on Alex's shoulder. Despite her better judgment, Alex untangled her arm and put it around Jill. Alex drew Jill closer, and Jill let out a contented sigh.

They lay like this for several minutes, neither speaking. A calm descended over Alex, and Jill stopped crying. Alex lightly ran her hand up and down Jill's back, and Jill held a fistful of Alex's shirt tightly in her hand. Their breaths soon synchronized and slowed, the connection between them restored.

Alex struggled, knowing they should talk, but words seemed to lead them down the wrong path. Jill had enough to worry about, so she didn't need to know how badly it stressed Alex having her here. Alex needed to put her own needs aside for now and be strong for Jill. Somehow, though, she needed Jill to stop baiting her.

❧❧❧❧

Jill felt Alex's breath become deep and rhythmic. She was pretty sure that Alex had fallen asleep, but didn't want to check for fear of waking her. Instead, she lay staring at the mesmerizing picture on the wall. It was a painting of two hands that appeared to be drawing each other. Alex loved MC Escher and had his paintings throughout her apartment, but this was Jill's favorite.

She loved being here with Alex, but wished that Alex would give her some indication that she felt the same. Alex seemed to be running away from her every time their relationship deepened. Sometimes, she was almost certain that Alex had feelings for her and just wouldn't give in to them. But Jill's mind kept wrapping back to the same answer; maybe Alex's feelings were simply pity. She certainly didn't measure up to the women Alex normally dated. Sure, Alex told her she looked pretty, but wasn't that the lie everyone told each other? Anytime someone posted a picture on Facebook, there were at least ten people who told them they looked pretty, even if they looked like they'd just stepped out of bed.

Or maybe Alex did just want to be friends, and Jill's constant flirting was starting to wear on Alex. She should stop baiting Alex, but every time she convinced herself that she would, she caught herself saying something leading. She'd caused Alex to turn red and practically sprint from the room several times. Whenever she received that reaction, it confirmed her suspicion that there was something between them.

Jill sighed and closed her eyes. The last thing she

saw in her mind before falling asleep was Alex's warm brown eyes.

❧❧❧❧

Alex woke with a start and looked around the room. Jill was sleeping peacefully in the crook of Alex's arm, her face showing none of its earlier strain. Alex shifted slightly, so she could see the clock. It was nearly midnight, so they'd been asleep for a couple hours. She'd fallen asleep before they could finish the conversation. Alex wanted nothing more than to close her eyes and go back to sleep with Jill in her arms, but she knew it was a dangerous choice. She laid there for several minutes, an internal battle raging, but her practical side eventually prevailed.

Slowly, she edged Jill's head from the crook of her arm and replaced her shoulder with a pillow. Jill stirred, but didn't wake. Alex deliberately slid from the bed, stopping every few seconds to ensure Jill remained sleeping. Once she was back on her feet, she took a blanket from the end of the bed and spread it over Jill, before she shut off the light and left the room.

Chapter Eighteen

Jill was going through her closet, picking out an outfit, when she heard Alex calling her name. "I'm in here."

Things between the two had improved over the course of the week. When Jill had awoken and found Alex gone, she had been disappointed, but knew it was Alex's way of asking her to stop pressing for more. Jill kept her vow to no longer flirt with Alex, even though it had been difficult. As the days went by, she'd noticed that Alex no longer seemed to be crawling out of her skin, nor had she mentioned moving out again either. The tension was replaced by a comfortable familiarity.

"What are you doing?" Alex asked, gracing Jill with a big smile. Her eyes twinkled and held the warmth that Jill loved.

"Trying to pick an outfit for my first day." Jill returned the smile. She interviewed with Jim's wife Nancy, and they immediately connected. Nancy offered her the job on the spot, and Jill accepted.

"You don't start until Monday."

"I know, but if I pick it out now, I won't have to worry about it all weekend."

Alex laughed. "Yeah, like that'll work. You'll pick out something now and change it ten times before Monday."

"Shut up." Jill playfully threw a pair of socks at

Alex.

"Just saying." Alex snagged the socks before they hit her in the chest and lobbed them back in Jill's direction.

"Get out of here, if you're not going to help." Jill tried to glower at Alex, but the corners of her mouth curled upward and her eyes danced.

Alex plopped down in the middle of Jill's bed. "What are your choices?"

"Oh no, I'm not taking your advice. You'll pick something that would hooch me up."

"I'm telling Michelle you said that she picked out hoochie clothes."

Jill looked at Alex stretched on her bed, a smirk on her face and a twinkle in her eye, and resisted the urge to go to her. Jill found Alex nearly irresistible when she was relaxed and playful. They'd been doing too well together for Jill to do anything to ruin the tentative peace they'd settled into.

"I have some good news and some bad news for you." Jill fought the temptation to join Alex on the bed.

"Words that nobody ever wants to hear." Alex covered her face. "Hit me with the bad first."

"Smart choice, good things are always worth waiting for." Jill was unable to resist baiting Alex just a little. Jill pulled two lightweight sweaters out of the closet and looked in the mirror while she held one in front of her.

"Let me be the judge of that. So, what's the bad news?"

"Well, um. I, well, I need to..." Jill's voice trailed off. Telling Alex was proving harder than she thought it would. She continued to look in the mirror, nervously switching between the two sweaters.

"What is it, Jill?" Alex propped herself up on her elbows, the earlier playfulness gone.

Jill heard the tone in Alex's voice and turned away from the mirror. "Don't look so scared. It's making me nervous."

"You're making me nervous." Alex sat up and dangled her legs off the side of the bed and looked at Jill expectantly.

"Trust me, once you get over your initial reaction, you'll be fine." Jill continued to face Alex, but unconsciously ran her fingers over the soft sweater.

"You don't know what my initial reaction will be, since you haven't told me anything."

"I'm pretty sure I can guess." Jill dropped one of the sweaters onto the bed, but continued to cling to the other.

"Are you going to tell me?"

"Promise you'll let me finish, before you start rampaging."

"Since when have I been someone who goes on a rampage?"

"When you're worried about me. When you want to protect me," Jill answered. She resisted turning back to the mirror.

"I'm not liking this. You remember the last time you asked me not to react until you were done, don't you?"

"I know, but it's not that bad this time."

"You're stalling."

"Yep." Jill flashed Alex a smile. She took a deep breath, straightened her back, and looked Alex in the eye. "Truly, it's not that bad."

"I'm waiting."

"Detective Barrett called this morning and wants me to meet with Steve tomorrow morning." Jill's words spilled out quickly, wanting to get them out before Alex reacted. She dropped the other sweater to the bed and held her eye contact with Alex.

"No way, there is no way you can do that. I can't believe she even asked you." Alex sputtered and flailed her arms around as she spoke. "What the hell is she thinking?"

"Yep, I had that reaction figured out." Jill grinned. "Just hear me out."

"What is there to hear out? That asshole shouldn't be allowed within ten miles of you. Has the detective lost her mind? And why are you just sitting there smiling at me like I'm an unruly child?"

"You're always watching out for me. Do you know how good, how safe, it makes me feel?"

"You're just trying to disarm me with compliments, aren't you?"

"Is it working?"

"Maybe, a little." Alex finally smiled. "At least you've stopped me from marching down to the station and shaking some sense into Detective Barrett."

"Well, that's a plus. I'd prefer not visiting you in jail." Jill smiled. She saw the tension in Alex's shoulders relax, so she continued. "Are you ready to listen to her logic?"

"Fine, but I think logic is a pretty generous word."

Jill ignored Alex's dig. "Steve has been asking to see me for the last couple of days. Apparently, he's playing the martyr and claims it is all a big misunderstanding."

"Are you kidding me? The stupid—" Alex stopped when Jill shot her a look.

"In typical Steve fashion, he's being manipulative and trying to charm Detective Barrett. She sees right through his charade, but he doesn't know that. She's let him think she's on his side in order to exploit the opportunity."

"The thought of you being anywhere near him makes me crazy, so I'm failing to see any opportunity."

"There is opportunity here. Apparently, he's told Detective Barrett if he were able to talk to me, he could clear everything up. She thinks he'll try to intimidate me and bully me into rescinding my complaint."

"That's exactly why I don't want you anywhere near him."

"Detective Barrett is banking on him being like most bullies." Jill picked up one of the sweaters and began folding it. "She thinks if I stand up to him that he'll back down. And if he does, he might agree to a plea bargain, which means we wouldn't have to suffer through a trial. It all hinges on whether I can do it or not."

"But what if you get in there and can't stand up to him?" Alex ran her hand through her hair.

"That's a risk we would be taking." Jill began refolding the sweater she'd just finished folding. "I think I can do it as long as you're there."

"He wouldn't agree to talk to you if I tagged along."

"No, you can't be in the room with me, but you can take me and be there when I'm done. I think I can do it just knowing you're nearby." Jill dropped the sweater and reached out her hand.

Alex took Jill's hand. "Are you sure you want to do this?"

"No, I'm not, but I have to give it a try. I think it's a big step on my path to healing,"

"As much as I hate the thought of it, I'll be there if that's what you want to do."

"Will you be okay?"

"No, I'll be a wreck the whole time. The detective may have to tase me." She looked into Jill's eyes and squeezed her hand. "If you're brave enough to do it, I can be strong enough to be there for you."

"Thank you." Jill squeezed Alex's hand in return. "Are you ready to hear the good news?"

"Hell, I almost forgot that there was good news. Why didn't you remind me of that earlier? I definitely want to hear it."

"Michelle called. Next weekend they want to take us out to celebrate my new job. Michelle mentioned some club, but damned if I can remember the name. It was something weird."

"Kasabooboo?"

"That's it."

"So, what's the good news?"

"That was the good news, grumpy."

"You don't want to go to Kasabooboo."

"It sounds like fun." Jill crossed her arms over her chest. "I told her we'd go."

"It's a gay bar." Alex frowned. "You don't want to go there."

"I do too," Jill said defiantly. She knew it wasn't fair, but added, "You're not refusing to go to my celebration, are you?"

"I'll go if you want me to." Alex sighed.

"Great, then you can help me choose that outfit too." Jill pulled her white shirt from the closet.

"Wonderful," Alex said, dramatically flopping back onto the bed and closing her eyes. Jill laughed, and Alex couldn't help but smile.

Chapter Nineteen

S o, what do you think?" Jill twirled around, showing off her outfit.

"I think I'm going to puke," Alex responded.

"That's not what I meant." Jill shot Alex a dirty look.

"I know."

Jill felt herself getting frustrated, but stopped when she noticed Alex's pained expression. She put her hand on Alex's arm and looked into her eyes for several seconds before she spoke. "It'll be okay, Alex. I promise."

"Shouldn't I be the one reassuring you?"

"Yes!" Jill playfully slapped Alex on the shoulder. The serious look lifted from Alex's face, and she smiled.

"That's better. So, what do you think?" Jill twirled in a circle again. She was dressed in a pair of black slacks and a bright red button-down blouse. Unlike her old clothes, they fit and accentuated her body. Since she met Alex, she'd put on a much needed ten pounds and could probably stand to gain another five. With the extra weight, she looked trim, rather than skinny.

"You look good."

"Good. Is that all I get?" Jill teased.

"You look very good. Is that better?" Alex smiled

and continued. "You look pretty, but still confident and in control. I think your dresses would have made you look too soft and vulnerable. This look kinda butches you up."

"Oh great, I wasn't really going for butch." Jill laughed.

"Well, butch may be too strong of word. It just makes you look more confident and assertive. I think the asshole looks at soft as a weakness, but this makes you look small but mighty." Alex hit herself in the forehead. "Oh my God, they did it. They made you one of them."

"I still have a couple inches on them," Jill said, winking at Alex.

⊰⊱⊰⊱

Alex pulled to a stop in the police station parking lot. She kept the conversation light and had Jill laughing through much of the trip, but Alex sensed Jill's apprehension as they got closer to the station. The last several miles, Jill began to play with her hair and ran her hand across her pant leg several times. Alex shut off the car, but did not remove the keys or open the door. Jill sat looking straight ahead and didn't make a move to get out. Her hands clenched and her jaw had a determined set to it. Her eyes were distant and her breathing was shallow. Alex wrestled with what to say, but Jill spoke first.

"I was doing so well this morning at home, but now I'm not. Did I make a mistake, Alex?"

Alex wanted to say yes, start the car, and drive away, but instead she said, "No, you didn't make a mistake."

Jill turned and looked at Alex. She fought back tears. "I can't cry in there, or I lose."

Alex touched the key in the ignition, but let her hand fall back to her lap. Her heart ached. Her eyes still held their warmth, but the rest of her face was hard. She took Jill's hand. "You won't be like that in there. You're safe here with me, that's why you can let down your guard, but in there, you'll be strong."

"I guess I'm as ready as I'll ever be. Let's do it."

"Just remember, once you're done, we get to spend the day with the girls."

"That's all the inspiration I need." Jill took a deep breath and reached for the door handle.

Once inside, they waited for Detective Barrett by the front desk. The station was eerily quiet, nothing like the bustling police stations portrayed on television. Detective Barrett appeared before the silence became uncomfortable. Alex stifled a giggle when Detective Barrett did a double take when she saw Jill. The transformation in just a few short weeks was amazing, but she thought cops were supposed to be like poker players and never give anything away. The detective recovered quickly, shook their hands, and asked them to follow her.

There were piles everywhere in Detective Barrett's office, files were stacked on the two chairs closest to her desk, and loose papers were strewn across her desk and on the floor. The messiness made Alex cringe, so she looked away. Unfortunately, everywhere she looked there was more disarray. The detective motioned for them to have a seat across from her desk, and then went around her desk to sit in her own well-worn chair. She absentmindedly pushed aside a stack of files in their line of sight. Some of the files toppled off the pile, but the detective didn't seem to notice. Alex sat on her hands, so she didn't reach out and straighten the file folders.

"You're looking good," Detective Barrett said to Jill. "I'm not sure I would have recognized you at first glance."

"Thank you," Jill said and averted her eyes.

"Are you ready?" The detective turned to Alex and smiled knowingly. "Or maybe I should be asking you that question."

"I think we're both ready, right?" Jill said, patting Alex's leg.

"Sure. Piece of cake."

"If you don't mind my saying, you have a different vibe about you," Detective Barrett said. "I'd hoped you could pull it off, but seeing you now, I'm almost sure you will. You seem so much more confident."

"It's amazing what new hair and makeup can do. Then add some new threads and I'm good to go," Jill answered.

"No, it's more than that. It's the way you're carrying yourself."

"I've had some amazing people in my corner, especially this one. She's helped me get stronger," Jill said, looking at Alex and smiling.

"Can I have some of that strength back?" Alex teased.

"We're both going to be strong." Jill locked eyes with Alex and squeezed her hand before turning back to Detective Barrett. "So, what happens now?"

"He should be here soon. I'd like to set the scene for you and describe what to expect. I find if someone can visualize the encounter first, it is a little easier."

The detective gave Jill a description of the room and the layout. Steve would enter the room first, be put in the seat furthest from the door, and his leg cuffs secured to a clip on the floor. The entire time his hands would remain cuffed. The detective assured Jill that he would be unable to touch her. Then Jill would be brought into the room and sit on the opposite side of the table. The guard would remain in the room with her the entire time. The detective would be watching behind the one-way glass, but wouldn't be able to hear the conversation. Alex would not be allowed to watch, which Alex knew was for the best. If, at any time, she became uncomfortable or fearful, she could ask the guard to escort her from the room.

Alex nonchalantly ran her hands down her pant leg, subtly wiping them off. Her palms had immediately begun to sweat as soon as the detective described the scene Jill would soon face. The detective had nearly finished when a knock on the door interrupted them. A young baby-faced police officer opened the door a foot, stuck his head in, and informed them the prisoner was ready. Alex's shoulders tensed, but she hoped Jill hadn't noticed.

"Are you ready, Jill?" Detective Barrett stood up from her desk.

Jill and Alex tentatively rose to their feet.

"I'll be okay, Alex." Jill touched Alex's chest then patted her own. "You're with me in here, so I won't be afraid."

Words escaped Alex, so she stepped forward and wrapped her arms around Jill, not caring they were standing in the middle of Detective Barrett's office. Detective Barrett kept busy, pretending to straighten her files. Alex had an intense look in her eyes when they broke their embrace.

"I know you can do this." Alex put as much conviction in her voice as she could. "Just remember, I'll be here waiting for you."

Jill hugged Alex once more, and then turned to Detective Barrett. "I'm ready now, Detective."

❧❧❧❧

Before the officer opened the door, Jill took a deep breath. He held it open and motioned her in ahead of him. She steeled her eyes, held her head high, and stepped into the room. Steve was sitting at the table in an orange jumpsuit, his hands shackled. Jill pulled her chair out, sat down, and looked him directly in the eye. His eyes held contempt as he sized her up. It was clear he didn't approve of her new look. His eyes narrowed and the cruel look she was accustomed to settled on his face.

"Hello, Steve." Jill looked directly at Steve, something she'd not done in years. His eyes widened. She knew he wouldn't have expected her to speak first or make eye contact, so she had already caught him off guard.

"Jill." He sneered. "I see you've been out spending my money."

She didn't take the bait. "How have you been?"

"Who the fuck do you think you are?" Steve spoke under his breath. "You come waltzing in here with your fancy clothes and new look. Do ya think that makes you someone? Well, it doesn't. You're still the same worthless piece of shit you've always been."

"It looks like you've lost a few pounds. Aren't you liking the food?"

"I get it. That big dyke is your sugar momma now. You giving her some pussy, huh? Is that it?"

"Any idea when the trial will start?" Jill was surprised how easy it was to maintain her composure. She saw him for the pathetic coward he was and his intimidation tactics were almost laughable.

"Just wait until I get out of here, you'll need to be reminded of what it means to be with a man." He looked down into his lap and thrust his hips a couple times.

"I've already hired a lawyer, who will be handling the divorce." Jill's face remained expressionless.

"Do you think a divorce is going to stop me from giving it to you? You'll need it extra hard and rough to cure you from whatever that lesbo is doing to you." His face continued to get redder.

Jill could tell he was losing control. It was almost as if he'd forgotten there was a police officer in the room. "Is there a lawyer you'd like the papers sent to?"

"Are you listening to me, you bitch? You won't be able to walk right for a week once I'm done with you."

His crude threats were making Jill's stomach lurch, so she decided she needed to end the conversation, soon.

"You'll need a real prick to put you back in line, and mine's getting hard just thinking about it." He laughed and sat back with a satisfied grin.

"Yep, you are definitely a real prick, but that's not what we're here to talk about."

"You cunt." Steve strained against his chains. He leaned as far forward as he could, trying to intimate her with his much larger physique.

Jill was tired of this game and his physical presence was beginning to make her uncomfortable, so she decided to deliver her knockout punch. A blow that the officer in the room wouldn't recognize as being one, which made it that much more perfect. "How has your mom been? Has she been here to see you? I'm seeing her and the girls after I leave here. Should I tell her you say hi?"

With that, he lunged at her and started screaming. His rant was incomprehensible other than his repeated threats.

❦❦❦❦

Alex thumbed through another magazine. Detective Barrett had given her a stack to keep her busy, but Alex found she couldn't focus enough to read. She picked up a new magazine with a bunch of Hollywood stars on the cover, and thumbed through it, looking at the pictures. She was on her second time through, only registering half of what was on the pages. Her stomach was in knots and her chest felt as if it might crush her heart. She was on her feet as soon as she heard the doorknob turn behind her. Alex was standing facing the door when Jill walked in ahead of Detective Barrett. She looked a little pale, but was smiling and otherwise looked good. Alex was sure she looked much worse than Jill did.

Before Alex could speak, Jill was across the room, touching Alex's cheek. She smiled and looked at Alex with compassion. "Oh, Alex, it's okay. I'm fine, see?"

As soon as Jill touched her, the release was immediate and tears escaped from her eyes. Alex embarrassedly swiped at her face. She hadn't intended to cry in front of Detective Barrett.

"Thank you for being here for me. I knew it would be hard for you, but now I see just how hard it really was." Jill wrapped her arms around Alex.

"Whatever gave you that idea?" Alex let go of Jill. She held her at arm's length and studied her, especially her eyes, wanting to be sure Jill wasn't putting up a front. When she saw the confidence was real, Alex smiled and pulled Jill to her.

"I am so proud of you. You did it."

When they finally let go, the reality of where they were hit them. Alex nervously looked around the room and realized Detective Barrett was no longer there. She must have quietly left the room, recognizing their need to be alone.

Detective Barrett entered the room as Alex said, "I can't believe you picked Oscar the Grouch over the Cookie Monster."

"I'm not even going to ask." Detective Barrett shook her head. "Is everything in here okay, now?"

"Yes, thank you so much for giving us that time," Jill said.

"Are you up to answering some questions about the meeting?"

"Sure."

"I have to satisfy my curiosity. What did you say that caused him to lunge at you like that?"

"He lunged at you? Are you okay?" Alex's eyes widened.

"I'm fine, Alex. You worry too much." Jill laughed and patted Alex's hand. Jill recounted how Steve was trying to bully and intimidate her. "I'd finally had enough of his crap, so I asked him how his mother was. Let's just say he has mommy issues."

"Ouch. Remind me never to piss you off."

Detective Barrett stifled a giggle and looked down at her notepad. When she looked up, she said, "I think that was the turning point in the meeting. After you held your ground, his body language completely changed, and it was evident you were the one in control. What did you say to make him cry?"

"Damn, you had him in tears?"

Jill smiled at Alex, her eyes showing a mixture of strength and softness. "As big of an asshole as he is, I don't want revenge. I'm not proud of the fact I had to reduce him to that, but I knew that in the end it would make everyone safer. I know how it feels to be driven to my knees, and I didn't want to have to do that to anyone, not even my worst enemy."

Alex smiled and her eyes danced. "You're an amazing woman and the incredible thing is I don't think you even know it."

"Stop it." Jill blushed and lightly pushed Alex in the shoulder. "I'm trying to give a report to Detective Barrett. She doesn't need to hear your commentary."

"Sorry." Alex winked at Jill.

"I don't think it was any one thing that I said, but more likely the direction of the conversation. I told him I was fully prepared to testify against him, as was everyone else. I think he realized that I'm not afraid, and I won't shrink back."

Detective Barrett nodded. "Now it's a waiting game. He'll more than likely take one of two paths. Either he'll try to shove you back and get the upper hand, or he'll fold. As well as you handled yourself today, I'd lean toward the latter. I expect he'll be demanding to talk to me soon, but this time he will get the bad cop."

Chapter Twenty

Alex stepped out of the shower and ran a towel through her hair. She chastised herself for the butterflies dancing in her stomach. *She was simply going out with three friends, nothing more,* she unsuccessfully tried to convince herself. If it were so simple, why had she changed her choice of clothes more than half a dozen times before she settled on what she would wear?

Now looking in the mirror, she was afraid she'd chosen wrong. The black ribbed tank top showed off her muscular build, but she wondered if she looked too casual. She eyed the faded ripped jeans hanging from the door, and her worry intensified. Jill would no doubt be dressed up, probably in a skirt, so they'd be mismatched. She angrily pulled the jeans from the hanger and slid them on. She certainly didn't need to think about how they would look together, since they weren't together. The chunky belt was difficult to pull through the loops of her jeans, but she finally succeeded and latched the large silver belt buckle. Alex sat down on the toilet lid and pulled on her black biker boots. She smiled to herself, knowing Sarah hated them because they gave Alex a couple more inches of height.

The past week with Jill had gone well. They had finally settled into their roles as roommates and friends. Granted, Jill was gone most of the time, settling into her new job, but the time they spent together had been without any awkward moments. Jill was buoyant every evening, excitedly filling Alex in on her day. With her new job taking center stage, Jill hadn't flirted with Alex once the entire week. This proved to Alex what she believed all along; once Jill was fully back on her feet, she'd have no interest in anything more than friendship with Alex. The realization caused a deep ache in her chest, but Alex would have denied it if anyone asked.

Alex stood and looked into the mirror again. She saw her nervousness and couldn't help but smile. She needed to stop looking like a deer in headlights, or everyone would notice her discomfort. It was hard enough being near Jill day after day, but being at a club with her was a new challenge that Alex wasn't sure she was ready for.

Alex ran her hand through her hair one last time before turning away from the mirror. Before she exited the bathroom, she took a deep breath to calm her shakiness. When she walked into her bedroom, she looked at the clock on her nightstand and saw that she still had fifteen minutes before Sarah and Michelle would be there. She debated staying in her room until the last minute so she wouldn't have to see Jill until the others arrived. *What was her problem?* She was acting like a junior high kid, hiding out in the bedroom, afraid to go to her first dance.

Alex grabbed her wallet and keys from her dresser and put on a confidence she didn't feel, before she pushed open the door. She immediately looked down the hall and noted the closed bathroom door at the end. Apparently, Jill was still getting ready, so she headed for the living room. Part of her wanted to see Jill before Sarah and Michelle arrived, so she could get past her initial reaction to Jill without an audience. The other part of her couldn't help but think it would be safer to have them there as a buffer. Now it wouldn't be her choice; it would depend on when Jill emerged.

Alex went into the kitchen and grabbed a handful of grapes. They'd already eaten dinner, so she wasn't hungry, but she needed something to do with her hands. She pulled a beer off the shelf, but replaced it. She hadn't needed a beer before she went to a club since she was in college. She needed to get a grip. She was nearly thirty-five years old, which was too old to be regressing. She giggled to herself at her own foolishness. In her bedroom, she was acting like a junior high kid; now she had at least matured to her college days. Maybe by the time they left, she'd be back to her own age.

≈≈≈≈≈

Jill crumpled the shirt she'd just taken off, making sure to wrinkle it so she wouldn't be tempted to put it on again and threw it into her pile of dirty clothes. She'd put it on and taken it off several times, but this time her decision was final. She would throw caution to the wind and take Michelle's advice. She zipped the tight black leather vest up over her bra, and examined how she looked without the shirt underneath. She fought the temptation to zip the vest higher to hide her ample cleavage. The necklace she wore lay on her chest a couple inches above.

She slid into her tight, intentionally torn jeans.

She'd been resistant to buying them, but now she was glad she did. It had been a long time since she'd been out to a club of any kind and was afraid she would look out of place, but Michelle assured her the ripped look never went out of style. She finished her outfit with a pair of black boots with three-inch heels.

She was surprised when she looked into the full-length mirror. For the first time in years, she was satisfied with how she looked. She stared hard, looking for the mousy woman she'd become, but she could see no traces of her. Her makeup was heavier than usual, especially around her eyes. The dark eyeliner and generous mascara highlighted her brown eyes, drawing attention to her best feature. She'd applied her blush to further accent her high cheekbones. Now she only needed to choose her lipstick.

Jill picked up three tubes, trying to decide on a color. When they rattled against each other, she realized that her hands were shaking. She couldn't remember the last time she'd been this nervous. Her hands hadn't been shaky when she went to confront Steve, but they were now. *How ironic*, she thought. The person she felt the most fearful of didn't illicit this kind of response, but the person she felt the safest with did.

The past week had gone well. Jill continued to keep her vow not to flirt with Alex, although it was difficult at times. At the end of a long day, she longed to be wrapped in Alex's strong arms. Other times, she watched Alex's lips move when she talked, wanting so badly for Alex to kiss her. In those moments, she focused all her energy on her new job and tried to share that excitement with Alex. She hoped Alex would see the positives Jill could bring to a relationship when she was back on her feet, instead of being the constant burden she had been. It was important to Jill that she prove to Alex that she could stand on her own. She wanted Alex to understand that she wanted her in her life more than anything, but it wasn't because she needed Alex to take care of her.

Jill wanted everything to be perfect tonight. Since Alex agreed to go, she'd daydreamed how the evening would play out. Alex would look at her across the club, and the guarded fearful look that was becoming commonplace would turn to hunger. Alex would approach her, ask her to dance, and take her in her arms. They would dance and the rest of the world would fade away. Alex's strong arms would hold her tightly as they moved to the music, their bodies molded to each other. When the music stopped, Alex would look into her eyes. Jill would offer a silent welcome, and Alex would devour her lips.

She needed to stop thinking about it, or she'd need another cold shower. She felt the pressure between her legs and tried to push it out of her mind. In the past month, her body was reacting in ways that she'd thought were long dead. She fussed with her hair, knowing it could be dangerous seeing Alex when she was feeling this charged. It would be safer if she waited to emerge after Sarah and Michelle arrived.

A smirk crossed her face and her eyes twinkled. She had been fearful for too long, for a much different reason, but she was not going to be tonight. She looked into the mirror one last time before she opened the door and emerged into the hallway. She noticed that Alex's door was open, but saw no sign of Alex when she passed.

❧❧❧❧

Alex heard the bathroom door open, so she stuffed the last few grapes she held in her hand into her mouth, chewed a couple times, and swallowed them practically whole. She almost choked but swallowed hard, hoping she wouldn't break into a coughing fit. She wanted to maintain her cool demeanor, and she knew choking would destroy that façade. Taking one last deep breath, she pushed through the door and went into the living room.

Alex froze when she saw Jill striding down the hall. Alex was glad she'd taken that last breath, because she didn't think she was breathing at all now. Jill smiled broadly, her eyes full of mischief. Alex felt her face redden when she realized she'd unconsciously looked Jill up and down.

Jill laughed. "So you like what you're seeing?"

"No, I mean…I'm sorry," Alex stammered.

"What's there to be sorry about?" Jill had a playful smile on her face.

"I just wasn't, well, expecting you to be dressed like that. I didn't mean to…" Alex's voice trailed off.

"So, you don't like it?" Jill smirked and then tilted her head and looked Alex up and down, nodding in approval.

"I just wasn't expecting…Well, expecting you to be dressed like that."

"You thought I'd be in a nice conservative skirt and sweater, didn't you?"

"Maybe."

"You didn't think I could pull off sexy?"

"I never said—" Alex stopped; her face felt like it was on fire. "I thought I might be under-dressed."

"So, you think I'm under-dressed?" Jill tried to feign offense, but the twinkle in her eye gave her away.

"God, no. You look amazing."

"Thank you," Jill said, accepting the compliment. She took several steps toward Alex. "You don't look so bad yourself."

"Thanks," Alex faltered. The closer Jill got, the more frantically Alex looked around the room, as if she were looking for an escape route.

"I think we'll look pretty good together." Jill stopped two feet from Alex. "Don't you?"

"Um, Sarah and Michelle should be here soon." Alex's eyes lighted on the clock. Alex was rattled, while Jill seemed to be gaining confidence.

"I think we have a few minutes." Jill locked eyes with Alex. "What do you say we have a practice dance?" She closed the gap between them and wrapped her arms around Alex's waist. Alex let out an audible gasp when Jill's breasts pushed against her. She hesitated for only a second, before she put her arms around Jill as well.

Jill moaned quietly as she ran her hands up Alex's back until her hands rested on her muscular shoulders. They swayed gently under the pretense of dancing, to a song that existed only in their minds. Alex felt every nerve ending in her body screaming, especially the ones between her legs.

Alex knew she should step away, but she couldn't. It felt too right having Jill in her arms to ever let go willingly. Jill shifted slightly, so she was straddling Alex's thigh and slowly moved against it. Alex could tell by her breathing that the motion was having an effect on Jill. Alex fought the desire to pull Jill against her and help Jill slide up and down her leg.

A loud banging on the door startled them, and Alex jumped back with a guilty look on her face. Jill's face was flushed, and she had an unfocused look in her eyes.

"We should answer the door," Alex stammered. She shook her head a couple times as if trying to clear her mind.

"I need to go freshen up." Jill hurried from the room.

Alex took a deep breath before opening the door, not knowing whether Sarah and Michelle had the world's worst timing or the best.

⁂

When Jill emerged several minutes later, she felt nearly composed. She still had a slight flush in her cheeks, but thought Alex would be the only one that noticed. Michelle immediately went to her, raving about her outfit. In typical Michelle fashion, she reached up and started messing with Jill's hair.

"Would you leave her be?" Sarah grumbled.

"You better be nice or your mop of hair is next," Michelle shot back.

"I think you've had your hands in it plenty today." Sarah raised her eyebrows.

"Ew, do we really have to listen to this?" Alex turned to Jill. "Didn't I tell you they were like a couple of rabbits?"

"And why, exactly, were you telling Jill about our sex life?" Sarah said with a devious smile. "Giving her pointers?"

Alex laughed. "That's it, I'm leaving. I call shotgun."

"You can't have my seat," Michelle whined.

"I need to go over a couple things on the Florida deal."

"No business tonight; we're celebrating," Michelle said.

"I promise, you let me talk business on the drive there, then I won't mention it again for the rest of the evening."

"Fine, as long as it's okay with Jill." Michelle turned her eyes to Jill.

"Do what you have to do, Alex." Jill hoped her tone didn't come out too sharp. She saw by the look on Alex's face that she caught Jill's double meaning. Alex was obviously retreating from their earlier moment, but Jill needed to hide her disappointment. Tonight was supposed to be a celebration, so the last thing she wanted was for Alex to avoid her. She hoped giving Alex a little space during the drive might help.

❧❧❧❧

Alex held open the door for Jill. The butterflies were back in Jill's stomach, the loud pulsing music a reminder that she was out of her element. Alex must have sensed her hesitation, because she smiled and held out her arm. Jill gratefully took it, thankful that Alex was always so attuned to her. Despite Alex's earlier discomfort at her apartment, Jill was relieved that Alex's natural inclination took over as soon as she sensed Jill's fear.

"Looks like we have a couple choices who to join," Sarah said.

"Great, does that mean we'll end up offending someone?" Alex groaned.

Jill recognized several of the women as regulars at the gym. She never thought about the public relation roulette that Alex and Sarah had to traverse until now. Obviously, the price they had to pay for owning a popular business.

"Look, there's an empty table back by the dance floor." Michelle pointed, but by the time the others looked, it was filled.

"Shit," Sarah said. "Any preference as to who you don't want to piss off?"

"It looks like it's someone's birthday at that table," Jill said, trying to be helpful.

"Good catch," Sarah said. "The birthday table is definitely the least likely to offend anyone."

"Lead the way," Alex said, letting her two much smaller friends go first. Jill still had her arm threaded through Alex's, so Alex squeezed gently, indicating they should follow.

"Sorry, I didn't know there would be so many people we know here." Alex spoke into Jill's ear, so she could hear her over the music. "We'll have to do some table hopping because God forbid if we miss talking to anyone."

Jill was excited to get the opportunity to get better acquainted with the women she'd only briefly met, but still felt disappointed that the setting inhibited any of the intimacy they'd had earlier. She wondered if Alex was thankful for the distraction, or happy to be surrounded by so many people. She didn't have much time to ponder it, before they were immersed in the crowd.

⚜ ⚜ ⚜ ⚜

Jill couldn't remember the last time she'd had so much fun. The group they'd joined immediately made her feel welcome. Alex took longer to relax, asking her every few minutes if the lesbian stuff was making her uncomfortable. Jill was enjoying the female camaraderie, and after all she'd been through, it was refreshing being with only women. She found that she was able to relax, instead of feeling constantly on guard.

Surrounded by so many lesbians seemed to bring out the protective side of Alex, which served Jill well. Alex couldn't remain distant when she was worried about Jill's enjoyment and comfort. Before long, Alex was sitting close to her, whispering commentary into her ear most of the evening. Alex was especially playful and had her laughing much of the time.

Sarah and Michelle loved to dance and tried to persuade Jill to join them, but she'd been hesitant until Alex encouraged her to enjoy herself. It didn't take long before Jill was comfortable with the other women at the table and found herself on the dance floor with them, as well. She'd hoped Alex would join them, but she stayed on the sideline. She longed for another moment like they had in Alex's apartment, but Alex seemed content sitting and watching.

As the evening went on, a couple women asked Jill for a slow dance, but she politely declined. She hadn't missed the relief that crossed Alex's face when she did. She contemplated accepting a dance in hopes that it would goad Alex into asking her, but she decided against it. She was having too good of a time to possibly ruin it by playing juvenile games.

It was just after midnight and the crowd was starting to become more boisterous as the alcohol flowed. The coupling ritual had begun. Jill noticed as the evening progressed that Alex sat closer to her, making sure to keep the other women at bay. It comforted her having Alex close; she only wished Alex would touch her the way she saw some of the women around her touching.

Alex nursed the drink sitting in front of her, as she had most of the evening. Jill likewise had little to drink. She wasn't a big drinker anyway, but was less so in an unfamiliar environment.

"The show is about to begin," Alex said, leaning into Jill. She looked at Alex, puzzled, so Alex continued. "Get too much alcohol into a group of lesbians, and you never know what might happen."

Jill smiled. "You'll protect me, won't you?"

"Of course." Alex smiled back. Before Alex could say more, Sarah and Michelle came off the dance floor, panting and laughing. They made a beeline to Alex and Jill. Sarah grabbed the beer Alex was nursing and took a large swig.

"Hey, get your own." Alex swiped at her beer in Sarah's hand and missed. Jill giggled, knowing Sarah was trying to annoy Alex.

"I was just helping you out. It's already turning to piss water since you've been milking it for so long." Sarah threw some bills on the table. "Order us another one when the server comes around."

"Why don't you do it yourself?"

"Because we just came to get your lovely date, since you don't seem to be taking her out to dance." Sarah took Jill's hand and helped her up from the table.

Alex glared at her. "Fine, I'll order the next round."

Sarah winked at Alex, before she and Michelle led Jill toward the dance floor. Alex watched them walk away, her eyes never leaving Jill.

Alex was mesmerized, watching Jill dance, oblivious to everything and everyone around her, so she failed to hear the voice behind her. She was startled when she felt someone snake their arm around from behind her and rest their hand on her breast. When she spun around, she looked into familiar pale blue eyes.

"Hey stranger," the stunning blonde said. Without warning, she leaned into Alex, pulled her close, and kissed her neck.

Alex recoiled and glared at the woman. "Hello Kristen."

"I've missed you." Kristen reached out, grabbed a handful of Alex's shirt, and tried to pull it from her pants.

Alex grabbed Kristen's wrist to stop the onslaught. "I see you've had a few too many."

"Who, me?" Kristen giggled and ran her other hand across Alex's stomach.

Kristen's actions forced Alex to take her other hand as well. "I thought you'd moved away."

"Keeping tabs on me, huh?" Kristen winked. "I moved back a couple months ago. I'm surprised I haven't seen you sooner."

"I don't get out much." Alex wanted to end the conversation as soon as possible, so she let go of Kristen's hands. She immediately regretted it when Kristen reached out and touched her face.

"Still as sexy as ever." Kristen caressed Alex's

cheek. Alex took a step back, but she bumped into the table behind her, nearly knocking over a couple beers. Alex turned to apologize, which gave Kristen the opportunity she needed. Kristen closed the gap between them and pressed against Alex. Being nearly as tall as Alex, their faces were within inches of one another. Alex started to speak, but Kristen covered Alex's mouth with her own.

When Alex pulled away, she found herself looking into a pair of hurt brown eyes. Alex pushed past Kristen. "Jill?"

Jill stood without moving, staring at Alex, not speaking. Alex put her hand on Jill's arm.

"Oh, I always loved your shoulders." Kristen grabbed them and started kneading them from behind. She looked past Alex, made eye contact with Jill, and smirked. "I especially liked feeling them when they were between my legs."

Alex remained facing Jill, but turned her head and looked over her shoulder. "Would you shut the hell up and take your drunken ass somewhere else?"

She felt Jill start to pull away and turned back, locking her eyes on Jill. The hurt was still there, but she also saw a questioning look as well.

"Mm…Alex, you're turning me on. You know I'm a sucker for the tough girl." Kristen moaned and continued caressing Alex.

Alex was surprised when she felt Kristen's hands suddenly come off her shoulders. She was relieved when she heard the familiar voice say, "She said you need to back off."

"Sarah, I see you haven't changed a bit." Kristen's voice dripped with contempt.

Alex tuned out the conversation behind her,

sure that Sarah and Michelle could handle Kristen. Her only concern was Jill. "Jill?" Alex said again. Jill still didn't answer, so Alex continued. "Jill, please talk to me."

"Is that her?" Jill asked.

"Yes, that's Kristen."

"She's gorgeous. Her picture didn't do her justice." Jill looked at Alex and then looked back at Kristen, as if trying to imagine them together.

"You know she means nothing to me, don't you?" Alex felt her panic rising. She realized her reaction was over the top if she and Jill were just friends, but right now, she didn't care. The only thing she cared about was erasing the fear and hurt in Jill's eyes.

"But you were kissing her." Jill's delivery was flat, devoid of emotion.

"No, she kissed me. You have to believe me. I didn't want her to."

Jill started to respond, but the loud conversation behind Alex stopped her. Three of Kristen's friends, who also appeared drunk, joined the heated conversation. Jill's eyes widened. "I think maybe you better help out Sarah."

"Stay here with me?" Alex took Jill's hand, afraid that she would disappear if she turned away.

Jill nodded. Alex gave her a smile before she turned, still holding her hand.

"This must be Alex," one of the women said.

"Look, Kristen, it looks like you were replaced by the girl next door," another of the women said, looking Jill up and down.

Kristen stepped forward and sneered at Jill. "This is the best you could replace me with?"

"She's ten times the woman you'll ever be."

"Come on, Alex." Kristen ran her hands down her own body. "Admit it. You'd love to have another piece of this."

"Alex, why don't you take Jill out on the dance floor and get away from this trash?" Michelle said, finally joining the conversation.

"Get your hands off me," Jill shouted. Alex spun around, forgetting everyone else in the room. It took Alex a moment to realize that Kristen's friend standing next to Jill had a handful of Jill's breast.

"I don't know, Kristen, these are pretty nice," the woman slurred.

"I said, don't touch me." Jill swung her arm up, knocking the woman's hand off her breast. Despite having several inches and at least fifty pounds on Jill, the woman took a step back.

Alex grabbed the woman by the shoulders and pushed her against a table. "Never touch her again." Alex's eyes blazed and she took a deep breath. It was taking all her control not to throttle the woman.

"Okay, okay," the woman said, shrinking back. "Relax already."

"Just take Kristen and get the hell out of here."

"Sure, we aren't looking for any trouble." Several women from the gym had encircled the group, and the drunken woman eyed them nervously.

"Get Jill out of here," Sarah said. "We've got things under control."

Alex hesitated for a moment, not wanting to walk out on her friends, but wanting to get Jill away from the unpleasant scene. When she felt the tremor in Jill's hand, she immediately made up her mind. "Would you like to dance?"

"Please." Jill offered a slight smile. Alex protectively draped her arm over Jill's shoulder before guiding her through the crowd. Jill leaned into Alex and threaded her arm around Alex's waist.

They were half way to the dance floor when Alex stopped. The music was pounding, so she leaned in close in order for Jill to hear her. "Are you all right?"

"I'm fine, Alex. You don't have to worry about me so much."

"But she had her hands all over you."

"For God's sake, I'm not a delicate flower." When Alex winced, Jill added, "I love how protective you are, though."

"But?"

"But I think I did a good job of putting her in her place."

"You did." Alex smiled. "I know you can handle yourself, but I'm not sure I'll ever be able to sit back and not react."

"I wouldn't want it any other way, but I don't break easy."

"That might be the understatement of the decade."

"Thank you for seeing my strength." Jill reached up and touched Alex's cheek. "Do you miss her?"

"No," Alex almost shouted. Her brow furrowed and she frowned. "There is nothing about her that I miss."

"But she's so pretty."

"Not in my eyes, she's not." Alex wanted to say, "She's not nearly as pretty as you."

Alex was sure Jill caught her unspoken words by the smile that spread across her face. Jill's smile faded. "What about the kiss?"

"She blindsided me. I certainly wasn't kissing

her back." Alex saw the concern in Jill's dark brown eyes, so she continued. "Please Jill, you have to believe me. I didn't want her to kiss me and I don't miss her."

"I believe you." Jill smiled. "Can I have that dance now?"

"Let's do it." She had been so focused on Jill that she hadn't noticed the music had slowed. Her pulse quickened. She'd already agreed to dance, so she couldn't back out now. She put her arm out and Jill took it, a large smile lighting her face. Her smile was contagious, and Alex smiled back.

When they got to the crowded dance floor, Alex took Jill into her arms. Jill nestled against Alex and put her head on Alex's shoulder. Unlike earlier at Alex's apartment, the embrace wasn't sexually charged but full of tenderness. Alex hoped that being in her arms would make Jill forget about Kristen.

Jill put her lips near Alex's ear. "I wish I could stay here in your arms forever."

Alex held Jill tighter, but said nothing. Her chest ached and she fought back tears. She wished she could tell Jill all that she felt but knew she couldn't. She vowed to herself that this would be the last time she held Jill like this.

Alex blinked back her tears and her body stiffened. She fought an internal battle. As much as she loved the feeling of Jill's body against hers, she knew she needed to shut down her feelings for Jill. She would allow herself to savor the moment, but after this dance ended, she needed to get a grip.

The song ended too soon and the tempo picked up. Reluctantly, Alex released Jill. When Jill stepped out of her arms, she looked up at Alex sadly. Alex's eyes were also full of pain, but she quickly hardened them. Jill took Alex's arm, but both knew the moment was over.

❧❧❧❧

They left Kasabooboo with Sarah and Michelle shortly after their dance. It was getting late, and Kristen's appearance had put a damper on the evening. Alex sat in the back seat with Jill, but she was quiet and distant. Alex gazed out the window, her body pressed against the door. Her mind was a jumble of thoughts and her heart ached. It was time to let Jill go, so Jill could go on with her life. The thought nearly brought Alex to her knees, and she fought back tears as she watched the lights from the passing cars flash past.

How could she have been so stupid? She knew how it would end, but every step of the way, she'd been unable to walk away. Tonight, Jill showed that she could take care of herself and didn't need Alex to protect her any longer. Alex convinced herself that Jill needed her, while she'd known all along that she needed Jill more. Her heart had been touched in ways it had never been before, and she knew Jill would take a piece of it when she left. *Would she be okay with such a huge piece missing from inside?*

While they drove, Sarah and Michelle rambled on about the evening. They tried to draw Alex and Jill into the conversation but with little success. If either were asked a direct question, they would answer, but then returned to their own silent thoughts.

"Are you listening to me, Alex?" Sarah said.

"Huh?" Alex said when she finally registered hearing her name.

"Did you hear a thing I just asked you?"

"Do you want to refresh my memory?"

"Didn't I tell you she was on another planet?" Sarah said to Michelle.

"Would you just ask me again?" Alex snapped.

"I asked what the stupid bitch said to you."

"I'm assuming you're referring to Kristen?"

"How'd you guess?"

"You usually reserve all your favorite terms of endearment for her." Alex giggled.

"Very true. So, what was up with the bitch?"

"I really don't want to talk about her. She's not worth my breath."

"You've got a point there."

Sarah pulled up outside the gym and left the car running. Alex's breath caught in her throat when she realized that soon she would be left alone with Jill. Panic threatened to overtake her, and her mind raced.

"Hey, you guys have to come in. I have something I have to show you."

"It's late, Alex," Michelle said.

"It's not that late."

"What is it?" Sarah asked.

Shit, Alex thought. She hadn't come up with a good reason, so she said the first thing that came into her mind. "I just got that new PS4 game I was telling you about, and you have to come up and check it out."

"Are you serious?" Sarah asked. "Don't you think it can wait until next week?"

Michelle studied Alex. "You know, I was really looking forward to playing."

Sarah turned to Michelle with a puzzled look. "When the hell did you start playing video games?" As soon as she met Michelle's eyes, she finished with, "I guess it's not that late."

Alex looked at Jill, but immediately looked away. Jill had to know that Alex didn't want to be alone with her, and she didn't want to see her reaction.

When they got inside, Alex asked Sarah to set up the game while she freshened up. Alex emerged dressed in a pair of boxer shorts and t-shirt, which was what she normally slept in. Sarah glanced at her out of the corner of her eye, but didn't comment on her unusual move. Michelle and Jill were talking on the other couch, but both stopped and looked at Alex curiously.

"Let's play," Alex said, and picked up her controller.

"You're going down," Sarah answered.

They'd been playing for only fifteen minutes when Alex set down her controller and stretched. "Ya know, I'm not feeling the best. I think maybe I should turn in." She jumped to her feet. "Thanks for a nice evening everyone. Goodnight."

❧❧❧❧

They all stared after her, too stunned to speak before she was gone down the hall.

"Sorry," Jill said sadly. "I'm not sure what's up with her."

"It's not your fault, sweetie." Michelle patted Jill's leg.

"She's my best friend, and I can't figure her out."

"Can I get you guys another beer?"

"Sure," Michelle said.

When Jill left the room, Sarah turned to Michelle with a puzzled look.

"I didn't want to leave her alone," Michelle said. Sarah nodded and hit the game reset button.

Chapter Twenty-one

Alex closed the box, tucking one flap under the other so that it would stay securely shut. She put it in the closet next to her suitcases and used her foot to push it further back. She needed to do a final sweep of the apartment to make sure she hadn't forgotten anything, so she wouldn't have to come back.

"So, were you even going to tell me you were leaving?" Jill said from behind her. Alex jumped, not realizing she'd come in. "Or were you just going to leave?"

"What are you doing home?" Alex asked, ignoring the question.

"I have my counseling appointment this evening and had something I wanted to discuss with you before I went. Sarah told me you were up here."

"What is it you wanted to talk about?" Alex inconspicuously shut the closet door with her elbow and smiled, hoping Jill would forget what she'd seen.

"You can't wait to get out of here, can you?"

"I'm sure that's not what you came here to talk about."

"No, but that's what I want to discuss now."

How could she explain to Jill that the ache she felt was becoming unbearable? Jill would brush past her and Alex could feel the electricity coursing through her body. Sometimes Jill didn't even need to touch her for Alex to feel the charge. It surprised her that Jill didn't catch on to her reactions, but at other times she suspected Jill knew perfectly well what she was doing. Being friends wasn't enough when she saw Jill every morning when she woke up and every night before she went to bed. Knowing Jill was across the hall in bed caused Alex several restless nights. Alex wasn't a bar cruiser, but she considered it just to satiate the constant tension in her body.

"It's not that I want to get out of here, but the girls will be here soon and I figured you'd want to get the apartment ready for them."

"And when were you planning on telling me, after you moved out?" Jill waved her hand at the closet door.

"I told you before that I was moving out at the end of the month."

"Almost a month ago, but you haven't mentioned it since. I thought things were better."

"I'm not moving because things are bad."

"I've left you alone like you wanted." Jill blinked back tears. "If you're tired of me, just tell me."

Alex stared at Jill, suddenly realizing why Jill seemed different the last couple weeks. Why she'd been remote since the night at Kasabooboo. She was afraid that she was pushing Alex away, so in order to keep her here, she'd stopped letting her needs be known. Alex took a step toward Jill and said softly, "No, that's not it at all."

"Then what is it, Alex?"

"It's just that, you know...It's best for you and the girls."

"Bullshit, Alex. Why don't you just tell me the

truth?"

"What do you want from me?" Alex looked down at the floor, unable to look Jill in the eyes.

"When are you going to ask me out?" Jill surprised Alex with her boldness.

"I'm not." Alex looked at her defiantly. She tried to put steel in her eyes, hoping to dissuade Jill from saying more.

"Why not?"

"You're straight."

"You're not serious, are you?"

"Jill, you're straight. I'm a lesbian. It's about time you get out there and find yourself a man."

"I can't believe you just said that to me." Jill no longer tried to hide her hurt.

"It's true. Maybe it's time you faced facts." Alex crossed her arms over her chest.

"Tell me you don't love me."

"You know I love you."

Jill's voice had been steadily rising during the conversation and it went up another notch. "Don't play semantics with me, Alex McCoy. Tell me you aren't in love with me."

"Come on. Let's not do this," Alex pleaded.

"No. Tell me you aren't in love with me. Come on, Alex, say it."

"Stop it, Jill. This isn't helping anything."

"I'm not letting you off the hook that easy. Go ahead tell me. Can you?" Alex stood saying nothing, so Jill continued. "What if I told you I was in love with you, then what?"

Jill's words made Alex's heart soar, but it plummeted moments later. She couldn't allow herself to believe anything more was possible, or the pain she already felt would become unbearable. Alex looked at Jill, knowing how vulnerable the revelation made her and didn't want to hurt Jill.

"I know you think you are, but you're not."

"Really? I'm glad I have you to tell me how I feel. If you aren't in love with me, at least have the courage to say it."

"It's not that simple. I'm telling you it's the Lone Ranger thing, nothing more."

"Oh, for God's sake, don't tell me you are going to hide behind that again. You know at the end of the day the Lone Ranger sleeps alone. Is that what you want?"

"Seriously, I rescued you. It's typical for someone to think they're in love with their rescuer, but it's not real. You should ask your counselor about it."

"Don't tell me what I'm feeling isn't real. I know I've never felt anything more real. It's easy for you to tell me how I'm feeling, but I haven't heard a damn word about how you feel. Why don't you tell it like it is, Alex? It's you; you're scared." Jill's face turned red and her voice cracked.

"Okay fine." Alex had kept her voice level, but she finally raised it. "One day, I don't know when. It could be next month or next year, but one day you'll wake up next to me and think, 'what in the hell have I done?' Then you'll get out of my bed. No, I guess it would be our bed, and you'll leave me and go back to being the straight woman that you are. And I'll lay there with my heart ripped out. I can't put myself through that."

"Oh, Alex." Jill's eyes softened. She took a step toward Alex, her eyes full of compassion, and put her hand on Alex's arm.

"No, Jill." Alex flinched and backed away. "You don't understand. I have to go now." Alex shoved her hands in her pockets and headed for the door.

"Alex, please don't go."

Alex turned, the pain in her eyes evident. "I have to. I'm sorry." Without another word, she left.

❧ ❧ ❧ ❧

Jill stood numbly in the middle of the room for several minutes and stared at the door. Finally, she went into the living room and sat on the couch. Before long, she curled up, hugging herself, sobs wracking her body. She was still crying when she heard the door open.

"Alex," Jill said and jumped to her feet.

"No, it's me," Sarah said, entering the room.

"Oh, I thought it was Alex coming back." Jill tried unsuccessfully to hide how distraught she was.

"I didn't mean to intrude. What's going on? Where's Alex?"

Jill tried to fight back her tears, but seeing Sarah standing there looking concerned was making it difficult. Sarah awkwardly approached Jill, put her arm around her, and led her to the couch.

"I'm sorry, I'm sure this is the last thing in the world you want to deal with. I'll be all right." Before Jill could continue, she began to sob. Jill fought to regain her composure, knowing that Sarah didn't handle emotions well; that was Michelle's role. It took her several minutes to stop crying and catch her breath.

"What happened?" Sarah finally asked.

"I can't drag you into this. You're Alex's best friend."

"Oh God, what did she do now?"

"No, she didn't do anything wrong. It was my fault. I pushed her."

"Where is she?" Sarah looked around the room as if she would see Alex standing in one of the corners.

"I don't know."

"What happened?"

"Are you sure you want to talk to me about this? I would understand if you didn't."

"It's better that I know what stupid thing she's done, so I can kick her in the ass." Sarah tried to bring some levity, but it fell flat.

"Honestly, it was my fault. I asked her when she was going to ask me out."

"Good for you. Oh wait, it obviously didn't turn out so good."

"She told me she wasn't going to ask me out."

"She's such an idiot." Sarah picked up her cell phone. "I'll just call her and tell her she needs to pull her head out of her ass."

"No, it got worse." Jill put her hand on Sarah's hand that held the phone. "I asked her if she was in love with me and when she wouldn't answer, I told her I was in love with her."

"I'm sensing that didn't go so well, either."

"She told me that I was a straight woman and one day I would wake up, realize it, and leave her with her heart ripped out. Then she ran out of here."

"Shit, Michelle warned me this was going to happen."

"I wish she would have clued me in." Jill offered a slight smile.

"She didn't want to be right, but she was worried Alex wouldn't know how to handle her feelings for you. You have to believe this, Jill. I know she has never loved anyone like she does you. She's scared."

"So am I." Jill's eyes filled with tears again.

"I know." Sarah awkwardly put her arm around Jill. Jill rested her head on Sarah's shoulder and let the next wave of tears overtake her.

❧ ❧ ❧ ❧

Jill's phone rang and she looked at the screen hopefully.

"Alex?"

"I'm sorry, Jill."

"Where are you?"

"I would have called you sooner, but Michelle wasn't finished chewing me out yet." Her voice sounded drained and was mixed with sadness.

"I didn't mean...Please don't think...Sarah showed up here or I wouldn't have said anything. I'm sorry. I shouldn't have talked about it with your friends."

"It's okay; they're your friends too," Alex reassured her.

"Thank you." There was silence on the other end of the line. "Alex, where do we go from here?"

"I don't know. I wish I did, but I don't."

"I didn't mean to push you. I'm so afraid, Alex. I can't imagine my life without you. I wish I could take everything I said back, if it's going to cause you to run away from me." Jill tried to fight back her panic. "Please tell me, I have to know, have I ruined everything?"

"No, you haven't ruined anything. We'll always be friends, Jill. Let's just pretend it didn't happen, okay?"

"Whatever you want. I just want you to come home. Or are you going to stay at Sarah and Michelle's?"

"I'm coming home."

Jill didn't realize she was holding her breath until the air forced its way out between her lips. "Soon?" Jill said without thinking. She chastised herself for her pushiness, but was relieved when she heard Alex giggle on the other end of the phone.

"I should be there in about fifteen minutes." There was a smile in Alex's voice. "Did you make it to your counseling appointment?"

"Yes." Jill was happy the conversation had taken a more casual tone.

"Are you going to tell me what you came home to talk to me about?"

"Of course I will, if you want to hear about it."

"More than anything. Have you eaten?"

"I wasn't very hungry."

"Do you want me to pick something up on the way home?"

"I'll throw on a couple burgers."

"That would be great."

Jill started to answer, but Alex interrupted. "Jill, I'm glad we're still okay with each other." When Jill didn't say anything, Alex said in a rushed voice, "We are, aren't we?"

"We are," Jill said softly.

⚓⚓⚓⚓⚓

The smell of hamburgers cooking caused Alex's stomach to growl as she approached the kitchen. She'd been so upset, she'd not eaten since she'd left, but now she was starving. Jill was standing over the stove with her back to the door. She flipped the hamburger and pressed down with the spatula. With her other hand, she separated the two buns and set them open faced on the plate. Alex enjoyed the fluid grace in which she moved.

"Smells delicious," Alex finally said.

Jill turned slowly. She had a tentative smile on her face when she greeted Alex. Her face was drawn, and she looked tired. Alex couldn't help but think she'd not seen Jill looking this rough since the night she'd brought her home from the hospital. Alex hesitated for only a moment, and then thought, *fuck it,* and moved quickly toward Jill.

Jill stood, not moving. Her right arm crossed her body and held onto her left arm, as if she were hugging herself. Alex noticed the defensive posture and stopped a couple feet from Jill. She couldn't blame Jill for being closed off, considering their last conversation. Maybe she should take Jill's cue and move on to the food, instead of saying anything more that could possibly send them in the wrong direction. The exhausted look in Jill's eyes was Alex's deciding factor.

"I could use a hug," Alex said. It was all the encouragement Jill needed. She quickly fell into Alex's arms. Alex felt her energy return the longer she held Jill; the overwhelming fatigue she felt earlier evaporated.

Alex squeezed Jill tightly one last time before finally letting go. Jill took a step back and her eyes met Alex's. Gently, Alex ran her thumb under Jill's eye, wiping away a tear. "I'm sorry."

"I am too. Is it wrong to tell you I missed you, even though you've only been gone a few hours?"

"No, it's not wrong. It seemed a hell of a lot longer."

"Tell me about it." Jill laughed. "God, we're pathetic."

Alex laughed too. "Speak for yourself. I'm just hungry."

"You came to the right place. Care for a burger?

"I thought you'd never ask." Alex picked up one of the burgers and took a huge bite. "Damn, that's good."

"Okay, stop being a cave person. What do you say we put them on a plate and sit down at the table?" Jill took the burger from Alex's hand.

"Fine." Alex tried to sound disgusted, but the twinkle in her eye gave her away.

⁂

After they finished eating and cleaning up the kitchen, Alex said, "Okay, now I can concentrate again. You have something to tell me?"

"I could use a beer; do you want one?"

"Uh oh, this conversation requires beer?"

"Maybe." Jill opened the refrigerator. "Do you want one?"

"Sounds like I better take one." Alex absentmindedly took both beers from Jill and opened them before handing one back.

When they went into the living room, Jill sat down on the opposite end of the couch. She was obviously trying to honor their agreement. Alex put her feet on the couch and turned her body fully toward

Jill. She took a big drink from her bottle before she spoke. "Okay, I'm all ears. What do you have to tell me?" Alex hoped Jill's revelations wouldn't send them back into a tailspin.

"I have a big decision to make."

"That sounds pretty serious." Alex tried not to let Jill hear the stress in her voice. *What if someone asked Jill out and she was trying to decide whether to go?* Alex wasn't sure she could handle that kind of revelation tonight, but she'd have to.

"Life changing." Jill paused and looked into Alex's eyes. "Promise you won't judge me until you hear me out."

"Now you're starting to worry me." Her chest tightened. She was becoming surer by the second that Jill was going to reveal a new love interest.

"I'm thinking about dropping my petition for custody of the girls." Jill's voice cracked when she delivered the line.

"Why?" Alex tried to hide her shock. *How could Jill be ready to give them up now, after she sacrificed her entire life for them?*

"You think I'm horrible, don't you?"

"No, I just don't understand. I'm just surprised after what you've been through for them."

"I don't want to, but I think it's the right thing to do." The pain in Jill's eyes was deep, but she forged on. "I talked to Stephanie's attorney today and she thinks Stephanie will be out of jail by the end of next month. She's their mom and she's going to need time to reconnect with them, without me around. I think it would be best if the girls lived with Stephanie and their grandma, as much as it kills me to let them go. They need to start seeing Stephanie as their mom, and

I'm not sure if they can do that if I am there all the time."

Jill stopped and lifted her beer to her lips. She took several long swallows before she continued. "In light of that, it would be silly to bring the girls to live with me until Stephanie gets out. They would probably only be here for a month or two before they would have to move out again. I wanted us to be a family, if only for a little while, but that would be selfish of me. They have settled in nicely with their grandma. You see how happy they are every time we visit. I'm afraid the back and forth would do them no good. The poor things have seen enough in their short lives. I want them to have stability for a change."

Jill took another drink from her beer. "Are you going to say anything? You think I'm a monster, don't you?"

"You may be the most selfless person I've ever met. You're definitely not a monster."

"You understand then?"

"Of course I understand. Jill, you've sacrificed yourself for those girls and you're continuing to. They are lucky to have you and it doesn't mean you'll never see them again."

"God, no, I couldn't take that. They're all I have." Jill stopped. "Well, all I used to have."

"You have nothing to feel bad about." The relief in Jill's eyes was apparent as Alex spoke. "I'm sure that your counselor told you the same thing."

"She did, but I really needed to hear it from you."

"Well, you've heard it. It's the right decision," Alex said with more conviction than she felt. Her chest tightened as she felt the loss of the family she never had, nor would now.

"Thank you." The weight of her decision weighed on her face.

"I know this has to be hard on you."

"Hardest thing I've ever had to do." Jill smiled, but it didn't reach her eyes. "It'll just hurt for a while...a long while. But it's what's best for them."

"I hate that you're still being hurt. You deserve better." In the moment, seeing Jill so sad, Alex forgot her vow to keep her distance. The only thing Alex could think about was finding a way to ease the pain in Jill's eyes. "Is there anything I can do?"

"I'll be okay." Jill reached up and twirled a strand of hair.

"Would a hug help?" Alex knew Jill would never ask after their earlier argument.

"Only if you're okay with it."

"I am," Alex answered honestly. Jill slid down the couch and settled into the familiar spot against Alex's chest. Alex wrapped her arm around Jill and held her close.

"All better." Jill closed her eyes.

Chapter Twenty-two

A lex pulled a bag of shrimp from the freezer and ripped it open. She poured the contents into a bowl of warm water, so they would thaw slowly. She planned to surprise Jill with stir-fry, one of her favorites. Jill had called to say she was leaving work to meet clients at the old shoe factory on her way home. The factory was only about ten minutes away, so Alex was hurrying to finish the prep work.

Alex was determined to make the weekend a special time, hoping to heal the wounds from their argument on Wednesday night. She couldn't blame Jill for being angry. She'd finally told Jill that she was leaving early Monday morning to close the Florida deal. Jill was astute enough to realize that Alex had known the date for some time, but failed to tell her about it until now. Jill's hurt grew when Alex revealed she would be staying in Florida in order to assess the personnel and arrange for any needed facility improvements. When Jill pressed for how long Alex would be gone, Alex was evasive and admitted it could be several weeks.

The conversation went downhill when Jill casually mentioned that she should look for her own apartment while Alex was gone. Alex could still see the hurt in Jill's eyes when Alex agreed that it was probably a good idea. Jill said little after that. Shortly afterwards, Jill excused herself, saying she'd had a long day and wanted to turn in early.

The tension was still thick on Thursday, and there was a strain in their usual easy conversation. Alex was encouraged when she'd talked to Jill a few minutes earlier. Jill was excited about the new clients she was going to meet. She'd been at her job for well over a month, and this was the first time clients asked for her directly. Apparently, they'd seen one of the flyers she'd done for the gym and liked it. Working for Nancy had been exactly what Jill needed; not only did they get along well, but Nancy was highly encouraging, helping Jill build her confidence daily. Jill was nervous about the meeting, but was determined to succeed in order to prove herself to Nancy.

Alex was both hopeful and nervous about the weekend. She wanted to heal the damage from their fight on Wednesday, but she knew she needed to be careful not to cross any boundaries. The thought of being away from Jill for an extended time left her feeling sad and empty. She longed to reconnect and get back some of the closeness they'd lost, but she knew it would be unfair to Jill. Since their talk nearly a month ago, Jill no longer initiated any physical contact. Alex knew Jill was honoring Alex's wishes, but Alex missed the familiar way Jill touched her. At times, Alex couldn't stand the chasm between them and would abandon her self-imposed distance. Jill never resisted; in fact, she seemed to relish the moments. After Alex would spontaneously hug Jill or put her arm around her, Jill always rewarded her with a huge smile and twinkle in her eye. To Jill's credit, even after Alex crossed the line she'd set, Jill never took it as a license to do so herself.

Alex's cell phone interrupted her thoughts. She

looked at the screen and smiled.

"Are you guys there already?"

"Yep," Sarah said.

"Jesus, how fast did you drive?"

"I went the speed limit." Alex heard Michelle in the background and Sarah said, "Well, almost."

"That's what I thought." Alex laughed. "So are you sure the old married couple can handle two nights alone in a cabin in the middle of nowhere?"

"Oh God, do you think I'll remember what to do?"

"Maybe Jill and I should drive up and join you when she gets home."

"We'd love to have you, but it's nearly a three-hour drive, so maybe you better not."

Alex laughed. "Are you sure Michelle really wants to spend all that time alone with you?"

"I'm pretty sure she does. I've been teasing her the last hour of the trip. I've got her so worked up I'm surprised she even let me call you." Alex heard a thunk. "Ouch, why'd you do that?"

"She is so full of shit," Michelle said, obviously having commandeered the phone. "For the record, I just woke up from a nice nap. You know how being in a car puts me to sleep."

"Don't put me in the middle of your feuds." Alex laughed.

"Speaking of feuds, is Jill talking to you?"

"I think so. I'm in the middle of making her a nice suck-up dinner."

"That's a good start. Now get out a bottle of wine and some candles. After dinner, take her in your arms, and plant one on her."

"Not gonna happen."

"God, when are you going to come to your senses?" Michelle said.

"Can't we talk about something else?"

"Fine. Hey, I almost forgot, we were talking on our drive up and I've been meaning to ask if you've heard from Detective Barrett."

"We haven't heard from her in over two weeks. Not since she called saying she'd convinced Steve to give her a statement. She thought it should speed up the court proceedings, but since then, nothing."

"Obviously a bureaucrat's definition of speed. Let's just hope it's over soon, so Jill can put it all in the past."

"Definitely! Is that Sarah I hear whining?"

"You noticed? And she said I was the horny one."

"Okay, that's it, you two go do whatever it is that you need to do, I have a meal to prepare."

"Okay, sweetie. We love you."

"I love you guys too. Have fun."

≈≈≈≈

Jill was singing along to the radio as she drove to the old shoe factory. The prospect of landing her first client was exciting, only made better by the genuine pleasure she'd heard in Alex's voice earlier. Alex made no secret of how proud she was of Jill's reentrance to the working world. The transition was easy when she worked for someone like Nancy. They'd immediately hit it off and their skills complemented one another. Even though the salary was low, the opportunity of getting in on a start-up company was exciting.

Jill nervously smoothed her skirt. She smiled,

thinking it must be her lucky day, or that she must be clairvoyant, since she'd dressed in one of her nicest outfits. She tried to push the reason she'd worn it out of her mind, but she couldn't. She knew it was one of Alex's favorites, even though Alex never told her that. She saw the way that Alex looked at her when she wore it, and she hoped to see that look in Alex's eyes when she got home.

It had been a difficult month, since Jill told Alex she loved her. Jill honored Alex's wishes to keep their relationship strictly platonic, but it had been hard on her. Jill found she spent a lot of time in the gym, trying to work off the sexual tension she felt, and couldn't help but laugh at the number of hours Alex was putting in as well. *If they continued to live together, they both would end up in the best shape of their lives,* she thought with a smile.

Jill wanted to carry her buoyant mood into the weekend and enjoy her time with Alex. Their argument on Wednesday temporarily put a damper on her spirits, but she was determined to put it behind them. The thought of Alex being gone for several weeks caused an emptiness in the center of her chest, but she refused to let it spoil their weekend. They had plans to take the girls to the zoo on Saturday, and tonight she was going to surprise Alex with Red Sox tickets for Saturday evening.

For weeks, Sarah and Michelle encouraged Jill not to give up on Alex, assuring her that Alex was acting out of fear. The feelings she had for Alex were deeper than anything she'd ever felt before. Just being around Alex was comforting and made her feel alive. They had such an easy interaction, and Jill always felt safe in her presence. It was beyond safety, though; it was more the connection. Alex always knew what Jill needed and just the right thing to say. She made Jill laugh when she needed to lighten up and provided tenderness when she needed to be calmed.

Jill hoped Alex would let down her guard and finally throw out the ridiculous rules she'd put on their relationship. It was up to Alex, though, because Jill would not break her promise and cross the line again. Every time Alex touched Jill, violating her own supposed wishes, Jill was hopeful that this would be the time Alex stepped over the line for good. Each time, though, Alex would pull back, leaving Jill with mixed feelings. Having Alex hold her, even briefly, caused her spirits to soar, but it also left her wanting more. As much as she wanted to initiate contact with Alex, she held back.

Jill had been so lost in her thoughts that she didn't remember most of the drive to the shoe factory, but she could see it ahead on the right. She looked around the rundown area, wondering what kind of business someone would want to put into such a godforsaken place. The area was once booming but now looked ugly and rundown. Jill couldn't imagine this industrial park ever looked attractive, but it surely didn't look this desolate when it was shiny and new.

Jill unconsciously shivered as she slowed and turned onto the street leading to the factory. The broken bottles, grown up weeds, and cracking pavement gave her the creeps. The sun was still above the horizon, and she hoped she'd be done before it set. She wasn't looking forward to being here in the dark. *Stop it*, she thought. She was being a coward. The most important thing was wooing the clients, not getting out of dodge before sundown. She looked around, wondering again why anyone would want to put a business here. If it were up to her, she'd tear down all the creepy buildings and put a nice park in their place. *Who knows*, she thought, *maybe that's what the developers were going to do.*

She pulled into the large parking lot and scanned the area. She glanced down at the email to ensure she'd gotten the right address, and read again that she was supposed to access the office area through the alley. A narrow lane was sandwiched between the factory and what appeared to be a warehouse. There were several rusty trucks parked in front, blocking most of her view of the building. She was too intent on the factory itself to notice the glint of newer metal just behind the broken-down trucks.

She slowly drove down the alley, looking around for a sign of life. Despite the sun still being up, it was dark in the alley, and her lights automatically came on. She was almost at the end of the alley, which was blocked by two large storage trailers, but she didn't see any signs of an office.

"Damn," Jill said to herself. She must be in the wrong place. When she reached the end, there was nowhere to turn around, so she pushed the gearshift into reverse. By habit, she looked into her rearview mirror and her palms went cold. A large pickup had pulled in behind her, blocking her exit. Her hands were shaking when she reached for her purse.

᪥᪥᪥᪥

Before Alex could set the phone on the counter, it rang again. She answered without looking at it.

"What do you want, Sarah? I don't want to hear

your side of the story."

Alex was startled when she heard a scream. It took her a couple seconds to key in on the voice.

"Alex," Jill screamed. "Oh God, I think it's a trap. I think it's Steve; he's got me cornered. Help! Alex, help!"

Alex held the phone, listening to the words with horror. Then she heard a loud crash that sounded like broken glass, followed by silence. Alex screamed Jill's name into the phone, but it was dead.

Alex grabbed her car keys, dialed 9-1-1 on her cell phone, and ran down the stairs. She tried to remain calm, but her panic threatened to overcome her. She repeated Jill's location three times to be sure the dispatcher got the right information. She threw her car into gear and shot from the curb. The dispatcher continued to ask her questions as she sped around the corner, nearly hitting an on-coming car.

"I'm trying to drive," Alex yelled into the phone. "Please contact Detective Barrett. She's been working this case. I think Steve Bishop has escaped from jail. I'm on my way there now and need to concentrate on my driving." Alex repeated the address one more time before ending the call.

Alex was oblivious to the tears streaming down her face as she skidded around the corner into the industrial park. She forced herself to slow her speed as she approached the turn for the shoe factory. Her natural inclination was to burst onto the scene, but she knew approaching quietly was the smartest tactic. There was a possibility he might have a weapon that he could use on Jill if he was alerted to Alex's presence.

Alex slowly turned into the shoe factory parking lot and quickly assessed the situation. She saw the pickup truck blocking an alley leading between the two buildings and immediately deduced that was where Jill's car was. She scanned the terrain and drove toward the debilitated trucks in front of one of the buildings. Alex parked behind the trucks and opened her door, closing it so it barely clicked shut.

Alex ran around behind the trucks toward the pickup and stopped dead in her tracks when she heard a scream. Her heart clenched at the sound of Jill's agony, but she knew for Jill's sake that she needed to approach carefully. Alex arrived at the pickup and peered over the back, looking down the alley. The buildings blocked most of the light, so her eyes struggled to adjust to the darkness.

She saw movement about forty yards away at the end of the alley and heard Steve screaming. She couldn't make out his words, but they seemed to be a string of incoherent rants. Alex slid around the back of the pickup and stayed close to the wall, making her way closer to Jill. When she was about thirty yards away, she began to make out the scene. Her stomach lurched into her throat.

Jill was on her knees and Steve clutched her hair with one hand; he raised his other hand and slapped her hard across the cheek. Alex heard the sound of flesh hitting flesh, but Jill did not cry out. Steve laughed and reached for his belt buckle.

"You're going to pay now, bitch," Steve said and laughed again.

Jill hunkered on the pavement, but Steve jerked her up. He fumbled with his zipper, and Alex knew it was time to make her move.

Alex sprinted down the alley and, when she was within five feet of Steve, she left her feet and launched herself at him. The impact was enough to send them both hurling against the chain link fence. Steve landed on his side with Alex on top of him.

It took several seconds for Steve to register what was happening, and in that brief time, Alex was able to land a punch to his jaw and send a knee toward his groin. He moved just in time, so the blow hit him in the thigh. Even though Alex missed her target, he still grimaced in pain.

Steve flailed his arm and connected with Alex's shoulder, but didn't have enough force to slow the blows that rained down on him. He stopped fighting, rolled into a fetal position, and covered his head with his arms. She went to send another well-placed knee, when she felt herself falling backward.

Alex instinctively reached for her neck, trying to determine why she was struggling to breathe. She was puzzled when she looked down at Steve still curled in a ball, protectively covering his face. *Why can't I breathe?* she wondered. Alex clawed at her neck and touched a large hairy forearm. Her lungs burned. She twisted and kicked, but the arm didn't release. She was getting dizzy, and Jill's face flickered in her mind. She tried to call out to her, but the arm blocked any sound she might make. Alex closed her eyes, trying to muster enough energy for one more push to free herself.

Before Alex launched her counterattack, she heard a noise and felt the arm loosen. Alex dropped to the ground and gasped for breath. She coughed violently, causing the contents of her stomach to come up. Somewhere, her mind registered the sound of another thwack and distant sirens. She fought to pick herself up off the ground. She had to find Jill.

Shakily, she staggered to her feet and frantically looked around the alley.

"Jill," Alex croaked, overwhelmed by the sight in front of her. Jill was standing over a large man, and she clutched what appeared to be a thick pipe. Unsteadily, Alex stumbled toward her.

"Oh my God, Alex, are you okay?" Jill cried out.

Before Alex could reach her, Alex fell on all fours, overcome by another coughing attack. Jill ran to her and dropped to her knees. Jill put her arm across Alex's back and ran her fingers through Alex's short hair.

Alex was finally able to catch her breath; with each inhalation, her mind cleared. She finally registered Jill's fingers running through her hair and started to speak, but was interrupted by Jill's scream.

Alex looked up to see Steve towering over Jill, who was trying to crab crawl away from him. He pulled back his leg and his boot swung toward Jill. In one swift motion, Alex did a roundhouse kick at his leg still firmly planted on the ground. Loud sirens and squealing tires at the other end of the alley drowned out Steve's scream. Steve landed hard on his back next to Jill, but still had enough fight in him to grab her already torn shirt and pull with all the strength he had left. Her shirt tore off in his hand, which seemed to give him renewed energy. He raised his fist to strike her, when Alex leapt between them and took a blow off her chin. Her body twisted in midair and landed facing Jill. Steve tried to reach around Alex to land a blow to Jill's head. Alex looked into Jill's frightened brown eyes and all she could think of was protecting her.

Alex drove her elbow back with all the force she

could generate and heard a crunching sound when her elbow contacted Steve's face. At the other end of the alley, doors slammed, and she heard shouted orders, but was having trouble making out the words. She heard Steve moan. He seemed further away but she couldn't be sure, so she crawled to Jill and wrapped her arms around her. Jill clung to Alex and buried her head against Alex's chest.

Alex was suddenly blinded when a bright spotlight flooded the alley, and a loud voice screamed, "Nobody move."

Alex held Jill tighter; she had no desire to move now that she had Jill in her arms.

The police swarmed the alley with their guns drawn. They quickly surveyed the scene. A large man lay unmoving off to the side with a gash in the back of his head, bleeding profusely. Another man sat with his back against the wall, whimpering quietly. His hands covered his face, and blood gushed between his fingers. The two women in the middle of the alley clung to each other, oblivious to everything but each other.

"Ladies, can I ask you to rise slowly to your feet?" the officer said. When they did not comply, he repeated it louder.

"Jill, do you think you can stand?"

"I'm okay, Alex." Jill squeezed Alex tightly before she let go and tried to stand. She was shaky but managed to rise without assistance.

Alex was having a harder time. She tried twice, but each time stumbled and landed back on the ground. Two officers grabbed her under the arms the next time she tried and lifted her to feet.

Once standing, she looked toward Jill and an

angry look settled on her face. "For God's sake, would one of you get her a jacket?"

The officer in front of her blushed and shouted orders at the young officer standing beside him. The officer headed down the alley in a sprint, and Alex pulled Jill to her.

"Ma'am, I'm afraid I need you to step away from her," the officer said.

Alex fixed him with an angry stare. "As soon as you give me something to cover her up, I'll do just that. She's been through enough already. She doesn't need to be exposed to the whole fucking world."

"Ma'am, I know you're upset, but I need for you to follow our direction."

"Go to hell." Alex pulled the shivering Jill closer to her.

"Ma'am, I will not tell you again." The officer's voice rose and he scowled.

"Peterson, I'll handle this," a familiar voice called from down the alley.

Alex looked up and saw Detective Barrett walking their way, carrying a blanket. Without a word, she handed the blanket to Alex and indicated to the officers that they should turn away.

Alex took a step back from Jill, grabbed one corner of the blanket, and let it cascade open. She shook it out and put it over Jill's shoulders. Alex pulled it tightly around Jill, covering her exposed breasts.

For the first time since the ordeal began, Alex really looked at Jill. Her face showed surprisingly little damage. Her eyes no longer held fear, just wariness. Alex reached out, gently touched her cheek, and smiled. Jill returned the smile and a sparkle danced in her eyes.

"Ms. Bish—Jill, I would like you and Alex to follow me," Detective Barrett said, interrupting their moment.

"How in the hell did he break out of jail?" Alex asked.

"Please, come with me and we can talk about this." Detective Barret motioned toward the flashing lights.

"Come on, Alex, I think sitting down would do both of us some good." Alex put her arm protectively over Jill's shoulder as they followed Detective Barrett down the alley.

The medics were still tending to Steve and the other man lying in the alley. The big man began shouting obscenities, apparently revived. Alex stopped in her tracks when she heard the man screaming threats at Jill. Alex removed her arm from around Jill and abruptly turned.

"Shut the fuck up." Alex started back down the alley toward him.

"No, please, Alex." Jill grabbed Alex's arm. The blood had drained from Jill's face, and she looked frightened again.

"Would someone get him out of here?" Detective Barrett said to the officers milling around, waiting for the medics to complete their checks.

"Who is he?" Alex asked Jill.

"I'll tell you once we get out of here. Please, Alex, I need you to come with me." The desperation in Jill's voice caused Alex to forget the man. Alex put her arm back around Jill and walked slowly with her down the alley.

The number of emergency vehicles, all with flashing lights, crowding the factory's parking lot, shocked Alex. Jill grabbed Alex's arm and pointed. "Look, that's the Channel 8 news van."

"Shit, we're going to make the nightly news." Alex pulled Jill closer, trying to hide her from the cameras.

"Ladies, if I could get you to come this way, it'll get us a little privacy." Detective Barrett steered them toward a large ambulance parked near the abandoned trucks. "You're both going to need some medical attention."

They followed the detective through the maze of cops and vehicles to the waiting ambulance. There was a team of paramedics standing nearby, seemingly waiting for them. The back door of the ambulance was open and an abandoned stretcher was just outside the door.

"Hey guys," Detective Barrett said to the team. "I'm going to need these two checked out, but I was wondering if they could sit here for a little bit before that."

"Sure, Detective, we'll be ready when you need us," the man standing nearest them said and moved away to give them privacy.

"Have a seat." Detective Barrett motioned to the back of the ambulance.

Alex led Jill to the open back door and helped her hold the blanket in place as she sat. Alex let out a gasp. "My God, Jill, what happened to your knees?" She immediately regretted it, when the scene of Jill being forced to her knees flashed in her mind. "I'm sorry, I didn't—"

"It's okay, sweetie. Come sit down." Jill took Alex's hand. Alex sat down hard, finally aware of how fatigued her body felt. Jill leaned against her and put her head on Alex's shoulder.

"I just need to get a couple things cleared up and then I'd like for you both to get checked out at the hospital." Detective Barrett stood in front of them, flanked by a fresh-faced young officer.

Detective Barrett started to ask a question, but Alex cut her off. "How in the hell did he break out of your jail?"

"He didn't." Detective Barrett maintained eye contact with Alex.

"What do you mean, he didn't? You mean you let him out?"

"I'm afraid so."

"And why didn't someone contact us?" Alex threw her hands up in disgust.

"Calm down." Jill squeezed Alex's knee.

"It appears we had a breakdown in communication," Detective Barrett said uncomfortably.

"A breakdown in communication. Jill could have been killed, and you call it a breakdown in fucking communication. How could something like this happen?"

"I've been off the last week and a half and apparently the communiqué concerning Mr. Bishop making bail went to only me."

"Jesus, you just go on vacation and nobody covers your shit? And they put you in charge?" Alex's face turned red and the veins in her neck throbbed. "Somebody needs to be held accountable for this."

"I'm sorry," Detective Barret said. "I take full responsibility."

"I would think you damn well should. First, you make her confront him, which obviously pissed him off. Then you drop the ball and let him wander around the streets without her being forewarned." Alex was angry and not willing to let the detective off the hook. There was no forgiving someone for putting Jill into this kind of danger.

"Excuse me, but you're out of line," the young officer said, glaring at Alex.

"Am I?" Alex jumped to her feet and moved toward the officer. "Do you understand what Jill just endured because of Detective Barrett's screw up?" Alex glared at the stunned officer and took another step toward her. "And if not for a couple lucky breaks, how badly this could have turned out?" Alex's voice cracked and she went pale as she delivered the last line, suddenly deeply aware of what could have happened.

"Alex, it's over now, I'm safe." Jill reached for Alex's hand and gently pulled her back.

"No thanks to our city's finest." Alex continued glaring at the two women in front of them.

"Her mother had a massive stroke a week and a half ago. She didn't just run out and ignore her duties. She's the best detective I've ever worked with, and I resent your attitude." The young officer took a step toward Alex, so they were standing only a couple feet apart.

"Officer Carter, enough. They have every right to be angry at me. There is never any excuse for neglecting our duty." Detective Barrett put her arm between the two and subtly encouraged the officer to step back.

Jill urged Alex to sit back down, before turning her attention to Detective Barrett. "I'm so sorry, Detective. Is she all right?"

"She's still in the ICU. Only time will tell. I appreciate your concern."

"Alex, apologize to the Detective." Jill gave Alex a look like she would have given Jenna or Trina had they behaved badly.

"No, she doesn't owe me an apology. It's me that owes both of you an apology. I cringe at what could have happened to you."

"It's okay." Jill nudged Alex with her shoulder. "Apologize."

"I'm sorry, Detective."

"There is no need to apologize. I don't blame you for being angry. If I were in your shoes, I'd be crazy angry myself."

"I am sorry about your mom," Alex said.

"Thank you. I apologize for everything that's happened. A perpetrator should never be released without the victim being notified."

"So how long has he been out?" Jill asked.

"Apparently, it was a week ago today."

"Oh God, so he's been watching me?" Jill shivered and Alex pulled her closer.

"If I had to guess, I'd say yes. I know this has been very difficult for you, but I'd like for you to tell me exactly what happened here."

"Certainly." Jill nudged Alex, who nodded in agreement.

In a strong voice, Jill began her story, beginning with the call to her employer requesting she meet clients at the shoe factory. Detective Barrett asked the questions, while Officer Carter took notes.

"I'm afraid I can't remember much after Steve broke my window and I saw Carl Foster standing behind him."

"So, you knew the man with him?" Detective

Barrett asked.

"Yes, he was the best man at our wedding." Jill's tone had turned monotone.

"Do you know where Mr. Foster lives?"

"He used to live in California, but I'm not sure now." Jill's answer came out in the same flat voice.

"When was the last time you saw him?"

"It will be four years ago this Labor Day." Jill's answer came without hesitation. Alex looked at her, but she did not turn.

"You seemed to be very sure about that date," Detective Barrett said.

"Yes."

"Can I ask about the last time you saw him?"

"No." Jill looked down at her hands.

"Excuse me?" Detective Barrett looked at Jill, puzzled.

"No, there is no need to talk about it. That was the past."

"I see. Would you like to give me a statement in private?" Detective Barrett glanced at Alex when she asked.

"Alex can hear anything I have to say, but the last time I saw him has no bearing on what happened today." Jill's breathing was shallow and Alex felt her body trembling.

Detective Barrett started to speak, but stopped. Jill's eyes had become unfocused, and they darted around, taking in her surroundings. Without warning, Jill jumped from where she sat on the back of the ambulance and disappeared behind the nearby trucks.

Alex and the detective made eye contact. With a slight tilt of her head, the detective acknowledged that Alex should follow Jill.

Alex jumped from her seat and hurried around the broken trucks. When she rounded the corner, she saw Jill doubled over, vomiting. Alex wrapped her arm around Jill to steady her and then held back her hair. Jill gagged a few more times and continued to dry heave. Each time she wretched, she became weaker, causing Alex to support more of her weight. Alex spoke softly, assuring her that everything was okay and that she was safe.

"Alex," Detective Barrett said, coming around the corner. "I thought this might help." The detective held out a towel and a bottle of water.

"Thanks. Mind setting them down on the bumper over there?" The detective complied and left without a word.

Jill coughed a couple more times, but for the moment seemed to be done throwing up. Alex helped her stand up straight and guided her to sit down. Alex picked up the towel and poured some of the water on one corner. She lightly ran the towel around Jill's mouth.

"Why don't you take a drink?" Alex held out the bottle. Jill took it and sloshed the water around inside her mouth before she spit it out. After she rinsed a second time, she took a big swallow of the cool water.

"I'm sorry," Jill finally said. "I don't know what got into me."

"Obviously something really bad happened the last time you saw this Carl."

"It was by far the worst weekend of my life, Alex." Alex reached out and brushed the hair away from Jill's face. She looked into Jill's eyes and her heart clenched at the pain she saw there. "I wanted to forget it forever."

"You don't have to talk about it if you don't want to."

"Detective Barrett is going to push for some answers."

"You don't have to talk about anything you don't want to, and I'll make sure she understands that."

"No, Alex, she's just doing her job. Let's go get it over with." Jill was unsteady when she got to her feet.

"Are you sure?"

"Yes." Jill gave Alex a weak smile. "As long as you're right there beside me, I'll be okay."

"You know I will be." Alex forced a smile, sensing Jill needed her to be strong.

Jill touched Alex's face and closed her own eyes. "You need to know that you're going to hear some things that are going to be painful for you. Are you sure you're up for that?"

"You lived through it, so I'm going to have to be strong enough to hear it." Alex steeled herself, knowing that, whatever she heard, her only concern was to support Jill. She would deal with her own emotions later.

"I'm ready then." Jill's voice was suddenly stronger.

"I love you," Alex said without thinking.

"Thank you," Jill said softly. A genuine smile parted her lips and reached her eyes before she closed them "I love you too, Alex."

*　*　*　*

"I never saw him again after that weekend," Jill said, finishing her story. Alex sat silently behind Jill, who rested her back against Alex's chest. Alex hadn't said anything the whole time she spoke; the only indication that she was listening was the way her arms continued to tighten around Jill after each revelation. Jill suspected that Alex was crying, but wasn't ready to look at her.

Detective Barrett stood listening to the story, showing little emotion. The young officer beside her was not faring as well, but no one drew attention to the horror on her face or the tears in her eyes. Jill never cried, but told the story as if she was a television reporter, simply reporting news of what happened to someone else.

No one spoke, so Jill continued. "When he left that morning, he grinned and said he'd see me next Labor Day. The next year, when August rolled around, I was a wreck, but he never came then or ever again. I always wondered if he and Steve had a falling out."

"Was there any reason to believe that they had?" Detective Barrett asked.

"I think that weekend was even too much for Steve; he didn't touch me in any way for well over three months. He even tended to me for a couple days afterward until I was back on my feet."

Alex shivered. Jill knew the images would be burned into Alex's mind for a long time, and regretted that she had to hear. Alex didn't speak, but words would have been inadequate. Her strong arms around Jill offered more comfort than anything she could say.

Jill turned in Alex's arms and brushed a tear from her cheek. "Thank you for being here. I know that was hard for you."

Alex's mouth dropped open. "Hard for me? What about you?"

Jill smiled. "It was easier to tell than I thought

it would be. It was another lifetime ago, Alex. Here in your arms, I realize that life is gone forever."

"Good riddance," Alex said. Jill smiled and tussled Alex's hair. Alex smiled.

"Does that mean that you'd be willing to press charges and testify against him about that weekend?" Detective Barrett asked.

"No." Jill's voice was firm. "I will never tell that story again."

"But—" Detective Barrett started to say before Jill cut her off.

"There is no negotiating this, Detective Barrett. There is no physical evidence. I'm smart enough to know that convicting him would be difficult at best. I will not sit on the witness stand, without Alex to lean against, and let a defense attorney humiliate me in front of a room full of people. Somehow, I think you probably have enough on him to put him away for some time."

"Okay," Detective Barrett relented. "Actually, we ran a check on him. The reason he didn't come back is because he was in prison. Apparently, he got out a couple months ago. There's a warrant out for his arrest."

"For?" Jill asked.

"Triple homicide. Apparently, he found the woman that he'd attacked that put him in prison in the first place. He broke into her home and killed her, her mother, and her child. They're still trying to determine if the child was his."

"Oh God." Jill's face turned pale, and she squeezed Alex's hand.

"I do need to ask how Mr. Foster ended up with his head busted open."

"I should have known that Alex wouldn't wait for the police to get here." Jill noticed the confusion on Detective Barrett's face and continued. "Steve was standing over me, then the next thing I knew he was flying across the alley. It took a few seconds for me to register that it was Alex. I panicked, realizing that she didn't know Carl was there. He came up behind her and was choking her. I was frantic. Then I saw this pile of rubble and picked up the biggest pipe I could find. I had to get him off her, so I swung with all my might and he crumpled."

"I'm pretty sure you fractured his skull."

"Good," Alex said, her eyes blazing.

"I think that answers everything I have for now. I'd like to accompany you to the hospital, just in case there is anything else."

"That would be fine." Jill sighed, suddenly feeling exhausted.

Detective Barrett waved to the emergency personnel. They insisted on putting both women on a gurney before they would transport them.

"Shit, I should call Sarah and Michelle. I'd hate for them to catch this on the news." Alex reached into her pocket. She pulled out her cell phone that had obviously been damaged in the struggle. "I'm afraid this one isn't going to do me any good. Can I borrow yours, Jill?"

"Steve threw it against the wall."

"Detective, would you please call them and let them know we are okay and tell them I'll call them later when we get home?"

"Of course, I just need their number."

Chapter Twenty-three

A lex sighed and closed the door. Jill looked at her and smiled. This time at the hospital, Alex had required extensive tests. She'd suffered some structural damage to her throat, but luckily her larynx had not been crushed. Her neck was a deep shade of purple that the doctor warned would look worse before it healed. The only damage Jill sustained was deep lacerations to her knees from the broken glass that littered the alley. Once the grime was washed away, her knees looked like ground hamburger, but the hospital staff had expertly treated them and they already looked better.

"How are you holding up?" Alex asked.

"Surprisingly well." Jill hugged Alex. "I could use a shower though."

"Me too. Then how about a drink?"

"Sounds perfect." Jill took Alex's hand as they walked through the house. When they arrived at the bedrooms, Alex reluctantly let go of Jill's hand at the entrance to her room.

Jill went into her own room and quickly stripped out of her clothes. She threw on her robe when she remembered she'd run out of shampoo that morning.

When Jill walked into Alex's room, she found her naked from the waist up. Jill stopped and stared, seeing Alex's muscular body for the first time. Alex's breasts were larger than Jill thought. Apparently, the sports bras she always wore served to flatten her chest. Her shoulders were well muscled and her stomach washboard flat. Jill felt her heart race.

"Um…I needed shampoo," Jill stammered as she walked toward Alex.

"I have extra in the linen closet." Alex moved toward Jill.

Before either knew what was happening, they were in each other's arms. Jill's face lifted toward Alex's and their lips met. The kiss started out softly, their lips lightly brushing, but soon they grew hungry. Their kiss intensified and Jill moaned when Alex's tongue parted her lips.

Alex drew Jill closer, as Jill ground her pelvis against Alex's thigh. Jill kneaded Alex's muscular shoulders, and slowly ran her hand down Alex's back. Alex slid her hand inside Jill's robe, her fingers brushing across Jill's stomach. Jill trembled at Alex's touch. She shifted her body, hoping Alex's hand would move higher. She closed her eyes and moaned again when she felt Alex's hand oblige.

Alex cupped her breast, but didn't touch Jill's nipple. Jill ached for Alex's touch and whispered, "Please touch me, Alex."

Alex moaned. Their kiss broke off when Alex lightly flicked her finger over Jill's nipple. Jill gasped and pressed harder against Alex, while Alex caressed her nipple. Jill felt the wetness between her legs and shifted so she was straddling Alex's leg. She pushed against Alex and felt herself throbbing.

"Jill!" Alex stopped abruptly.

Jill opened her eyes, but they were unfocused. She was trying to process what was happening, but desire was making it difficult for her to think straight. She thought she'd heard Alex's name called, but that made no sense. She blinked her eyes, realizing that Alex had stopped and was saying her name.

"I think someone is here." Alex grabbed her shirt, closed Jill's robe, and secured the drawstring. Alex took a step back and called out, "Sarah? Michelle?"

"Where are you guys?" Sarah said.

"We'll be there in a second," Alex answered.

"Are you guys okay?" Michelle asked.

"Fine, we're coming." Alex quickly pulled her shirt over her head.

Jill looked at Alex with a big smile and took a step toward her. "Damn, they have bad timing. We'll have to finish this later." She was suddenly frightened when she saw the look in Alex's eyes. "Hey, are you okay?"

"No." Alex stepped back. "I'm so sorry."

"For what?"

"For what I just did to you." Alex grabbed her keys off her dresser.

"You mean for not finishing what you started?" Jill said teasingly, hoping that Alex would stop acting so strange.

"For taking advantage of you." Alex jammed the keys into her pocket. "I'm so sorry."

"What? You certainly weren't taking advantage of me. I was definitely responding to you. Do you want to feel how much I was responding?" Jill opened her robe.

Alex's eyes widened in horror, and she whispered another sorry before she ran from the room.

༄ ༄ ༄ ༄

"Is that you, Alex?" Michelle said.

"Yes." Alex walked into the living room. Sarah was lightly snoring, where she laid fully reclined in Alex's favorite chair. Alex's chest clenched when she looked at Michelle, who was sitting on the couch, Jill's head lying on her lap. Michelle was lightly running her hand through Jill's hair. Jill was breathing rhythmically, her face peaceful in sleep.

"You've been gone for over two hours." Michelle's eyes held a mixture of relief and anger.

"I'm sorry."

"Are you okay?"

"No, I'm not sure I'll ever be okay again," Alex answered honestly.

"Oh, Alex, would you just stop beating yourself up? I don't know where you got this Lone Ranger shit from, but it's not working for you anymore."

"Don't you get it?" The pain was etched on her face. "I betrayed her trust."

"And how do you think you did that?"

"She was hurting. She was vulnerable. I was like a fucking bird of prey and swooped down when she was at her weakest."

"Is that really what you believe?" Michelle's eyes softened.

"That's what I know."

"No, Alex, just because you believe it doesn't make it true." Michelle's voice was firm.

"No, this one was all on me, don't you understand?"

"Hey, maybe Jill was preying on you." Michelle rolled her eyes. "See how absurd that sounds, Alex?"

"Don't you understand that I promised to

protect her?" Alex's eyes shifted to Jill's face. Her chest ached and tears spilled from her eyes.

"And you have. My God, Alex, you've completely protected her. Why can't you see that?"

"I didn't protect her from me."

"And why in the hell do you think she needs protection from you?"

"She was vulnerable, scared, and all alone. She needed a friend, not someone lusting after her. Don't you see what a betrayal that is? She just got attacked in an alley, for God's sake. Then I go and attack her in my bedroom."

"Really? I don't think she felt attacked. You love her, Alex, that's all you're guilty of. You've loved her better than anyone ever has."

"Sure, and how do you know that?"

"She told me," Michelle said softly. The pain in Alex's eyes deepened and she looked down, no longer able to meet Michelle's eyes.

"I can't, Michelle." Her voice came out in a whisper. "She's straight. Maybe it would be different if she were a lesbian."

"Why are you so hung up on labels? This is what I know. You're head over heels in love with her, but you're either too stupid or afraid to do anything about it." Alex started to protest, but Michelle interrupted and continued. "She's the best thing that has ever happened to you. I would venture to guess you're the best thing to ever happen to her too. She's in love with you and you rejecting her is more painful than anything Steve could ever do to her."

Alex's eyes narrowed and lost their warmth. She glared at Michelle, contemplating a response.

"No, Alex, don't give me that outraged look.

You know it's true. I can't make you do the right thing, but I'm sure as hell not going to let you pretend you don't know the truth. The truth is you're hurting her. Whatever you decide to do, you do it knowing the truth. That's it. I'm done. I've spoken my piece. Now the ball is in your court."

"But—" Alex started to say, but Michelle cut her off.

"No, I'm done."

"Fine. Would you guys stay here with her tonight?"

"And where are you going?"

"Can I borrow your house to crash?"

"No, Alex, you're not leaving here. We'll stay here with her, but you are going to stay too. Once you go into your room, I'll wake her up. But I want you in this house."

"Why?"

"She was a wreck when you left. She wanted to go looking for you, but we convinced her to give you a little space. She finally fell asleep about fifteen minutes ago after crying herself out. She deserves to know you are back and safe. If you're the woman I think you are, you'll help me wake her up and at least tell her good-night."

Alex stared at Michelle for several seconds before she looked away, Michelle's intensity too much for her. "Okay," Alex finally said.

"Jill." Michelle gently shook her. "Sweetie, Alex is home."

Alex walked to the couch and knelt at the other end, several feet away from Jill. Groggily, Jill opened her eyes and immediately they landed on Alex. She sat up abruptly. "Alex, are you okay?"

"I'm fine, sweetie," Alex lied. "Are you okay?"

"Physically or emotionally?"

"Let's start with physically."

"Then I'm fine." Jill smiled. "Alex, we need—"

Alex held her finger to her own lips. "Shh, please, Jill, I can't right now. We're all exhausted. Maybe by the light of day everything will look better."

"Okay."

"Michelle said she'd help me get you to bed."

"Are you staying?"

"I'm staying. I'll be here in the morning when you wake up." Jill visibly relaxed with Alex's promise.

Alex stood up and reached her hand out to Jill. She took it and rose to her feet. She gasped, and reached down to her knees.

"What's wrong?"

"I think the scabs on my knees tightened up. Will you walk me to bed?"

"Yes, we will." Alex made sure to include Michelle.

Jill was unsteady and leaned against Alex as she walked slowly down the hall. Michelle trailed along behind. In Jill's room, Michelle pulled back the covers and Alex started to lower Jill to the mattress.

"Wait, can I get a hug from both of you?" Michelle stepped up and hugged her first. Jill whispered a thank you to her before she let go. Jill looked at Alex hopefully and stepped into her arms. They both held on for some time, before Alex finally released her.

"Good night, Jill," Alex said and left the room.

Chapter Twenty-four

Alex smelled coffee when she walked down the hall. She entered the kitchen and found Sarah and Michelle sitting at the table, enjoying a cup.

"Damn, you look rough," Sarah said.

"Thanks," Alex murmured, pouring herself a cup of coffee and sitting down at the table with her friends.

"Did you forget to sleep last night?"

"Something like that." She rubbed her eyes, trying to wipe the sleep out.

"Did you sleep at all?" Michelle asked with concern.

"Not much. I had a few things on my mind."

"I didn't sleep very well on that lumpy chair of yours," Sarah complained.

"Seriously, you looked pretty comfortable when I got home last night. Not only were you snoring, but you were drooling all over my chair." Alex was grateful that Sarah was trying to lighten the heaviness in the room.

"I left a little puddle just for you." Sarah let a spit string dangle from her mouth, until Michelle slapped her.

"Great, thanks."

Michelle went to the sink and rinsed out her cup. "We should probably think about heading home."

"You're leaving?" Alex felt panic rising in her.

"Yes."

"But..." Alex started but her voice trailed off. She knew her friends would tell her she needed to handle the situation with Jill on her own. She knew they would be right, but she still wished they'd stay. "Okay. Thanks for everything last night."

"Things will be fine, if you follow your heart," Michelle said.

"Good advice. She should know better than to follow her head, since there's nothing up there," Sarah said.

Alex pretended to glare at Sarah and said to Michelle, "Remind me again why I chose her as a best friend."

"Because you love me," Sarah said dramatically.

Alex rolled her eyes, but said nothing.

❧❧❧❧

Alex was sitting on the couch, flipping through a magazine when Jill finally emerged from the bedroom. She looked much more rested than Alex, but her eyes were tentative.

"Are Sarah and Michelle gone?"

Alex looked up from her magazine. "Yeah, they left about an hour ago. How are you feeling this morning?"

"A little stiff, but not too bad." Jill extended her arms over her head and stretched.

"That's good." The polite conversation was strained and Alex searched for something more to say.

"How are you?" Jill sat down on the opposite end of the couch.

"Okay."

"You look tired."

"I didn't sleep very well."

"Oh."

"You look well rested."

"I have a tendency to sleep when I'm upset."

"Oh."

"Did you finish getting everything together to close the Florida deal?"

"Yeah, I think I'm ready to go."

"That's good."

"Do you have a counseling appointment on Monday?"

"How long are we going to keep up this inane conversation?" Jill's eyes darkened and she put her hand against her forehead. "Do you think we can talk about what happened last night?"

"There's really not much to talk about. I'm sorry. I promise I won't let it happen again."

"What if I want it to happen again?"

"Damn it, Jill, you don't."

"Really? And you know that how?" Jill's voice dripped in sarcasm.

"How many times do I have to remind you that you're straight?"

"Apparently, you feel the need to remind me of it quite often." Jill glared at Alex. "How many times do I have to remind you how I feel about you?"

Alex laid her head back against the couch, closed her eyes, and let out a loud sigh. When she opened her eyes again, they were distant. "We need to get off this rollercoaster we're stuck on."

"I couldn't agree more. Does that mean you're going to finally give in to your feelings?"

"My feelings are that we need to be friends, nothing more."

"You can't tell me you don't feel something more for me," Jill said, the frustration evident in her voice.

"That's not the point."

"That's exactly the point. You have feelings for me, but you're blinded by this false sense of right and wrong." She looked at Alex and said slowly, enunciating each word, "You are not taking advantage of me."

"Well, that's a point we can't seem to agree on."

"Who the hell put you in charge of determining that for me? Sometimes you frustrate the shit out of me, Alex, and then other times I just want to hug you and make you understand." Jill's eyes blazed as she stared at Alex, waiting for a response.

"You're weak and vulnerable right now. Someone has to look out for you, since you don't seem to be doing it for yourself," Alex said matter-of-factly.

"God, you piss me off sometimes." Jill threw her arms in the air, before she pointed at Alex. "Don't you dare tell me that I'm weak. I'm so sick of everyone treating me like I'm a delicate flower that might blow over at the slightest breeze." Alex started to protest, but Jill stopped her and continued. "No, you will listen to me. I have lived through hell and survived, so don't tell me I'm weak. Do you hear me, Alex?" Jill fought back her tears.

Alex sat stunned, not saying anything in case Jill had more to say. Alex was glad she waited when Jill continued. "I'm a survivor and maybe it's about time you give me credit for the strength it took to come through what I have. I might have been broken, but I am not shattered. Yes, having you by my side has made it so much better, but I can survive with or without you."

Alex stared at Jill and thought, *but will I survive without you*? Jill looked at Alex with tears in her eyes and finished. "But even though I'll survive, it will be with a broken heart. You need to know that. I'm not going to let you get away with pretending you're being gallant and protecting me, when it's you that's hurting me. It is you that's breaking my heart." She put her hand over her face and let the tears fall.

Alex sat not moving, her heart heavy in her chest. She longed to go to Jill and wrap her in her arms. To tell her everything that she felt. To apologize for hurting her, but she sat paralyzed by her fear. She wished she could explain to Jill how frightened she was. Explain how deeply Jill had gotten inside, where no one else ever had. As much as she wanted to say those things, she couldn't get past the fact that Jill had never been with a woman.

"I wish you could understand," Alex said. Her voice was soft and her eyes vacant. "You're straight, Jill."

Jill looked up and her eyes flashed. "After everything I just said to you, that's what you have to say to me?"

"Why do you keep acting like it's not important?"

"Because it's not."

"Then let me ask you, have you ever been attracted to a woman before?"

"Not that I can recall."

"So why should I believe that your attraction is anything more than the fact that I helped you?"

"Oh Alex—" Jill started, but Alex held up her

hand.

"One more question," Alex said. "If you had met Joe Blow in the grocery store that day, would you be attracted to him?"

"I didn't meet Joe Blow. I met you."

"Humor me, if I'd been a man would you have been attracted?"

"Probably," Jill admitted, looking down at her hands. "But I don't think it's fair because being a woman is part of what makes you you."

"The fact remains, you're straight, and I won't set myself up to have my heart ripped out."

"Oh Alex, don't you understand I would never hurt you that way?"

"You don't think you would, but it would happen." Alex saw the anger start to return to Jill's eyes, so she quickly forged on. "It wouldn't be on purpose. I know you believe what you're saying now, but that day would come once you heal."

"Nothing I say or do is going to make you believe different, is it?" Unconsciously, Jill reached up and twirled her hair around her finger. A sharp pain ripped at Alex's chest; it had been a long time since Jill had done that with her. When they first met, Jill played with her hair frequently, but as her confidence grew, she rarely did it.

"One day you'll thank me for not letting you make a huge mistake."

"Or maybe one day, you'll believe in me." Jill got to her feet.

"Wait, Jill."

"There's really nothing more to say, is there?"

"I suppose not. So, what happens now?"

"What do you want to happen, Alex?"

"I'd like to spend the weekend with my friend Jill before I leave for Florida on Monday."

"Not fair, Alex. You haven't even told me how long you're going to be gone."

"I don't know. It all depends on how things go." Alex knew she wasn't being fair, but didn't know how else to handle it. "Can't we just enjoy our last weekend together?"

"Okay." Jill's eyes were full of sadness. "You win."

The words cut into Alex, and she started to protest, but Jill held up her hand. "No, Alex. I can't talk about this anymore. We better get moving because the girls are expecting us at ten."

⁂

Jill and Alex sat on the couch Sunday night, drinking a beer. The weekend flew by much too fast. Alex looked at Jill, not wanting to go to bed despite needing to be up by five am to leave for the airport. The pain in her chest was back, knowing she'd not see Jill for several weeks.

It was a testament to their feelings for each other that they were able to salvage the weekend. Both were able to put aside their argument in order to enjoy their time together. It was easy being together and despite the pain both were feeling, the weekend had been full of laughter. The only uncomfortable moments came when they were alone at the apartment. Alex felt Jill's distance. Jill hadn't casually touched Alex all weekend, which was unheard of from the usually affectionate Jill. Alex didn't blame her; Jill had to be tired of putting her heart on the line only to have Alex push her away.

Heaviness descended now that the weekend was nearly over. Alex knew there was so much to be said, but if neither had until now, it was likely to remain unspoken. Alex reluctantly finished the beer she'd been milking for nearly an hour. The bottle made a loud thud when she set it on the end table harder than planned.

"Done?" Jill said.

"Yes," Alex answered.

"Want another?"

"I probably shouldn't. I have to be up early."

"Yeah," Jill said, her face falling. "You don't want to have a hangover at the closing."

"I'm thinking I should be safe, since this is only my second." Alex held up the beer and smiled.

"I don't know, you are a lightweight." Jill gave Alex half a smile. "I guess you better get to bed then."

"Yeah."

"Will you call to let me know you got in safely?"

"Of course." She picked up her bottle and took it to the kitchen. "I suppose I better turn in," she said when she returned to the living room.

"Good night." Jill had a slight tremor in her voice.

"Good night." Alex walked down the hall. She got to her bedroom door and turned around.

Jill was still sitting on the couch, sipping her beer and staring at the television that wasn't turned on. Alex cleared her throat and Jill looked up. "I just wanted to tell you." Alex stopped and weighed her words. "I need for you to know that I'll miss you."

"Thank you." Jill smiled. "I'll miss you too."

"I'm sorry about everything that's happened."

"No, Alex, let's not go there again. You'll be gone in a few hours and I can't take you leaving after another argument."

"Okay, we'll leave it on a high note." Alex's limbs suddenly felt heavy and her chest ached.

"Good night."

Alex stood looking at Jill, realizing that Jill wouldn't go against what Alex asked of her, which meant it was up to Alex. Even though she knew she should simply turn and go to bed, she couldn't leave it like this. "Can I have a hug good-bye, since I won't see you in the morning?"

Jill was up off the couch in an instant and in her arms. Alex felt the tension drain from her body as she held Jill. The tension was replaced by an ache of desire, but the terrible pain in her chest was gone for the moment.

After several minutes, Jill stepped back from the embrace. Alex immediately felt the loss. Jill put her hand on Alex's cheek and looked deeply into her eyes. Jill let her hand drop. "I love you, Alex." Before Alex could reply, Jill left the room.

"I love you too, Jill," Alex said to the empty room. She went to her bedroom, shut the door, and fell onto her bed without bothering to take off her clothes.

Chapter Twenty-five

"Couldn't you get an earlier flight?" Sarah asked. "It'll be fine. I should be in by three and the banquet doesn't start until seven. Plenty of time," Alex answered. She looked around the sterile office, missing the comfortable sitting area in her own office. She'd been busy the last few weeks after closing on their new acquisition, so she'd taken no time to personalize the space she was using.

"Michelle still isn't happy you aren't coming home earlier."

"I know, but she'll get over it."

"Should I tell her you said that?"

"Hell no."

"That's what I thought." Sarah laughed. "Big and bad until you're dealing directly with her."

"She should be glad I even agreed to do this at all."

"She would never forgive you if you didn't come."

"That's not what I meant. I wouldn't miss the banquet for anything. I just don't see why she keeps setting me up on these damn blind dates."

"Are we going to have to argue about this again?"

"No. I get it. She's the guest of honor, so you two will be tied up for a while. I still think I can entertain myself. Who knows, maybe I'll meet a nice single woman. One I pick out myself."

"You did pretty well with the last one you chose, but you're just too stupid to realize it."

"I'm not having this conversation with you."

"Fine. Besides, if you were alone, Michelle would worry about you."

"She's going to be more worried about me being unsupervised. She's afraid I might do something inappropriate." Alex giggled.

"You've got a point. Nice email you sent her." Sarah laughed.

"Did you laugh when she showed you?"

"Not while she was standing there with her hand on her hip, I didn't."

"Which part was your favorite?" Alex opened the email. "I'll make sure to do it."

Michelle:

I wanted to make sure I behave appropriately on the blind date. You know how much I am looking forward to it. Please review my top ten etiquette questions and advise. I want to make sure not to embarrass you.

1.   If she leaves food on her plate that looks tasty, is it okay if I reach over and grab it with my hand or should I use silverware?

2.   If she is talking about something I find extremely boring, is it okay if I let my head fall into my mashed potatoes? I'll tell her I'm narcoleptic if it would help.

3.   If she has especially nice boobs, is it okay to ask her if they're real?

4.   When the alarm on my watch goes off,

can I jump from the table and scream, "Oh my God, I forgot to bring my meds. Is there a Walgreens around?"

5.   In order to impress her, would it be okay if I show her how I can drink beer up my nose? Or is that better saved for a second date?

6.   Is it okay if I ask her if she has the local U-Haul on speed dial? And if she doesn't, should I offer to give her the number?

7.   If she asks me to pass her a roll, is it okay to jump up from the table, get in a football stance, and hike it to her? Or would you prefer I do a Michael Jordan fade away shot?

8.   If I offer her a piece of gum, can I say, "Here, you better take two. You could use them."?

9.   If she asks me any personal questions, is it okay to look at her nervously and tell her my therapist prefers I not discuss these things with strangers?

10.   Can I tell her I'd like her to meet my parents, and then have the limo driver take us to the cemetery?

Most importantly, when I'm sitting across from her and the only face I see is Jill's, is it okay if I burst into tears?

Looking forward to the evening. Tell Sarah hi for me.

Love ya both,
Alex

"She'll shoot you, but I especially liked the therapist question." Her tone changed and she said, "But the last question was the only true one, wasn't it?"

"Didn't I just tell you I wasn't going to have this conversation with you?"

"Does Jill know you're coming home?" Sarah

said, ignoring Alex's question.

"Not yet. She called and left me a message earlier. I was planning on calling her back tonight."

"Why don't you ask her to go with you to the banquet? I'm sure Michelle would be more than happy to cancel your blind date."

"Do you think we can talk about how things are going with our latest acquisition?"

"One more message from Michelle, then we can get down to business."

"Great, go ahead, let's get it over with."

"You have an appointment tomorrow to get fitted for your tux. Apparently, she has everything all worked out. All you do is show up at the appointment and get measured and poof, the tux will be waiting here at your apartment next Friday."

Alex considered asking questions about the logistics, but realized she didn't care as long as she didn't have to worry about it herself.

"Tell her to send me an email with where to go and when. Now can we talk business? I have five candidates for the director position and hope to have someone picked before I leave here next Friday."

"Does that mean you'll be coming home to stay?"

"The first candidate..." Alex said, launching into her analysis.

❧ ❧ ❧ ❧

"Hey stranger," Jill said, trying to sound upbeat.

She missed Alex. The physical distance was painful, but the emotional distance was even more so. Alex had been gone over a month, and as time went by, Alex seemed to become more remote. Even though Jill was miserable, she vowed not to let Alex know. If Alex was going to come around, it wouldn't be because she felt sorry for Jill.

"Hi, Jill. You sound good," Alex said with a little more formality than she intended.

"So, what have you been up too?"

"Boring gym business. And you?"

Jill winced at Alex's professional tone; they sounded like two people that didn't know each other. Jill took a deep breath and forged on as if she hadn't noticed. "I've been working a lot. The job has been my saving grace."

"That's great. I guess that must be the reason I came into your life, so you could meet Jim and Nancy." Jill was weighing her words and remained silent. "Are you still there?"

"I'm here," Jill answered softly. The distance was becoming unbearable. An internal battle raged inside Jill. On one hand, she'd made it clear to Alex how she felt and didn't want to keep exposing herself to rejection. On the other hand, she didn't want to keep up this charade of a conversation

"I'm sorry, I didn't mean it the way it came out."

"I've missed you, Alex."

After several beats, Alex said, "I miss you too."

Jill's heart soared, but she stopped herself from responding too enthusiastically in fear it would push Alex away. She was careful to choose her next words carefully. "Are you coming home any time soon?"

"That's the reason I called. I've been meaning to tell you that I'll be home next weekend."

"Really? Great. How long will you be here?" Jill already knew Alex was coming home, but was relieved that Alex told her herself.

"I'm not sure. It depends on how much work I still have here."

"Will I get a chance to see you?" Jill braced herself for Alex's response. She wished Alex would invite her to the banquet, but as of yet, Alex hadn't mentioned the banquet at all.

"I have to go to Michelle's banquet on Friday night, but after that I'm wide open."

"I'll keep my weekend free."

"Are you going to the banquet?"

"Who would I go with?" She wanted to kick herself for such obvious bait. Alex didn't bite.

"What do you want to do on Saturday?"

❧❧❧❧

"Hey Alex," Michelle said into her phone.

"Are you ready for your big day?"

"As ready as I'll ever be. Did Sarah tell you they expect me to give an acceptance speech?" Michelle grumbled.

Alex recognized the front Michelle was putting on. She was excited about the award, but didn't want to show it in fear of appearing arrogant.

"Michelle, it's an honor. It's okay to be proud. I still don't know how you manage to run a successful business and still have time to give so much back to the gay community."

"So, you don't mind I'm dragging you back from Florida?"

"I wouldn't miss it for the world. You know that, don't you?"

"You've been throwing such a fit, I wasn't sure you really wanted to come."

"If I ever made you feel that way, I am so sorry. Please believe me, I really want to be there. It's the blind date thing that I'm throwing a fit about."

"I know you're pouting, but there's still time for you to get your own date."

"You know, you're right. Do you think Tanya would want to go with me?"

"Very funny. You know who I'm talking about. There's still time for me to cancel your date."

"I've thought about asking her a million times, but I can't."

"I don't understand you. She's easily the best thing that has ever happened to you. Why can't you see that?"

"I do see it. I just can't," Alex said miserably.

"I know how you feel about her, so why are you going to let her slip away?"

"It's not that simple."

"It's simple if you let it be."

"I was the Lone Ranger coming in to save the day. It was never about me; it was about her needing to be rescued. Once she's fully back on her feet, she'll have a real choice and I won't look so good to her anymore. And one day, soon, she'll realize she's made a huge mistake."

"Do you really believe that? I hope not, because if you do, you're an idiot. You should give Jill more credit than that. She's been through so much and it pisses me off you're putting her through more. Damn it, Alex, she deserves better. You both deserve to be happy. If you'd pull your head out of your ass, you'd see how perfect you'd be together."

"So how do you really feel?" Alex hoped to lighten the conversation.

"I think all this resistance is pure fear. You're so scared of losing her that you aren't going to allow yourself to have her in the first place. I know you, Alex. You've never felt like this about anyone before."

Alex didn't want to cry, but was near tears. She wanted to stop feeling the pain that crushed her chest whenever she thought about Jill. It was easier to become defensive than feel anything else.

"Why do we have to keep having this conversation?" Alex snapped.

"We need to keep having this conversation until you do the right thing. I see her every day, Alex. She's hurting. I look into her eyes, and all I see is sadness and pain. Then I hear your voice and I hear that same sadness and pain. She loves you, Alex. I don't understand why you slapped her down like that."

"That's crossing the line, Michelle. Don't ever use that word when referring to me, not after what he did to her."

"Hit a nerve, did I? Well good. I'd be willing to argue that his punches hurt her less than she's hurting now. What do you say to that, huh, Alex?"

"I can't believe you just said that." Alex tried to maintain her anger, but she was too exhausted to continue.

"I don't want to be hurtful, but I don't know how else to get through to you. We love you both, and it's tearing us apart watching this play out."

Alex's shoulders slumped and her anger entirely disappeared. In her mind, she saw the sadness in Jill's eyes, the sadness she caused. The lump in her throat made it hard for her to speak.

"I know you're only trying to help, but I can't talk about this anymore."

"Okay, I'll back off. You've had enough for today. Please, just think about it."

"I will." Alex didn't want to end the conversation on a sour note, so she said, "Besides, I'll probably fall madly in love with my blind date, so then you won't have to worry about this anymore."

"Pretty likely," Michelle answered, trying to sound light hearted.

"I'll see you soon. I love you."

"I love you too, Alex."

≈≈≈≈

"Hey Sarah, I wanted to call and give you my flight info. I have my first staff meeting in ten minutes."

"Let me get a pen." Alex heard the sound of shuffling, as Sarah must have been rifling through her desk. "Okay, give it to me."

Alex gave her the information and then said, "I think I've chosen the candidate for director and wanted to bounce it off you before I announce anything at the staff meeting."

"Didn't you say your meeting is in ten minutes? Don't you want to have the new director there so you can introduce them to the staff?

"That's the plan."

"But everyone you interviewed for the position is outside the company. You already offered the job to someone, didn't you?" Sarah's voice held an edge of defensiveness. "As long as we've been partners, we've always made the big personnel decisions together."

"No, I haven't offered the job to anyone, yet."

"Then how will they…" Sarah's voice trailed off. "No, Alex. No, this is not fair calling me, dropping this bomb on me, and expecting me to give you my blessing. No, you're not making any decision until after you come home. We'll talk about it then. Tomorrow is Michelle's day and I won't let you ruin it. No, Alex, absolutely not. I can't—"

"Okay, okay. You can't blame me for trying," Alex said, interrupting the tirade. She'd expected reluctance from Sarah, but hadn't expected the angry outburst. "Take it easy. It was just a thought."

"A bad one. You will not introduce yourself as director. You are not leaving us and moving to Florida, do you hear me?"

"Loud and clear. I didn't mean to upset you. Can we just pretend this conversation never happened?"

"That's a good idea. I want to have a good time tomorrow night and not have to worry about my best friend running away from home."

"We'll have fun. My goal is to see if I can accomplish at least half the list I sent to Michelle." Alex hoped to erase the tension she'd caused.

"Make sure I'm around when you ask the boob question."

"I swear you're fixated on boobs. But I'll make sure I put it in my repertoire."

"I'll see you tomorrow, Alex."

"Looking forward to it," Alex said before hanging up.

❧❧❧❧

Alex was disappointed when she got Jill's voicemail, but the disappointment soon turned to anger at herself. Did she expect Jill to be anxiously awaiting her call? After how she had been acting, she wouldn't blame Jill for never wanting to talk to her again. She started to hang up, but on impulse she decided to leave a message.

"Hey Jill, it's me. I'm about ready to get on the plane and will be home soon." Alex hesitated, but continued. "I just want you to know, I've really missed you, and...and um, I'm really looking forward to seeing you."

She stopped and listened to the airport announcement.

"Jill, they just called for my flight to board. But I need you to know, I'm sorry. I'm sorry for the pain I've caused you. It's the last thing in the world I ever wanted. I did everything I could to keep you safe, then, like an idiot, I'm the one hurting you."

Alex walked toward the boarding line; her stomach churned but she continued. "Jill, please don't give up on me. It was never you; it's all me. I'm just scared to death of how much I love you. I know telling you all this on voicemail isn't the way it should be, but I'm freaking out here. I can barely breathe. I keep thinking when I get there, you'll be gone. I'm terrified of losing you. Please be there when I get back."

Alex took a deep breath. "Jill, there's one more thing I need you to know. I feel like I'm betraying you, but it was all just a huge mistake. I just hope you can forgive me. I'm not telling you this to hurt you. I just can't stand the thought of keeping something from you. Jill, I have a blind date tonight for the banquet. I was an idiot, I should have asked you, but I was afraid. Now, more than anything, I wish I had. Please believe me, the whole time I'll be thinking of you and wishing you were there with me. This date means nothing to me and it will be the first and last time I'll ever see this woman. I promise you."

Alex glanced at the people in front of her and said, "Jill, I don't have much time left, I'm almost to the boarding gate. I'm sorry I've been rambling. I need to go, but please know I'm speaking from the bottom of my heart when I tell you again; I love you. No, I don't just love you; I'm madly in love with you. I've been in love with you for a long time, probably longer than you even know. I'm coming home and if you're still willing, I want to give us a try. I hope to see you soon, Jill. I love you."

Alex ended the call and looked at her phone as if it was a snake in her hand.

"Excuse me ma'am, but I need your ticket." Alex absentmindedly held out her cell phone.

"I need your ticket," the woman repeated. Alex looked down at what she was holding and blushed. "Oh yeah, sorry," Alex stammered. She fumbled through her computer case and came up with a ticket. She handed it to the ticket taker and blindly moved on.

Chapter Twenty-six

Sarah pulled up to where Alex was standing and popped the trunk. Alex tossed her suitcase in, jumped into the car, and said, "Damn, that was easy. Why did I bother parking and going in when I picked you guys up?"

"Probably because we weren't on a time crunch. Hopefully the traffic isn't bad or we'll be cutting it close."

"It's only quarter till four. We'll be fine. The limo doesn't pick us up until six."

"We'll be lucky to get to your place by four-thirty. Then we still have to get ready."

"What's up with you? Are you upset with me?"

"What do you think?"

"Hey, I'm sorry. I was just being stupid. I know running away isn't the answer, but it somehow seemed like the easiest solution."

"If you do it, it'll be the biggest mistake in your life."

"I know that. We don't need to talk about it anymore. I'm officially withdrawing my name from consideration."

"Seriously?"

"Seriously, I was just being stupid. Now can we drop it?"

"All right, now the night will be perfect."

"Perfect," Alex said with less conviction. She'd checked her phone twice since landing, but there wasn't a response from Jill. She didn't want to ruin the night for her friends, so there was nothing she could do until tomorrow.

"That didn't sound very convincing. I think tonight will be fun. After all, how often do a couple gym rats get the opportunity to get all dressed up? It's kinda like we are going to prom or something."

"Sure, but you're going with the prom queen. I'm just the loser who couldn't get a date. One of those girls who had to go with their cousin Melvin."

"Make that your cousin Melody. We wouldn't make you go with a guy."

"Gee, thanks. Michelle won't tell me anything about my date, so anything is possible. Have you met her?"

"Yes."

"So, what do you think of her?"

"What does it matter what I think? Every time you look at her, you'll only see Jill."

"You're right. I guess that's why Michelle won't tell me anything. Speaking of Jill, do you think she might be there tonight?"

"It's a LGBTQ+ event."

"Yeah, you're right. I just hoped maybe she'd be there. I had plenty of time on the plane to build my own little fantasy of the way the evening would go."

"What kind of fantasy? All mine have sex involved, so this could be good."

"Why does that not surprise me?" Alex laughed. "No, I'm more of a romantic. I see her across the room and our eyes meet. I get up from the table, cross the room, and without a word, we kiss."

"Oh man, do you have boring fantasies. Now if you did her right there on the dance floor that would be more interesting."

"You know if you were a man, you'd be a pig. Wait, it doesn't matter, you're still a pig." Alex laughed.

"Oink, oink. And in this fantasy, what do you do with your date?"

"That's a bit of a problem. I was thinking maybe she'll come down with food poisoning or malaria, or something like that."

"Sure, that's pretty realistic. I hear there's been a huge outbreak of malaria in the city."

"Hey, whose fantasy is this anyway? Do you think Jill will be at the apartment when we get there?"

"I wouldn't get my hopes up, she's been working a ton of hours."

ꔷꔷꔷꔷ

Alex adjusted her bowtie in the mirror. She enjoyed wearing a tuxedo; it made her feel a little like James Bond. Michelle had taken care of the details for her, and chosen a black tux with a midnight blue vest and tie. Her body was built for a tux, and she always felt confident when she wore one, but tonight her swagger was gone.

Sarah had been right; Jill wasn't there when they arrived. She was being stupid, hoping that Jill would rush home when she'd heard Alex's message. Alex was preparing herself in case Jill decided not to return to the apartment while Alex was home. Alex may have pushed her away too many times, and Jill wouldn't want to risk getting back on the rollercoaster after Alex had been away for so long.

Alex had looked around the apartment, drawing comfort at the telltale signs that Jill had recently been there. She smiled when she noticed the haphazard placement of Jill's towel on the rack, and all her products lining the shelf in the bathroom. When Sarah was showering, Alex went into Jill's room, hoping to catch a whiff of her scent, and wasn't disappointed. In every room, she was able to find evidence of Jill, which alleviated some of her edginess.

Alex's phone dinged. She looked down and saw it was from the limousine company. She adjusted her tie one last time, before leaving the bathroom. "The limo is here," Alex called to Sarah, who was still in the other bathroom. "I swear you're being such a girl tonight. You've been in there primping forever."

"Hey, I'm under pressure. I'm going to have the guest of honor on my arm. I'm not going to be with my buck toothed cousin Melody."

"Oh, so now she has buck teeth, huh?"

"That's one of her better features." Sarah opened the door and held her arms up. "So, perfection?"

Sarah wore a white tuxedo, which was a striking contrast to her dark tan. She wore her long blonde hair down, the natural curls cascading around her shoulders. She'd applied a touch of makeup that accentuated her features. Alex sometimes forgot how attractive her friend was and couldn't help but take a second look. Sarah noticed Alex's double take, so she strutted past Alex and did a pirouette.

"Checking out the goods, are you? Like what you see?"

Alex blushed. "Let's go, Tattoo, the limo's waiting."

Sarah laughed and punched Alex on the arm.

"You don't look so bad yourself. You clean up pretty good. You and Melody will be a cute couple. I just hope she remembered to Nair her mustache and trim her nose hairs."

The driver was standing outside of the car and opened the door for them. As soon as they were in the limo, Sarah started playing with the gadgets and opening all the compartments. Before they pulled away, Sarah opened the sunroof and stood up in the back with her head out.

"Hey, weren't we supposed to call Michelle and tell her we're on our way?"

"Go ahead." Sarah was preoccupied with the remote control she was using to open and close the sunroof.

Michelle answered on the first ring.

"Are you as edgy as your partner?" Alex asked.

"Why?"

"The phone didn't even ring. Were you sitting on it?"

"No, we were just waiting for you two. Are you on the way?"

"Yep."

"Where's Sarah?"

"Let's see, she was hanging out of the sunroof, but now the mini bar seems to have grabbed her attention."

Sarah yelled toward the phone, "Tell Melody to be sure she braided her armpit hairs."

"Who's Melody and what is she muttering about?"

"Oh, that's the name she's given my date. Just ignore her. She's hanging out the sunroof screaming, da plane, da plane."

"Have you two been drinking?" Michelle asked suspiciously.

"No, there's a bottle of champagne chilling, but we haven't opened it, yet."

"And you better not, not until afterward." Michelle's scolding was ineffective, since Alex could hear the smile in her voice. "You sound like you're in good spirits."

"It's hard not to be with Sarah around, but Michelle, I need to ask you something before we get there."

"Why don't I like the change in your tone?"

"Nothing bad. I want this day to be perfect for you, but after the banquet, would you be too upset if I just wanted to go home?"

"We have the limo until three. I thought we'd go have some fun."

"Then I'm going to ask you for a huge favor. Could we take my date home and it just be the three of us? I don't mean to put you on the spot, but I made a gigantic mistake. I was an idiot for not inviting Jill. I promise I'll be a decent date. I just can't stand the thought of running around the city in a limo with another woman. I'm sorry, Michelle. Please tell me you understand."

"I understand. Everything will be okay; you just need to relax."

"I'll try. I'm afraid this will hurt Jill. I'm worried she'll feel betrayed by all of us because of this stupid blind date."

"Hey now, Melody isn't stupid. The coke bottle glasses just give her that appearance. I hear she has an IQ of 180," Sarah said. Alex giggled, happy for the diversion.

"Everything will be fine. How long before you get here?"

"Probably about ten minutes."

"Okay, go play with Sarah. I'm sure she's missing her partner in crime. Just don't piss off the driver. We need him. Things will be fine, sweetie."

"I'm going to trust you on that one. See you soon."

≪≪≫≫

Walking up to the house, Sarah jumped on Alex's back.

"Michelle is going to shoot you if you wrinkle either one of us."

Michelle opened the front door and scowled at them. "If either of you mess up your clothes, you are in big trouble."

The duo laughed and Sarah jumped down. She hurried the rest of the way up the walk and took Michelle's hand.

"Wow, you look beautiful," Sarah said, a big smile lighting her face.

Michelle smiled and drew Sarah to her. They stood on the front porch and kissed.

"Excuse me, guys, we have a banquet to get to." Alex tapped her wrist, as if she wore a watch.

"I have all the banquet I need right here." Sarah raised her eyebrows a couple times and gave Michelle a cheesy grin. Michelle playfully slapped her on the back of the head.

"Ready to meet your date?" Michelle asked, turning to Alex.

Alex groaned and followed the two into the

house. Alex looked around the room, but it was empty.

"What did you do, hide her in the closet?"

"No, she's upstairs, putting the finishing touches on her makeup." Michelle walked to the open staircase and yelled up, "Hey, Melody, they're here."

Alex looked toward Michelle, her brow creased. Did Michelle really just call her date Melody? Alex looked back and forth between Sarah and Michelle, but couldn't read the look on their faces. She started to say something, but she caught a movement out of the corner of her eye. She turned toward the stairs and looked up.

She saw a high-heeled shoe, attached to a shapely ankle. The dress above the ankle was a vibrant royal blue. Her eyes moved higher. Alex stood motionless for a second, and without a word, bounded up the stairs, taking them two at a time. Jill was only a third of the way down the staircase when Alex reached her. Alex stopped on the step below her and looked up. Tears welled in both their eyes. Alex lifted her hand twice to touch Jill, but stopped both times. She stood, unsure what to do. Jill carefully stepped down next to Alex, so they were standing face to face.

Jill reached out and touched Alex's cheek and Alex returned the gesture. Their lips met. The kiss started softly, but the urgency increased. The passion both felt spilled over and the kiss continued. Alex wrapped her arm around Jill's waist and the other rested lightly on her back. Jill put one hand on Alex's hip and the other held the back of her head. They were both breathless when they broke the kiss.

"Do you two need to get a room or would a cold shower do?" Sarah asked. Alex blushed and Jill laughed.

"By the way, they're real," Jill said. Without thinking, Alex glanced down at Jill's cleavage. She turned even redder when she realized what she'd done. Alex started to say something, but was at a loss for words. "If you're a good date, maybe later you can see for yourself." They all laughed at Alex, who still hadn't found her voice.

"If this is the way the whole evening is going to be, I'm opening the champagne when we get to the limo," Alex threatened.

"Speaking of the limo, we better get going." Sarah looked at her watch.

Alex looked into Jill's eyes and held out her hand. "Would you be my date for the banquet tonight?"

Jill smirked. "I thought you'd never ask."

≈≈≈≈

On the way to the car, Alex stopped Jill. "Did you get my message?"

"Yes, thank you." Jill put her palm against Alex's cheek. "Michelle and I were getting our hair done when you called. It made the afternoon so much easier, definitely easier for Michelle. I've been so scared you would react badly when you saw me." Alex closed her eyes, fighting back tears, the pain obvious when she reopened them. "Alex, what's wrong?"

Alex turned and fully faced Jill. She put one hand on the back of Jill's arm, just below the elbow and with her other hand took Jill's hand. "Jill, I'm so sorry. I want to kick my own ass for making you feel that way. What can I do to make it up to you?"

"Just love me, Alex. That's all, just love me."

Alex wrapped her arms around Jill and pulled

her close. "That's easy. I love you and have since shortly after I met you. Even when I was being an idiot, I never stopped loving you. You know that, don't you?"

"I do, but I'll never get tired of hearing it."

"I love you, Jill," Alex said again. Alex leaned forward and their lips met.

Sarah put her head through the sunroof and yelled, "Hello, we have an event to get to. It wouldn't be cool if the guest of honor was late."

Reluctantly, they broke their kiss. "It's your own damn fault, setting me up with such a sexy blind date." As they climbed into the limo, Alex smiled at Michelle. "Finally, you got it right. I can't keep my hands off her."

Michelle opened the bottle of champagne and poured four glasses. She handed Alex and Jill a glass and Sarah grabbed one.

"Now, I think we have reason to celebrate." Michelle held up her glass. "To Jill and Alex. May their love continue to grow."

"To Alex for removing her head from her ass." Sarah held up her glass.

"You be nice." Michelle playfully slapped at Sarah, who looked around, faking astonishment, and then settled on a look of innocence.

"Let's not forget, to Michelle, the reason for this evening. We're proud of you." Alex held up her glass.

Jill reached up and touched her hair, knowing she should say something. She had come a long way from the nervous insecure woman she once was, but for some reason, everyone's eyes on her made her self-conscious. Alex recognized her unease, so she took her hand and gave her an encouraging smile. Jill smiled shyly.

"To the three people who have changed, no, saved my life. I'm indebted to you forever." They clinked glasses and took their first sip. Alex instinctively put her arm around Jill when she leaned against her.

"Okay, now that the niceties are over, I have a bone to pick with all of you. You guys lied to me." Alex tried her hardest to scowl at the others.

"Nope, we never did," Sarah responded.

"You did so, you told me Jill wasn't coming tonight."

"I think you better check your facts," Michelle piped up. "It was kind of a fun mind game trying to make sure we didn't give ourselves away while at the same time never telling you a lie."

"But all of you said Jill wasn't going to be there tonight. And you told me you weren't going." Alex gave Jill an accusatory look.

"I never told you that. When you asked me if I was going, if you recall, I asked you who I would go with." Jill laughed.

"Damn, you're right. But what about you two?"

"When you asked me, I told you it was a LGBTQ+ event and never answered your question directly," Sarah said.

"But you kept trying to get me to invite Jill. Why do that if you knew she was already coming?"

Michelle smiled at Jill. "She was a hard sell. She would have preferred you ask her yourself."

Alex puffed up. "Well, I did." They all laughed.

"She almost backed out on us a couple times. Your smart-ass email saved us in the darkest hour, when we didn't think she would go through with it. She was afraid you'd be upset we tricked you. We had to juggle both of you. It was like herding cats. No wonder Michelle had to open the bottle so early," Sarah said.

"Keep it flowing. I feel like a celebration." Alex kissed Jill again. Alex felt her body reacting to the kiss and broke it before the ache became intolerable. They were both flushed and desire burned in their eyes.

"Whoa, the sexual tension in here is going to start a fire." Sarah ran her hand up Michelle's leg. Michelle slapped it.

"What would you rabbits know about sexual tension? These two feel deprived if it builds up for more than forty-eight hours. They would have spontaneously combusted by now."

"I think I might too." Jill's eyes were full of desire.

"Okay, you can't give me that look or I won't make it through this evening."

"Driver, step on it," Sarah said.

❧❧❧❧

It was after midnight when they walked out of the banquet hall. The humidity from the day was gone, replaced by a slight chill in the air. Jill and Michelle carried their shoes, their feet tired from dancing. The cool air and bare feet caused Jill to shiver. Alex removed her tuxedo jacket, put it over Jill's shoulders, and drew Jill to her.

"Are you okay?" Alex noticed that Jill's eyes were glistening in the moonlight.

"Flashback, but the good kind." Jill smiled. "Remember the last time you gave me your coat? It seems like a million years ago. It still makes me feel cared for and safe."

"That's my goal." Alex pulled Jill closer.

The driver saw them coming, leapt from the limo, and held open the door for them. They piled into the car and Sarah grabbed the second bottle of champagne. She opened it in one fluid motion, took a swig from the bottle, and handed it to Michelle.

"Time to celebrate," Sarah said. Michelle took a drink and passed it on to Alex, who took her slug and passed the bottle to Jill.

"So where to now?" Sarah asked.

"Remember, Alex asked that we take her home after the party," Michelle said.

"But that was before she knew we had Jill. That changes everything." Sarah passed the bottle again.

"No, I don't think so," Michelle answered.

"Of course it does." Sarah gave Michelle a puzzled look.

"Sarah," Michelle said with exasperation. She looked toward Alex and Jill and motioned with her head for Sarah to look. Jill and Alex were snuggled together, looking into one another's eyes.

"Oh, I get it. I guess they've waited long enough to be alone, huh?"

"We may be lost in each other's eyes, but we can still hear you." Alex giggled. "And that answer is yes, I would like to be alone with my date. If it's okay with her."

"Please." Jill reached out and touched Alex's face.

"You heard the woman, get us home." She brushed Jill's hair back off her face and lightly kissed her lips. Jill's breath caught; she pressed harder against Alex and the kiss intensified. Jill broke the kiss first.

"Whoa, okay, I need a time out." She saw the

fear in Alex's eyes. "It's okay, Alex. I'm just feeling the kiss in my toes and a few other places. I think in the interest of being civilized, we need to stop until we get home."

"I think someone's horny." Sarah danced in her seat and pointed at Jill and Alex. Michelle slapped her on the back of the head.

"Thanks, Michelle," Alex said.

"What'd I do?" Sarah feigned innocence.

Alex ignored Sarah and said to Michelle, "You were awesome tonight. I don't think I got the chance to tell you, but I'm so proud of you."

"Your speech was inspiring," Jill added.

"Thanks. But you know, the biggest surprise of the night was Detective Barrett. Who would have guessed she is a big dyke?" Michelle asked.

"Oh my God, yeah, I just about fell over when she approached us," Sarah said. "Her wife is a hottie, though."

"She's actually a sweetheart," Jill said. "She handled everything with the case so well."

"By the way, I meant to ask you what she meant." Alex looked at Jill.

"Whatever do you mean?" Jill said, blinking her eyelashes.

"When she said it took everything she had not to break her professional code and tell me what you said in your interview. What is it she wanted to tell me?"

"Oh, that. Do you really want to know?"

"Yes," the other three answered together.

"I told her I was in love with you." Jill looked down at her hands.

"No way." Alex laughed. "I told her the same

thing."

"What, that I was in love with you?"

"No, that I was in love with you." Alex hugged Jill closer. "You were already in love with me then, too?"

"Duh," Sarah said. "I think everyone but you had it figured out."

"So, when did you know?" Alex asked Jill, ignoring Sarah.

"I'm not sure. In some ways, I could say I fell for you the first time I met you, but actually in love, I don't know. The first time I knew was the day I told you about Steve, but I'm pretty sure it happened much earlier than that."

"Boy, you two were stupid, wasting all that time. I know Alex was mooning over you the first time she met you. She was like a lovesick cow, all sad eyed and pathetic."

The light-hearted mood continued. They were soon laughing so hard that tears rolled down their cheeks. They continued to banter, laugh, and drink champagne for the rest of the trip to Alex's apartment. Alex and Jill were quick to say their goodbyes when they arrived. Sarah jokingly asked for an invitation for a nightcap. Both Jill and Alex shouted no in unison.

❧ ❧ ❧ ❧

Alex fumbled with her keys when she went to unlock the door. Jill put her hand on Alex's hand to steady it and their eyes met. They temporarily forgot the door. Alex put her hand against Jill's cheek.

"I can't believe we're finally here together," Alex said.

"You're scared, aren't you?"

"No...yes. Did my trembling hands give me away?"

"That, coupled with the sweat on your forehead." Jill grinned and wiped Alex's brow.

"Aren't you scared?"

"No. How could I be when I'm here with you? It'll be okay, Alex."

"Shouldn't I be the one reassuring you?"

"You've been doing that since we met. It's my turn."

"Be gentle, then." Alex smirked.

"You bet." Jill unlocked the door and pushed it open.

When they were inside, without a word, Alex drew Jill to her and softly kissed her lips. Jill leaned into Alex and hungrily returned the kiss. Alex put her hand on Jill's hip and slowly ran it up the length of her body, while Jill ran her fingers through Alex's short hair. Alex eased back against the door and Jill pressed into her. Jill moaned when Alex ran her tongue over Jill's lips and slowly sucked her bottom lip. Unconsciously, Jill rubbed her pelvis against Alex's leg and Alex gasped. Their kiss intensified and their hands roamed each other's body. Jill kneaded Alex's shoulder, enjoying the feel of her rock-hard muscles, while Alex cupped Jill's buttocks. Alex pulled Jill tighter against her leg and then released her. Alex continued the rhythm, helping Jill grind against her leg. Their breaths were ragged, the yearlong sexual tension bubbling to the surface. Alex broke the kiss and reluctantly stopped the motion that had Jill on the brink. Jill looked at Alex, the need palpable in her eyes.

"Jill, I don't want our first time to be shoved up

against the front door. I want it to be perfect."

"Then you better get me into the bedroom quick because I can't stand to wait much longer."

Alex started to kiss Jill and thought better of it. She took Jill's hand and, without turning on any lights, led her to the bedroom. Alex stopped beside the bed and flipped on the nightstand light. She held both of Jill's hands, but took a step back so she could see all of her. The dress hugged Jill's narrow waist and shapely hips. The dress was low-cut and Jill's ample breasts pushed together, creating a deep cleavage.

"I told you I'd let you see them," Jill said playfully.

Alex bent down, kissed the top of each breast, and let her tongue trail between them. Jill moaned and put her hand behind Alex's head. Alex cupped one breast and lightly brushed her thumb across Jill's hardened nipple. Jill stepped back, breaking contact.

"I've got to get out of this dress before one of us rips it off. Help me with the zipper."

Alex moved behind Jill, lifted her hair, and pulled the zipper down. She leaned down and kissed the back of Jill's neck, while she helped her release her arms from the dress. Jill let it slide down her body and drop to the floor. Alex continued to kiss her neck from behind, reached around front and ran her hand across Jill's smooth stomach, right above the band of her underwear. Alex let her pinky snake under the band and lightly brushed the top of Jill's pubic hair.

Jill reached back and ran her hand up and down Alex's leg. Alex continued lightly running her hand under Jill's waistband, making her way lower with each pass. Jill put her hand over Alex's, stopping her from going any lower.

"Is everything okay?" Alex said with concern.

"More than okay, but I know you'd be disappointed if I came standing here half-dressed before we even made it into bed." She stepped out of her dress. Alex picked it up, carried it to the dresser and carefully draped it across the top. When Alex turned back, Jill was already in bed. Alex unbuttoned her own shirt, leaving it hanging open, took off her pants, and tossed them aside.

When Alex got into bed, Jill reached for the light, but Alex stopped her. "I don't want to do this in the dark. I want to be able to see you."

"But I don't want you to see the scars."

Alex touched Jill's face and looked into her eyes. "They're part of you, it's okay. I just need to see your beautiful face and those eyes."

"Do you know how much I love you?" Jill's eyes got misty.

"No, why don't you show me?" Alex's eyes twinkled and she smirked.

"I plan on it."

Jill rolled on top of Alex and they started again with a kiss. Alex had one arm wrapped around Jill and with her other hand, she ran her fingers through Jill's hair. Jill straddled Alex's leg, while Alex slowly moved it back and forth, heightening Jill's excitement. Alex could tell by the change in Jill's breathing that she would not last much longer if Alex continued. Alex forced herself to stop and break the kiss. She started to turn Jill over, so she could explore her body, but abruptly stopped.

"What's wrong, Alex?" Jill said, sensing the change.

"Is this okay?"

"It's not okay to stop, but I don't think that's

what you're asking me."

"I don't want to be on top of you, if it will make you feel trapped. You know, after everything that's happened to you."

"You're so sweet, always concerned with how I am." Jill touched Alex's cheek. "You always make me feel safe, so with you on top of me I'll only feel safer." Jill's eyes turned seductive. "All this talking is getting me frustrated, though. It's time you do something about this ache you've created, or I may just spontaneously combust."

"I've got it covered." Alex gently finished turning Jill onto her back.

She unhooked Jill's bra and removed her own shirt and bra before she lowered herself onto Jill. The feeling of their breasts touching for the first time increased their urgency. Their kiss resumed, but soon Alex's kisses moved down Jill's chin to her neck. Jill turned her head slightly, so Alex would have better access to the sensitive spot on her neck. Alex found the spot and lingered, running her tongue lightly in circles. Alex's willpower was gone and soon she moved further down, needing to taste Jill's breasts. She kissed in a circle around Jill's nipple, and then slowly ran her tongue around it as well. Jill arched her back and tried to move so Alex's tongue would hit the spot. Alex moved with Jill, never letting her mouth touch Jill's nipple. Sensing Jill's need, Alex finally let her tongue roll over Jill's nipple and heard a sharp intake of breath. Before long, Alex was flicking her tongue over Jill's hardened nipple and gently sucking it into her mouth. Jill grasped Alex's head and held it to her breast. Alex noticed that Jill was slowly moving her pelvis against Alex, so she reached down and rubbed her entire hand over the crotch of Jill's underwear. Jill closed her eyes and moaned as Alex continued to run her hand over the area that was screaming for attention.

"Are you ready?" Alex asked.

"Oh God, yes."

Alex kissed Jill's breast one last time, before her kisses trailed down Jill's stomach. Alex kissed several scars on the way down, but did not stop to draw attention to them. When she arrived at her destination, she left Jill's underwear on. She kissed and licked Jill's thighs around the leg bands. Jill squirmed and ran her hand over Alex's hair. Sensing Jill could wait no longer, Alex pulled Jill's underwear off. Alex positioned herself between Jill's legs and began to kiss her thigh again. While Alex ran her tongue up the crease of Jill's thigh, Alex ran her finger between Jill's lips and felt her wetness. Gently, Alex pushed first one finger then another inside Jill. Another moan escaped from Jill and she rhythmically thrust against Alex's fingers. Alex eased her fingers out of Jill and pushed them inside again. Alex abandoned Jill's thigh in search of the spot she was craving. Alex slowly licked the spot directly above Jill's clitoris, the entire time continuing with the slow motion of her fingers entering and withdrawing. Jill's breathing was becoming more and more rapid and her need for release was evident. Alex flattened her tongue and for the first time ran it across Jill's clitoris. Jill let out a loud groan, which was all the encouragement Alex needed. She began to flick her tongue faster over the spot that was causing Jill so much pleasure.

"Alex, that feels so good." Jill gasped for breath. She said no more before an orgasm wracked her body and she screamed out Alex's name.

Alex ran her tongue lightly over the spot a few more times, making sure Jill was spent. Alex crawled up next to Jill and put her arms around her. Jill lay panting, her eyes closed. After a few seconds, she opened her eyes and looked at Alex.

"I love you," Jill said.

"I love you too."

"You have to be ready to explode." Jill lightly squeezed Alex's nipple. Alex closed her eyes and moaned. "I think you need to be taken care of."

"That would be nice," Alex answered, the throbbing between her legs nearly unbearable.

"I'm afraid I'm not as skilled as you are, but I'm a quick study." Jill smiled before sucking Alex's nipple into her mouth.

"Oh God, Jill. This isn't going to take long. I think a couple strokes in the right spot and I'm gone."

Jill reached her hand between Alex's legs, while she continued her assault on Alex's nipple. Jill ran a finger slowly over Alex's clitoris and heard Alex gasp. Jill wanted to explore Alex's body, but knew there was time for that later; for now, Alex needed relief. Jill rubbed Alex's clitoris faster and after only a few passes of her finger, she felt Alex's body tense. Alex cried out, exploding in an overpowering orgasm.

Alex collapsed on the bed beside Jill, closed her eyes, and tried to catch her breath. Jill rolled over and burrowed under Alex's arm, resting her head on Alex's shoulder. They'd laid this way in the past. Without clothes, the intimacy was even greater. Jill rubbed Alex's chest and Alex ran her hand over Jill's back.

"You're going to think I'm a light-weight. What,

I lasted about thirty seconds?" Alex said.

"I'd say more like fifteen. And you're the one with all the experience."

"No, I can tell you, I've never had an experience like this."

"Me neither. I'll give you a pass though, I'm thinking a year of foreplay was quite long enough."

"You've got a point there." Alex laughed and hugged Jill tighter.

"If I'd known it would be this good, I wouldn't have let you make me wait a year."

"So, are you saying you might want to do this again sometime? Should we put it on our calendar for the same time next year?" Alex pretended to reach for her cellphone.

Jill playfully slapped Alex. "Not funny."

"I'm guessing being with a woman didn't freak you out, then?"

"You were worried about that, weren't you?"

"Nah..." Alex said playfully. She looked into Jill's eyes and could feel the tears welling in her own. Alex's face changed and her voice took on a serious tone. "You'll never understand how terrified I was and still am."

"Why?" Jill put a hand against Alex's cheek. "Please help me understand, Alex. When I see you in so much pain, it makes my heart ache." The normally strong and confident Alex was struggling with her words and blinking back tears. Jill sat up in bed, propped a couple pillows behind her, and motioned for Alex to rest her head against Jill. Alex lowered her head to Jill's chest and Jill put her arm around her.

"Okay, I can't have this conversation with your nipple poking me in the cheek. It's distracting," Alex said teasingly, trying to regain some of her swagger.

"Wimp." Jill pulled the sheet up between Alex's head and her breast. "Is that better?"

"Less distracting, not sure if it's better though." Alex raised her eyebrows a couple times.

"Are you going to talk to me about this?" Jill said, her tone more serious.

Alex fought against her natural inclination to change the subject or downplay her feelings, but that wouldn't be fair to Jill. At the end of the day, Jill was stronger because she let herself be vulnerable and put her heart on the line. For Alex, this was uncharted territory. She'd never allowed herself to need anyone, always the Lone Ranger. It went a long way in explaining why she'd always chosen superficial women. They were all interchangeable, but Jill was different. Jill made her feel things that no one else had. At that moment, Alex knew Jill deserved an explanation.

"You could hurt me."

"Yeah, you could hurt me too," Jill replied, not fully understanding what Alex was trying to say.

"No, you could really hurt me. You could drive me to my knees. You could devastate me. You can reduce me to tears quicker than anyone I know."

"Sweetie, I'm not trying to be ignorant, but that's a part of being truly in love with someone."

"I vowed I'd never give anyone that power over me again, but it's too late. You have it. I thought if we didn't do this, if we never crossed the line, then I was safe. In the end, you got inside my heart long before today. Before I could fool myself and pretend it wasn't so, but now there's nowhere to hide."

Jill rubbed Alex's head. "You don't need to hide

from me. Here all along you've been trying to make sure I felt safe with you, but I never thought about you needing to feel safe too. Did Kristen hurt you that badly?"

"No. I never let her into my heart, so she only hurt my pride. I never let any of them in. I don't know how you slipped through the cracks."

"I guess it's lucky for me you thought I was safe. I guess being married with two kids served me well."

"I think you're right. If you were a single lesbian, I would have run screaming from you, as soon as I realized how I felt."

"Well then, I'm glad I had Steve."

"You can't mean that," Alex said, searching Jill's face.

"I think I do. If going through everything I did lead me here, then I wouldn't change a thing."

"I don't think you even know what you just said or did for me." Alex smiled. "If you're courageous enough to accept all that's happened to you and feel fortunate to be here with me, who am I to let my stupid fears stand in the way?"

"I think I'm missing something. If Kristen didn't hurt you and you never let anyone else in..." Jill's voice trailed off and a strange look crossed her face. "It was Michelle, wasn't it? You were in love with her and she broke your heart."

"Oh God, no." Alex laughed. "I barely knew her then. I thought she was cute and I asked her out. Nope, we can't hang this one on her."

"Thank God." Jill giggled. "It would feel strange for all of us to be together, if I thought you were secretly pining for her."

"No doubt. Besides, Sarah would kick my ass

or at least bite my ankles if that was the case." They both laughed at the image and continued from there. They weaved a more and more outrageous tale of the devastation Alex's secret longing for Michelle would cause in all their lives. They were laughing so hard Jill snorted and sent them into a fresh round of laughter.

After the laughter subsided, Jill said, "Are you ever going to tell me who broke your heart so bad?"

"Yes," Alex said softly and looked into Jill's eyes for reassurance. Jill kissed her forehead and then Alex began to speak. "Remember how I told you that I met Sarah during Christmas break at school and that I'd spent the holidays there? Well, there was a reason for me staying there."

"Yeah, you told me your family was mad because you chose to go to the University."

"Well, that was only partially true. When I was eighteen, two weeks before I left for college, my parents caught me making out with my girlfriend. They kicked me out of the house and told me I was no longer a part of the family. I had embarrassed and disgraced them."

"Oh, Alex." Jill held her tighter. "But that was a long time ago; didn't they get over it?"

"Nope. I never spoke to them again."

"But surely, now after this many years, they'd be receptive. They probably just don't know how to break the ice, but you could."

"No, I can't."

"Why not?"

"Mom's dead and Dad might as well be."

Without emotion, Alex told Jill the rest of the story. Alex's mom died of breast cancer when she was a senior in college. She didn't know about it until two weeks after the funeral when she received a letter from her mom's lawyer. During her illness, her mom had written her a letter, apologizing for everything that'd happened. Alex never had the opportunity to respond. Alex knew her dad, who was the local minister, didn't know about the letter and would never have let Alex and her mom talk anyway. Then three years ago, her father sent her a letter out of the blue. When Alex saw who it was from, her initial reaction was one of hope. The letter was full of hatred and blamed her for the death of her mother and the terrible life her sister led. Alex kept both letters in her desk drawer, never able to discard either.

"Here I put myself through school and became a successful business owner, while my sister has been married four times, lost two children to family services and is an alcoholic. However, I'm the bad one. I'm the disowned one, just because who I chose to love. How fucked up is that?" Alex said, finally showing some emotion.

"I'm so sorry. Why didn't you tell me?"

"I was embarrassed. I've never told anyone besides Sarah and Michelle. I'm an adult now. It shouldn't really matter. Here I am feeling sorry for myself for something that happened so long ago, while you're the one who's been through hell. I don't understand why you've bounced back so easily and I can't."

"But it does matter and is still causing you pain." Jill ran her fingers through Alex's short hair. "It was your family. They are the people who are supposed to protect and support you no matter what. Sure, I got into a bad situation with Steve, but I still had the foundation my parents set. I know how to love and be loved. You never had that, Alex."

"It's over, though. I should just move on and stop letting it hold me back. I guess maybe that's what I've accidentally done. You've gotten in far enough that you have the power to rip my heart out, too."

"I have a newsflash for you." Jill grinned. "I'm not the first."

"Huh?" Alex looked puzzled.

"There are two other people in this world that already have the power." When Alex looked at her blankly, Jill continued. "Sarah and Michelle."

"But that's different; they're just friends." Alex's brow wrinkled.

"No, Alex. They're your family." The truth of Jill's words sank in and the expression on Alex's face changed. "For some reason, maybe just to keep yourself from being afraid, you fooled yourself by putting them into a different category. If you said they were just friends, it somehow made it safe. That's why you were okay being friends with me. You thought you were safe, but ironically, you weren't. You've never been safe; you just thought you were." Tears ran down Alex's face, and Jill reached up and brushed one away with her thumb. "It's okay, Alex. It's not so bad to love someone completely and give them your heart. Unfortunately, the very people that should've always been there burned you. But unknowingly, for the past fifteen years, you weren't as sheltered from possible pain as you thought."

"How did you get to be so smart? And why did I miss it?"

"You didn't, really. You just selectively ignored it. By your reaction, I can tell it really doesn't come as much of a surprise."

"You know what this means, don't you? It means I have more practice at this than I thought. It means I don't have to be terrified of you, although I think that may take a while for me not to be." Alex smiled.

"I'm not really all that scary, just don't piss me off."

"I'm ready, Jill. I am willingly handing my heart over to you. Please be gentle."

"You know I will be. Alex, I love you more than I have ever loved anyone. Do you understand that?"

"I'm beginning to. I'll make you a deal. I won't keep protecting you, but we'll protect each other. No more Lone Ranger."

"Deal." Jill kissed Alex on the lips. Alex returned the kiss. They held each other tightly and their kisses intensified.

Alex broke the kiss and looked at Jill with a twinkle in her eyes. "There are a few other parts of my body, besides my heart, that would like your attention too."

"I think that can be arranged." She started to say more, but Alex sucked one of Jill's nipples in her mouth and slowly rolled her tongue over it.

༄ ༄ ༄ ༄

Jill's thoughts were lost, but she didn't mind. All she cared about at the moment was being here with Alex, the woman she loved. She let her body relax and felt how good it could be to let someone you loved and trusted completely have all of you, without barriers and without fear.

About The Author

Rita Potter has spent most of her life trying to figure out what makes people tick. To that end, she holds a Bachelor's degree in Social Work and an MA in Sociology. Her favorite pastime is crawling around inside peoples' brains. Her loved ones are grateful that she now has characters whose minds she can explore, so maybe she'll stay out of theirs.

Rita's writing reflects her belief that in some way we are all damaged and must conquer our demons in order to create a fulfilling life. Being an eternal optimist, she maintains that the human spirit is remarkably resilient and can overcome even the most challenging obstacles. That optimism is the wellspring of her life goal- to provide encouragement and support to help people thrive.

In her spare time, she enjoys the outdoors. She is especially drawn to the water, which is ironic since she lives in the middle of a corn field. Her first love has always been reading, which has spurred her writing. She rides a Harley Davidson and has an unnatural obsession with fantasy football. More than anything she detests small talk, but can ramble on for hours given a topic that interests her.

She lives in a small town in Illinois with her wife, Terra, and their cat, Chumley, who actually runs the household.

Rita is a member of American Mensa and the Golden Crown Literary Society. She is currently a student of the GCLS Writing Academy 2021.

www.ritapotter.com

If you liked this book?

Reviews help an author get discovered and if you have enjoyed this book, please do the author the honor of posting a review on Goodreads, Amazon, Barnes & Noble or anywhere you purchased the book. Or perhaps share a posting on your social media sites and help us spread the word

Other books by Sapphire Authors

The Dragonfly House: An Erotic Romance - ISBN- 978-1-952270-14-7

On the outskirts of a small, picturesque Midwestern town, sits a large, lovely old Victorian house with many occupants. This residence, known simply as The Dragonfly House, is home to Ma'am, the proprietor, along with several young women in her employ. One such woman, Jame, is very popular among the female clientele. One such client, Sarah, fresh from a divorce and looking for a little adventure, as well as some gentle handling, becomes one of Jame's repeat clients. Once Sarah enters the picture, Jame and Ma'am, as well as the brothel, will be forever changed.

The Coffield Chronicles – Hearts Under Siege: Book One – ISBN – 978-1-952270-12-3

The year is 1862. The war between the states has been raging intensely for a year now. The country is in complete and utter turmoil, and brother is fighting brother to the death, dying for what each believed. It seems it's all the townsfolk of New Albany, Indiana can speak of, and Melody Coffield is paying attention. Through a series of heartbreaks and sorrow, she settles on the decision to cut her hair and don men's attire. Going under the alias of Melvin A. Coffield, she leaves her childhood home, the only home she had ever known, and enlists in the United States Army. Chewing tobacco and drinking liquor were ways of men, and she learns quickly how to behave like one. She would soon know the horrors of battle, and what was called the glory of war, through roads that led straight to Vicksburg, Mississippi. However, her biggest concern was making sure she was not detected by the others. Keeping her secret would not only be challenging, but trying as well. Will she remain in this solitude the rest of her life, never allowing anyone into her heart again? Or will she find love, once more, in a world that was intolerant and unaccepting of who she truly was?

Keeping Secrets – ISBN – 978-1-952270-04-8

What would you do if, after finally finding the woman of your dreams, she suddenly leaves to fight in the Civil War? It's 1863, and Elizabeth Hepscott has resigned herself to a life of monotonous boredom far from the battlefields as the wife of a Missouri rancher. Her fate changes when she travels with her brother to Kentucky to help him join the Union Army. On a whim, she poses as his little brother and is bullied into enlisting, as well. Reluctantly pulled into a new destiny, a lark decision quickly cascades into mortal danger. While Elizabeth's life has made a drastic U-turn, Charlie Schweicher, heiress to a glass-making fortune, is still searching for the only thing money can't buy. A chance encounter drastically changes everything for both of them. Will Charlie find the love she's longed for, or will the war take it?

CPSIA information can be obtained
at www.ICGtesting.com
Printed in the USA
LVHW090910180421
684835LV00009B/117

9 781952 270222